150.1952 F889m
Freud's case studies :
self-psychological
perspectives
54403

WITHDRAWN

FREUD'S CASE STUDIES

FREUD'S CASE STUDIES
Self-Psychological Perspectives

edited by
Barry Magid

1993   Hillsdale, NJ   London

Copyright © 1993 by The Analytic Press, Inc.
All rights reserved. No part of this book may be reproduced in any form, by photostat, microform, retrieval system, or any other means without prior written permission of the publisher.

Published by The Analytic Press, Inc.
365 Broadway, Hillsdale, NJ 07642

Set in Garamond by Lind Graphics, Inc., Upper Saddle River, NJ

Library of Congress Cataloging-in-Publication Data

Freud's case studies : self-psychological perspectives / edited by
  Barry Magid.
    p.   cm.
  Includes bibliographical references and index.
  ISBN 0-88163-132-9
  1. Psychoanalysis—Case studies.   2. Freud, Sigmund, 1856–1939.
  3. Self psychology.   I. Magid, Barry, M. D.
  [DNLM: 1. Freud, Sigmund, 1856–1939.   2. Models, Psychological.
  3. Psychoanalysis.   4. Psychoanalytic Therapy—case studies.
  5. Self Concept.   WM 460 F8923]
RC509.8F74   1993
616.89'17—dc20
DNLM/DLC
for Library of Congress   92-48915
                                                              CIP

Printed in the United States of America
10 9 8 7 6 5 4 3 2 1

TABLE OF CONTENTS

Contributors   vii

Introduction   1
 Barry Magid

The Unmirrored Self, Compensatory Structure, and Cure:
 The Exemplary Case of Anna O   9
 Marian Tolpin

Did Freud Understand Dora?   31
 Paul H. Ornstein

Little Hans: His Phobia and His Oedipus Complex   87
 Anna Ornstein

The Two Analyses of Dr. L: A Self-Psychological
 Perspective on Freud's Treatment of the Rat Man   107
 Sandra Kiersky and James L. Fosshage

The Restoration of Schreber's Stolen Self   135
 Donna M. Orange

Self Psychology Meets the Wolf Man   157
 Barry Magid

The Homosexual Identity of a Nameless Woman   189
 Barry Magid

Index   201

CONTRIBUTORS

James L. Fosshage, Ph.D.—Cofounder and Board Director, National Institute for Psychotherapies, and Core Faculty Member, Institute for the Psychoanalytic Study of Subjectivity; Faculty and Supervisor, New York University Postdoctoral Program in Psychotherapy and Psychoanalysis.

Sandra Kiersky, Ph.D.—Coordinator for Training, Institute for the Psychoanalytic Study of Subjectivity, New York City; Faculty, National Institute for the Psychotherapies, New York City.

Barry Magid, M.D. (editor)—Supervisor and Faculty Member, Postgraduate Center for Mental Health and Institute for Contemporary Psychotherapy, New York City.

Donna M. Orange, Ph.D., Psy.D.—Institute for the Psychoanalytic Study of Subjectivity, New York City.

Anna Ornstein, M.D.—Professor of Child Psychiatry and Codirector, International Center for the Study of Psychoanalytic Self Psychology, University of Cincinnati Department of Psychiatry; Faculty member, Cincinnati Psychoanalytic Institute.

Paul H. Ornstein, M.D.—Professor of Psychiatry and Codirector, International Center for the Study of Psychoanalytic Self Psychology, University of Cincinnati Department of Psychiatry; Training and Supervising Analyst, Cincinnati Psychoanalytic Institute.

Marian Tolpin, M.D.—Faculty Member and Training and Supervising Analyst, Institute for Psychoanalysis, Chicago; Professor of Psychiatry, Chicago Medical School.

FREUD'S CASE STUDIES

Barry Magid
INTRODUCTION

> Even *gold* dust in the eyes will cause blindness.
> —Zen saying

Kohut (1981a) called empathy "vicarious introspection" and compared patients' reports of their inner mental landscapes with astronauts reporting their observations of the lunar landscape back to their earthbound colleagues (p. 528). In a similar fashion, he suggested, we can read the chronicles by the classical historians in order to understand vanished civilizations, all the while keeping in mind what we know of their biases, their allegiances, and the limitations of the explanatory tools at their disposal.

In this same spirit, we now return to the original case studies of Sigmund Freud. We hope to sift vicariously and empathically through his clinical data, examine the theoretical framework he used to organize the material, and be cognizant of what we know of his overarching didactic and polemical agendas as he made his presentations. And just as earthbound scientists will make one kind of sense of the astronauts' data if they use it to explain the origin of the lunar craters by means of a theory of vulcanism (the eruption of violent forces from within the moon itself) versus a theory of meteoric impact (a record of the moon's exposure and vulnerability to its astronomical surroundings), so will Freud's data yield up a different story when organized within the framework of self psychology.

In the practice of psychoanalysis we hear the stories of our patients' past, told and retold; and with successive tellings, and in the light of ever-increasing understanding, the stories gradually take on new meanings. So it is with the story of psychoanalysis itself. Each generation tells once again the story of Little Hans or the Wolf Man, and with each new telling old truths are acknowledged and new meanings emerge.

But the reinterpretations do not come easily or without a struggle. Freud wanted the stories told in just *his* way and in such a way as to stress the inseparability of the clinical data from his theoretical organization. "Either everything fits together exactly as I have stated it, or else the whole thing is nonsense from beginning to end," he challenges us in the Wolf Man case.

Our reassessment of Freud's cases will nonetheless attempt to separate out what Kohut (1984) called the "time-bound elements of certain contributions . . . from those elements that have a more enduring validity" (p. 41). Freud's attempt to ground his psychological data in a biological foundation of drive theory has increasingly proved to be the most "time-bound" and contested part of his legacy. The very pursuit of "foundations" outside the realm of a pure psychology of complex mental states is, as Goldberg (1990) delineated, fraught with philosophical pitfalls. Kohut (1981b) bemoaned the intrusion of this "foreign body," this "vague and insipid biological concept into a marvelous system of psychology" (p. 553). Furthermore, Kohut believed drive theory grafted onto psychoanalysis not only an outdated biological theory but a covert moral value system as well. This was, he argued, the inevitable result of a system that exhorted the renunciation of the pleasure principle in favor of knowledge and independence values. A *moral,* rather than objective or scientific, stance is generated by drive theory's view of man as "reluctant to give up his pleasure aims, however nonadaptive, and thus 'resisting' therapeutic analysis; a conception of man seen as unwilling to allow his aggressive-destructive aims to be tamed, and thus engaging in wars and/or prone to self-destruction" (p. 556). Thus Kohut's rejection of Freud's attempted bridge to the biological sciences was in part based on the recognition that it had, paradoxically, resulted in a stance that was both unscientific and moralistic.

How do we understand Freud's legacy, then, if we remove from it an element that he himself felt to be absolutely central and crucial? Much of the scientific community into which Freud wanted to integrate psychoanalysis still refuses to consider his legacy "scientific" at all (Grünbaum, 1984). Kohut (1984) himself certainly shared Freud's view of psychoanalysis as a science, but he grounded his definition in the scientific objectivity of the analyst-observer who must be willing to assess the effect of "the influence of the observed

Introduction

on the observer and, especially, the influence of the observer on the field that he observes" (p. 40).

I suggest that more and more we have come to understand Freud's legacy in terms of a field of observation (within which Kohut would radically alter the *stance* of observation), rather than in terms of any specific content that Freud claimed to have uncovered. Freud's genius and scope of inquiry were so great that no preexisting branch of science could encompass them; and, from the beginning, psychoanalysis has had both the blessing and curse of being *sui generis*. Unlike Einstein, who always remained identifiably a physicist within the ongoing field of physics—even as he radically upset its most fundamental assumptions—or William James, who sought to bring the whole range of the phenomena of consciousness systematically within the scope of experimental psychology—Sigmund Freud may be most remarkable, after all, for singlehandedly creating a whole new mode and practice of inquiry, one that drew from the psychology, psychiatry, and neurology of his day, but that was containable by none of them. Though many of us find a valuable grounding in the role and ethics of the physician, psychoanalysis has, for better or worse, not been containable within the medical model. The creation of a new profession to engage in such an unprecedented, sustained, and structured inquiry into our mental lives is, I believe, Freud's truest and greatest legacy.

Like theoretical physics, in which the fundamental concepts relating energy and matter, causality and indeterminacy, have all undergone radical shifts over the last hundred years, so that even a seemingly straightforward word like "electron" no longer means today what it meant at the turn of the century, so psychoanalysis continues to use words like transference, defense, and resistance that no longer mean to us what they meant to Freud. And yet physics is still physics. Kohut strove to maintain a similar sense of continuity for psychoanalysis. And the reexamination of these cases thus also serves to enhance that sense of continuity; to maintain our own sense as psychoanalysts of the continuity and cohesiveness of our professional selves over time, despite change and evolution.

Throughout this volume we will see the changes that have occurred in how we use the most basic psychoanalytic concepts since they were inaugurated by Freud. The very meaning of the "meaning" of a symptom has undergone a fundamental shift. Preeminently, for Freud *meanings* were to be located in *origins,* and the therapeutic and interpretative processes are ultimately grounded in uncovering the buried past. It is now a commonplace to observe that the excitement of these case studies is much like the excitement of a good detective story, as one by one the clues are unearthed and at last the oedipal crime scene is revealed. Fish (1989), writing on the Wolf Man case from the perspective of a literary critic, has analyzed how Freud so masterfully maintained the narrative tension in the case report, now withholding, now revealing just those elements necessary to propel the story towards its dramatic denouement. If, as Fish concludes, there is in the performance as much rhetorical genius as there is scientific, nonetheless we are in the hands of—or at the mercy of—a master of his craft. Certainly the Wolf Man himself remained for his entire life enthralled by Freud in both the positive and negative senses of that word, and generations of readers have likewise been similarly and as ambiguously enthralled. Some of what follows is necessarily intended to break that spell, or as Wittgenstein (1953) put it, to show the fly the way out of the fly-bottle, which was his metaphor for the bewitchment of our reason by language.[1] The conflation of meanings with origins is one such bewitchment. In reading Freud it is such a natural and automatic outgrowth of his theory that it is difficult to conceive an alternative, or even consider what alternative is either possible or necessary.

But in "The *Psychogenesis* [italics added] of Homosexuality in a Young Woman" (Freud, 1920), we see how self psychology enables us to evolve beyond this fundamental assumption. For Freud, the meaning of her homosexuality lay exclusively in whatever infantile conflict or biological predisposition *gave rise* to it. For us, its meaning is now to be found in the *function* it serves in maintaining a variety of selfobject needs and pursuing the consolidation of her sense of identity. Alas, much of the still-current debate about the nature of homosexuality is still mired in this question of origins; as if whether a person is in some sense *born* homosexual rather than made so by whatever constellation of interpersonal events somehow affects whether we will view it as a form of pathology or not. What really should be at issue is how gender roles and object choices function (or fail) to promote a mature selfobject milieu.

Thus, inevitably the meaning of these cases for us will also center on the use to which we put them. Kohut (1984) himself acknowledged that it is "impossible to separate the aims of the objective

---

[1]For Wittgenstein, the crucial confusion was between meanings and names. He argued that a word's meaning is its *use* in *language*, but that we reflexively think of words as labels stuck on objects, *naming* them. And, lest it appear that this critique applies only to Freud's use of language, I note that Wittgenstein also cautioned against analogies that equate reports of inner "objects" of experience with reports of external objects, as Kohut does in his description of empathy as vicarious introspection.

historiographer from the aims of a man who wants to lay the groundwork for a reform" (p. 40). And the chapters that follow argue for the superior efficacy, coherence, and even objectivity of a self-psychological approach to Freud's data. For the case reports themselves, as well as our responses to them, were conceived with a broadly didactic intent, seeking through their compelling narratives to give unassailable testimony to the theoretical framework that underlay them. We are inevitably, then, drawn into the issue of how Freud shaped his presentation and forced to consider what subsequent research has shown about the processes by which he included and excluded data. Marian Tolpin's review of the case of Anna O and the "Poor Breuer Myth" reveals how Breuer's contribution was distorted and maligned by the creation of a psychoanalytic myth—a creation myth for psychoanalysis, if you will—in which Breuer's alleged flight in the face of the sexual origins of the case and the transference is contrasted with Freud's supposed unyielding courage in the pursuit of the truth. Bertha Pappenheim's (the real-life Anna O) subsequent life story, one that Tolpin shows to have been animated by a profound sense of compassion for the victimized women of her day, needs also to be redeemed from earlier accounts that reduced her values and ideals to a mere disguise for her repressed sexuality.

Attuned as we now are to the vicissitudes of the fragmentation products that signal their disruption, we can no longer accept Freud's imposition of the inevitable oedipal scenario on the wide variety of personalities and problems represented in these cases as illustrating the broad explanatory range of his theory as he originally intended. Rather, we feel ourselves to be witnesses to a difficult Procrustean operation, with all the painful stretching and bloody stumps of truncated experience that that image implies. Even in the Schreber case, where Freud analyzes the autobiography of a man whose father turns out to have literally been a modern-day Procrustes, what we find is not an exploration of how such grossly unempathic manipulations affected the poor boy Schreber, so much as an attempt to channel the narrative into evidence to advance Freud's theses linking paranoia to homosexuality. Freud made no secret of his preoccupation with his evolving theory: "I am not basically interested in therapy," he confessed to his analysand Abram Kardiner, "and I usually find that I am engaged—in any particular case—with the theoretical problems with which I happen to be interested at the time" (Mahony, 1984, p. 97). And when the interests of theory and his patient diverged, Freud seems all too readily to have come down on the side of theory. The forced termination of the Wolf Man seems born of Freud's frustration and his determination to extract from his masochistic patient some theoretical satisfaction. And when the dreams of his homosexual woman patient strike him as unexpectedly hopeful and positive, he accuses the dreams of lying.

These case studies thus serve as an important reminder of how theory bound all clinical observations necessarily are. And if Freud's impositions of his theory on his data now seem crude and forced in the light of our current knowledge, we must not smugly imagine ourselves to be immune to the same process. Self psychology, with its emphasis on the patient's subjective experience and its abdication of the role of arbiter of objective reality, certainly has tried to build in safeguards against the more egregious ways analysts are tempted—or even encouraged—to impose their world-view on the patient in the name of "reality testing." But we must always beware of the attendant temptation to view our own observations as a pure phenomenology. A focus on the patient's subjective experience does not preclude the imparting of our theoretical organizing principles to the patient as part of the groundwork of our interpretations.

To the extent that interpretation partakes equally of understanding and explaining, our explanations will inevitably entail the linking together of material, both dynamically and chronologically, by means of a theoretical apparatus, which at least in part must be learned by the patient for the interpretation to be understood. When Kohut (1977) includes the image of a gastric fistula, such that no matter how much food is eaten, no true satiety or nourishment can be achieved, as part of his interpretation of the effervescent nature of defensive self-stimulation as an attempted antidote for an empty, enfeebled self, he is instructing his patient in a model of the mind and psychic functioning that will be part of what enables the patient to feel understood. Bateson (1979) has characterized all explanation as the "mapping [of data] onto tautology" (p. 48)—a self-contained, internally consistent set of organizing principles. To feel that our experience makes sense, is organizable by some system, and is not random, chaotic, or so alien as to be incomprehensible is a large part of what we mean by feeling understood.

The remission in the Rat Man's symptoms, as Kiersky and Fosshage point out, may be attributable to the uninterpreted selfobject functions Freud performed in the course of the elaborate deciphering of his patient's obsessional symptoms and fantasies, undertaken in the context of an analytic relationship remarkable for its degree of gratification and transference enactments. It is the one case in which Freud's scrutiny and intense interest reassured, rather than intruded upon, his patient, and it is the most successful in its outcome.

Much of what has been included under the rubric of the "therapeutic alliance" consists of the patient's prideful participation as coexplorer and coexplainer of his or her psychic reality. Freud was a master at creating a sense of participation in the cutting-edge of psychoanalytic research as part of the therapeutic experience, and his charismatic involvement of his patients in his discoveries surely forged the powerful idealizing and twinship selfobject ties that overrode the empathic failures attendant on his theory-driven interpretations. The Wolf Man in particular developed a whole new psychoanalytic identity around being Freud's famous patient. The Rat Man sought out Freud after reading *The Psychopathology of Everyday Life* and eagerly provided the sexual history he thought Freud expected. Little Hans's father likewise seems to have proudly enlisted in the nascent psychoanalytic movement. Anna Ornstein describes how the misinformation eagerly imparted to Hans in the guise of the most up-to-date and scientifically correct parenting ("maybe widdlers *do* bite") may have actually worsened the boy's conflicts. The two most prominent treatment failures, those of Dora and the young homosexual woman, both involved patients who were brought to treatment under duress by their fathers. In each case Freud allowed himself to be caught up in the fathers' agenda for their daughters, who proved impervious to Freud's charisma. The young homosexual woman in particular, unimpressed by Freud's interpretative prowess, dismissed his erudite, but experience-distant and unempathic interventions with a wryly contemptuous, "How very interesting." Dora, on the other hand, seems to have felt that her father was once again passing her off to another man, the better to pursue his own affairs, and Freud's sexual inquiries were felt as intrusive rather than illuminating.

Finally, I hope that all this attention paid to Freud's limitations and the strictures placed on his therapeutics by the "time-bound elements" in his theory is seen as part of the respect we pay his legacy by continuing to grapple with it. Thus we treasure the pure gold of his psychoanalysis without being blinded by it. As Kohut (1981a) said in his last public address in Berkeley the week before he died: "Freud was a genius . . . [He] has to be respected for what he gave us, and what we can see about the shortcomings of what he did, from our vantage point. And I think that is the respectful attitude toward a genius of some time ago."

REFERENCES

Bateson, G. (1979), *Mind and Nature.* New York: Dutton.
Fish, S. (1989), Withholding the missing portion. In: *Doing What Comes Naturally.* Durham, NC: Duke University Press.
Freud, S. (1920), The psychogenesis of a case of homosexuality in a woman. *Standard Edition,* 18:145–172. London: Hogarth Press, 1955.
Goldberg, A. (1990), *The Prisonhouse of Psychoanalysis.* Hillsdale, NJ: The Analytic Press.
Grünbaum, A. (1984), *The Foundations of Psychoanalysis.* Berkeley: University of California Press.
Kohut, H. (1977), *The Restoration of the Self.* Madison, CT: International Universities Press.
_____ (1981a), On empathy. In: *The Search for the Self,* Vol. 3, ed. P. Ornstein. Madison, CT: International Universities Press.
_____ (1981b), Introspection, empathy, and the semicircle of mental health. In: *The Search for the Self,* Vol. 4, ed. P. Ornstein. Madison, CT: International Universities Press, 1991.
_____ (1984), *How Does Analysis Cure?* ed. A. Goldberg & P. Stepansky. Chicago: University of Chicago Press.
Mahony, P. (1984), *Cries of the Wolf Man.* New York: International Universities Press.
Wittgenstein, L. (1953), *Philosophical Investigations.* London: Basil Blackwell.

Marian Tolpin
THE UNMIRRORED SELF, COMPENSATORY STRUCTURE, AND CURE
The Exemplary Case of Anna O
(Studies on Hysteria, 1893–1895)

THE UNMIRRORED SELF—BREUER'S CASE HISTORY OF ANNA O

"At the time of her falling ill (in 1880) Fraulein Anna O was twenty-one years old" (Breuer and Freud, 1895, p. 21). Dr. Josef Breuer (who had probably been the family physician for several years) (Hirschmuller, 1989, p. 101) saw her in late November for an extremely intense, persistent cough, weakness, appetite loss, and anemia. Her father lay dying of a subpleural abscess or peripleuritis (the most likely cause of both at that time was tuberculosis [Hirschmuller, 1989, p. 101]). According to Breuer (Doc. 23, p. 1), the patient "compensated" for what he considered a deprived and sterile life (I discuss this point later) by "revelling in her . . . gifts of poetry and fantasy" and by "passionate fondness for her father who spoils her . . ." (cited in Hirschmuller, 1989, p. 276). Not surprisingly, then, since the night of July 17, when he became gravely ill and a surgeon operated on the abscess, Anna O, at the same time, reveled in fantasy and "devoted her whole energy to nursing [him]" (Breuer and Freud, 1895, p. 23). Now, her mother with whom she shared the nursing duties, and her dominating 20-year old brother, a law student at the University, excluded her from the sick room, declaring her too ill to continue to care for him. Soon she was excluded altogether, "suffered deeply from pining for him" (p. 283) and took to listening at his door late at night. They lied to her when he was dying and prevented her from seeing him one last time (pp. 283–284). (Their disregard of her made her feel "cheated" and alienated from mother and brother and was the precipitant of a narcissistic furor for which she required medical supervision.)

In early December, Breuer saw Anna O's condition change abruptly: "She was split into two personalities" (Breuer and Freud, 1895, p. 45); she had two distinct selves, two alternating states of consciousness. These were present side by side. One self was melancholy and anxious, but relatively normal and lucid; although she complained of profound darkness in her head, of not being able to think, of becoming blind and deaf, of having a real self and an evil self. The second self had frightening hallucinations of black snakes, was rude and naughty, "lost" time (there were gaps in her train of conscious thoughts) (p. 24), and lost the ability to think or speak in German—eventually she spoke only English, or, at times, a jargonlike mixture of the five languages she knew. In the course of treatment, Breuer learned that the multiple personality disorder and the bizarre somatiform symptoms were only apparently new. They had been present, in transient forms, since her father became acutely ill. But no one had noticed. In fact, no one had noticed her "passing into illness" for years, for lack of "solid nourishment," as Breuer saw it (Hirschmuller, 1989, p. 1).

BACK TO THE FUTURE OF PSYCHOANALYSIS

In this chapter I shall ask you to accompany me back to the future of psychoanalysis and the talking experiment that absorbed Breuer and Anna O for 18 months. The object of the journey is a reassessment of Anna O and her treatment with Breuer and of her subsequent life course. Through the lens of self psychology, the case history of Anna O exemplifies the unmirrored, or unrecognized and unvalidated, self, and the severe emotional demands, for the patient and therapist, of a not yet known transference, the selfobject transference. It is a virtual certainty that Anna O and Bertha Pappenheim, social worker and feminist reformer, were the same person (see Edinger, 1968; Jensen, 1970; Jones, 1953; Hirschmuller, 1989; for an important dissenting view see Ellenberger, 1970, 1971). We shall also revisit The Poor Breuer Myth (my name for Freud's and Jones's largely disproved accounts of the ending of the treatment and its aftermath). The case history of Anna O exemplifies a 19th-century example of the unmirrored self. Bertha Pappenheim's life course exemplifies the largely overlooked idea of compensatory structure—for example, the revitalization of childhood needs by selfobject functions; the laying down of structure, which strengthens one sector of the self in depth; and a far-reaching change in the self, which deserves to be considered a valid form of cure. The story about Breuer and his patient is an example of a defensive myth used first by Freud to affirm himself and used subsequently by generation after generation of analysts to affirm the insecurely established group-self of psychoanalysis. This study of the beginnings of psychoanalysis is not simply academic. The unmirrored (unrecognized) self is a prevalent disorder that characteristically derails adolescents' and young adults' development—it is a disorder that particularly stunts the development and consolidation of ambitions and life goals. Judging from the current psychiatric literature, florid self disorders like Anna O's are seen with increasing frequency (Kluft, 1985), while less dramatic forms, originating in chronic selfobject failures (including abuse and neglect) appear to be near epidemic. The application of the essential idea of compensatory structure holds promise for the treatment of patients with such disorders and has yet to be explored.

And now back to the future of psychoanalysis and the talking experiment. To participate vicariously with Breuer and Anna O, we shall keep one foot in the cathartic treatment that absorbed them for an entire year and a half and the other foot in highly important new information about both participants (see especially Hirschmuller's 1989, recent work) and self-psychological insights into the conditions necessary for revitalization of the self.

THE TALKING EXPERIMENT

What Breuer Saw in Anna O

My reassessment of Anna O and Breuer is based mainly on his two case histories, both remarkable sources of primary clinical data. The first, unfinished (in Hirschmuller, 1989, pp. 276–292), was found by Ellenberger (1972) in the hospital file of Bertha Pappenheim at Bellevue Sanitarium, Kreutzlingen, where Breuer arranged for her to be admitted on July 12, 1882. It contains Breuer's views on the family dynamics and their bearing on the illness; Breuer had deleted this material from the later version, probably for reasons of confidentiality. The therapeutic action of catharsis, as Breuer saw it in 1880, was to get affects unstuck, to rid the psyche of excessive quantities of excitement and "imaginative products," which were traumatic unless discharged. To do this, Breuer prompted the patient when she went into an autohypnotic state and he heard her muttering. He echoed her words, and she began to narrate stories to him. The second case history, based on the first, is the more extensive and more theoretical version (it includes the hypnoid hypothesis), written approximately 11 years later. It is the well-known chapter by Breuer in *Studies on Hysteria*. In many ways the published case is more difficult and much more confusing because it is more theoretical and was written at a time when both Breuer and Freud were stumbling around in the dark.

This is what Breuer saw in his patient: she had a powerful intellect that was deprived of the "solid nourishment" ("mental pabulum") it needed by limited educational opportunities (her formal schooling ended at 16) and by her restrictive, "puritanical parents" (her father, the founder of a *shul* in Vienna, required her to adhere to his strict form of Orthodox Judaism); her "serious" mother could not respond to her daughter's vitality, was hypochondriacal about her health after the loss of two other daughters to tuberculosis years earlier, and could not be an alternative to the more dominant father. Breuer told the director of the hospital where she was to be admitted that she was confined to doing "excessively regimented lessons" on how to be a Jewish homemaker, which offered no outlet for her natural vitality; "*she sought compensation in passionate fondness for her father, who spoiled her and revelled in her highly developed gifts of poetry and fantasy*" (see case history compiled by Breuer, and the report of her treatment in Bellevue Sanitarium, in Hirschmuller, 1989, p. 276; italics added). Breuer's view of the unmirrored self could not be more different from Freud's: where Freud saw repressed sexuality in Anna O, in his young women patients like Dora, the 18-year-old he described in "A Case of Homosexuality in a Woman" (Freud, 1920), and in his daughter Anna, Breuer saw thwarted needs for what he described impressionistically as "solid nourishment." (Since Kohut's work we have known that psychological "nourishment" consists of the whole variety of parents'/others' selfobject functions that fit together with a growing child's valid self needs. For example, Anna O needed the gleam in a parent's eye that would validate her capacities and foster her making use of these for self-fulfillment.)

While Anna O outwardly complied with her father's wishes and devoted herself to trying to please him, she was inwardly irreligious. Silently she opposed his orthodoxy and struggled against his goals for her. A passionate relationship with him, an attempt to make up for the lack of ingredients to grow, "replaced" her capacity to fall in love and accounted for her sexuality remaining "astonishingly undeveloped" (cf. her later views on the strictures placed on a Jewish girl whose parents expected her happiness to come from being married and carrying on Orthodox traditions for women in Edinger, 1968). In her private theater she was continuously absorbed in living out fairy tales to embellish her monotonous life as she went about her chores as a future (Orthodox) homemaker. Everyone thought she was attending because she discharged her household duties and was always alert when she was spoken to. No one was aware of her daydreaming. In fact no one was aware of her thwarted needs and the measures she took to try to enliven herself.

For all that, Breuer also saw a young woman who was good natured, had a lively compassion (Hirschmuller, 1989, p. 277); was energetic, tenacious, and persistent (sometimes reaching the point of obstinacy, which gave way only out of kindness and regard for other people [Breuer and Freud, 1895, p. 21]); and possessed a critical common sense that made her completely unsuggestible and only willing to listen to arguments: He saw "essential character traits," "like capacities to greatly assist herself by being able to look after . . . poor, sick people" (p. 21). Breuer was certain, especially after the treatment with him ended, that her good natured, lively compassion "is the drive she needs to exercise at the earliest" and that nursing and caring for others would benefit her.

Anna O's lonely absorption in the private theater in which she lived her invented life was replaced by the unseen, not-yet-known transference to the willing audience. Breuer, the eminent internist and experimental scientist, now looked with the keenest interest at the most microscopic details about her inner life. He was fascinated by the new set of unfathomed data he was collecting by listening to this highly intelligent, articulate, and expressive young woman talk to him *about* her symptoms. Without knowing it, he and his listening created a climate of selfobject functions that temporarily provided the stunted self of his patient with oxygen. An essential part of the climate that led to the transference was his enthusiasm about the very attributes of the patient's self that were destined, much later and in a very different life context, to be reorganized in a transformation from paralyzed self to pioneering social worker, feminist, and social reformer (see Schonbar and Beatus, 1990). At the same time, Breuer was fostering a selfobject transference that was bound to be traumatically disrupted. Every time he went away or every time the patient was injured by her mother and her brother, her newly improving cohesion was once again disrupted. She was not only addicted to Breuer's cohesion-fostering functions, she was also literally addicted to the chloral he used to calm her down when she was in a narcissistic furor. (She was also to become addicted to the morphine he used when she developed convulsions. The etiology of the convulsions is unclear. She also had a recurrence of an earlier trigeminal neuralgia.)

The Not-Known Transference: Symptomatic Improvements and Traumatic Disruptions

The treatment was the source of the clinical data that led Breuer to his view of the patient's disorder. This is how the catharsis went: every day, in Breuer's presence and in a regular order, Anna O went into a somnolent state in the afternoon; after sunset she went into deep autohypnosis; then, when he echoed her "mutterings," she narrated stories or described her self-states, physical symptoms, and hallucinations. The routine was unvarying, for the most part, for 18 months—the same cycle was repeated day after day, except during a four-month confinement under medical supervision.

"Getting affects unstuck" by narrating her stories, talking about her symptoms and the feelings connected with their onset had a truly astonishing therapeutic action for Anna O: the state of her selves and her symptoms changed: when she fell into her autohypnotic state and told Breuer sad, often charming, fairy-tale-like "stories" about herself once removed—a girl sitting by a sick-bed—her speech gradually went from multilingual jargon to correct speech, and she finally awoke, calmed down and comfortable. When Breuer recognized that her symptoms made psychological sense and he "guessed," to cite one of many examples, that she had become mute and then aphasic because she was "greatly offended" and "mortified" by a "scolding" from her father, he insisted that she talk about the injury. "She was then better able to speak, though only in English, without knowing she was doing so. This happened at the same time as the return of movement to the left extremities" (Hirschmuller, 1989, p. 282; also see Greenson, 1950, on the inability to use the mother tongue). Breuer also understood that she had withdrawn because of the narcissistic injury, and he decided not to ask after her father any more.

With Breuer as resonating witness to her narcissistic injuries, balm for her terror and dread that her father was going to die, oxygen for her depletion depression, glue for her fragmentation (dissociation), Anna's symptoms abated. After four months of treatment (four days before her father's death on April 5, 1881), she got out of bed. She was no longer completely paralyzed; she no longer had to lift her head manually; she was able to walk. Her mother and brother, however, excluded her and lied to her and deceived her at the time of her father's death. She went into a dissociated state of narcissistic rage and despair and was alienated from everyone but Breuer. She grew worse with one of his brief absences and when he brought in a consultant (to whom he showed off her linguistic abilities in her dissociated state). Breuer did not deceive her, but on June 7, 1881, an important date for the patient, he forcibly removed her from home and had her confined under medical supervision near a sanitarium at Inzersdorf.

This is how it went for the whole of the 18 months. The patient's recovery from her agitated, dissociated states, and her symptomatic improvement, depended wholly on her talking to Breuer. At Inzersdorf, Breuer could see Anna O only every third or fourth day (visits necessitated a trip from Vienna). The transference disruption was, however, eventually repaired by his visits, and the improvement that came with talking to him was reestablished as part of a regular three- or four-day cycle: After his visits she was calm; the next day she was agreeable, easy to manage, industrious, and even cheerful; on the second day she was increasingly moody and contrary; and on the third day she was worse yet. The dramatic link between talking and her improvement was noted by the patient herself—she called the experiment the "talking cure" (Breuer and Freud, 1895, p. 30) (Jokingly, she also called it "chimney sweeping.")

The transference was disrupted again when Breuer took a five-week summer holiday in 1881. On his return, Anna O was "wretched, inert, unamenable, ill-tempered, even malicious" (p. 31). With the idea of providing a release for affects by making up for lost time, the talking treatment was intensified: Breuer brought her back to Vienna for a week in the autumn (the family had moved after the father's death) and then permanently. It is now known that he wanted to hospitalize her again (Hirschmuller, 1989); his feel of overburdenness may have intensified from this point on (see Breuer's own account in Cranefield, 1958).

In December, 1881 (the anniversary of the day she took to bed in 1880), Anna O and Breuer began to talk twice a day, morning and evening, so that she could go through a "year of re-living" the affects that had accumulated before her treatment with Breuer began. In a unique fragmentation (dissociation) in time and space one self lived in the present and one self lived out again, day by day, everything that had happened to her and all her symptomatic responses during her father's illness. Now it was the patient who insisted on getting back to the origin of every one of her attacks of blindness, deafness, hallucinations, and speech disorganization. With the reliving of the illnesses, her father's and her own, the transference to Breuer intensified even more.

The reliving was exhaustive and exhausting. To do it they hit on a new method of working together that became another unchanging daily routine. For the first time in the treatment, Breuer hypnotized the willing patient in the morning so that she could concentrate her thoughts on the symptom "we were treating at the moment." She told of all the occasions on which it had appeared (p. 36), rapidly and under brief headings. He took notes. "During her subsequent evening hypnosis she would then, with the help of my notes, give me a fairly detailed account of these circumstances" (p. 36). For example, Breuer would actually count up all the instances when the patient did not hear when she was spoken to.

> Not hearing when someone came in, while her thoughts were abstracted. 108 special detailed instances . . , mentioning the persons and circumstances, often with dates. One of the instances of deafness was when she thought her father was choking to death; one was when her brother found her listening at her father's door at night—she was pining for him—and her brother shook her. The first instance of deafness was not hearing her father come in [p. 36].

Their lists of when, where, how, with whom the symptoms occurred were truly exhaustive. It is not an exaggeration to say that the patient was addicted to Breuer's functions—he had replaced her father.

All the symptoms were traced back, including the very first set of symptoms, which appeared on the night of July 17, 1880, when her somnolent father appeared to be dying and she waited with him for the surgeon to come. With the reliving of that scene she was cured—her hallucinations were gone, and so was her inability to think and talk in German. (The dissociation helped her to remove herself from her dread that her father would die.) The treatment ended on June 7, 1882, by mutual consent (Breuer and Freud, 1895). Not unexpectedly, Anna O's vulnerability to disruptions in her tie to Breuer was greater than ever after the year of reliving.

In fact, the treatment did not end when Breuer said it did. The ending repeated the many earlier disruptions of the patient's unseen transference tie, now with an added factor: she was addicted to the morphine given her for convulsions. Although Breuer was definitely overburdened (Cranefield, 1958)—the treatment was too much for a general practitioner of medicine—he did not run away to Venice with a jealous wife and conceive a baby there on a second honeymoon, as Freud, and Jones (1953) embroidering Freud's myth, had it. Breuer corresponded with the director of the sanitarium where he arranged to send his patient (she was not admitted until July 12). In his letters he described her agitation, semiparanoid symptoms, convulsions, morphine addiction, and delirium tremens when he withdrew chloral.

In other words, Breuer continued to function as a conscientious physician until Anna O traveled to the Bellevue Sanitarium in Kreuzlingen, Switzerland where she remained for three months, until October 29, 1882. Breuer sent his case report as soon as she was admitted. On the way there she stopped to visit her maternal aunt, first cousin, and a distant cousin in Karlsruhe. Alienated still from her mother, she was accompanied by her cousins to Bellevue. She required chloral and morphine for her continuing addiction. She also continued to have dissociated states and "time missing," especially when her head hit the pillow. She no longer talked in German.

THE POOR BREUER MYTH

Why was Breuer so interested in his young woman patient? The answer Freud reconstructed retrospectively, five decades after Breuer had treated Anna O, accorded with his views of the nuclear oedipal complex as the chief motive force in development, a theory under siege at the time. Thus, relying on the theory that he was trying to preserve, Freud reconstructed an unconscious sexual (oedipal) transference to Breuer, Breuer's unconscious sexual (oedipal) countertransference to the patient, and an interruption precipitated by fear of sexuality and an oedipal baby fantasy (see Freud, 1932, pp. 412–413; for his earlier published references, see Freud, 1914, 1924). Everything fit together—Breuer had terminated the treatment, panicked, and fled when called back to find the patient in a hysterical labor; he later was reluctant to publish the case and collaborate on *Studies on Hysteria* and finally turned away from the truths about sexuality and denied and abandoned Freud and the field of psychoanalysis he had helped to create.

Jones (1953) embroidered Freud's reconstruction with a fanciful account of his own. His myth is complete with jealous wife, panic and flight, a second honeymoon in Venice, where a baby girl was supposedly conceived and was said to have committed suicide in New York 60 years later, and so on. (For more complete accounts, see Ellenberger, 1970, 1972; Reeves, 1982; Hirschmuller, 1989; for transmission of the myth in popular lore, see Freeman, 1972.)

The facts are these: The Breuers' baby, Dora, was born in March 1882, three months before the reported end of Anna O's treatment; Breuer vacationed with his family near Vienna that year; Dora took poison when the Gestapo came for her in 1936 and she died in a Viennese hospital; and so on with all the elements of the myth that have been disproven. Freud's "guess" about a pregnancy fantasy, "long after the break" in his relations with Breuer, can neither be proved nor disproved. However, this much is certain: it is highly unlikely that Breuer would have been surprised by an erotized reaction of the patient to her physician. The phenomenon of erotization of the relationship to hypnotists was so common in Vienna in the early part of the 19th century that a commission had been appointed to investigate the phenomenon, and hypnosis had come into disfavor. (Hirschmuller, 1989; Ellenberger, 1970). It was just beginning to become scientifically respectable again in 1880.

The "Poor Breuer Myth" affirmed Freud and minimized Breuer at a crucial time in psychoanalytic history—Freud was very near the end of his career; the first questions about the psychology of women, which he had formulated with his "eager band of collaborators," were being raised, only for him to dismiss them; and his whole concept of oedipal development was being challenged. Jones, who questioned Freud's psychology of girls' development in the 1930s, later became the faithful biographer in the 1950s and embroidered the myth into the version analysts still learn at their collective mother's knee, so to speak. In Jones's hands, Freud's reconstruction became a myth that acts as a kinship bond to affirm the insecurely established group-self of psychoanalysis. Prior to the publication of Hirschmuller's (1989) work on Breuer (first published in German, 1978), virtually every psychoanalytic study of Anna O, Breuer, and the relationship of Breuer and Freud was based on unquestioning acceptance of the Poor Breuer Myth. (Some examples are the influential methodological studies of Gedo et al., 1964.)

The Freud–Jones myth left no room for three potent reasons for Breuer's reluctance to publish the case: he knew the patient had not been well for many years; there was a problem of confidentiality—the family was well known and it was well known that he made daily visits from 1880 to 1882; and he was too skeptical to accept Freud's overgeneralizations and premature closure on theoretical matters (sexuality was not one of them). Breuer also had three characteristics that possibly constituted the chief motive force for the talking experiment with Anna O: his scientific curiosity about her remarkable pathology; his enthusiasm about what Kohut (in Miller, 1985) described as "the leading edge," the health, of the personality; and powerful personal motives that belonged to his own self-development—he deplored the orthodox upbringing that had deprived her of what she needed. Perhaps he needed to save the unmirrored self from psychological undernourishment. (I shall come back to the significance of the *ad hominem* myth in my conclusion.)

Summing Up

Long before her acute illness, Anna O had responded to her neglected girlhood needs to be an independent center of her own initiative much as Mr. Z (Kohut, 1979) responded to thwarted boyhood needs a century later. She all but relinquished her own needs. Instead of being able to pursue her own ambitions and goals and to use her skills and talents, she was organized around her father's desires. Her normal needs (the leading edge of her development) atrophied by nonrecognition. Now her need was to "embellish" herself, first by satisfying her father and his strict Orthodox requirements that she learn to be a Jewish homemaker (she did this entirely by rote while she was inwardly oppositional) and be happy by being married (she turned away from this goal of her father's altogether); and second by constructing a fantasy life in which to construct a self, so to speak. Fragmented and disrupted by her father's illness, organized around him as she was, excluded from his presence during the illness, and without goals after his death, the paralyzed self had no place to go.[1] After the cathartic treatment ended she still had no place to go. In the hospital, however, she formulated a plan to take a nursing course and prepare herself for purposeful work in accord with her ideals (Hirschmuller, 1989). On discharge from the sanitarium, she returned to her relatives in Karlsruhe, where she saw the impressive social welfare programs of the Baden Women's Union and took the nursing course. She did not complete it and did not return for the practicum. In Karlsruhe, she was also encouraged by her cousin to become a writer. It is now known that three more hospitalizations occurred between 1883 and 1887. For the rest, there is a complete gap in her history until November 1988. Edinger (1968) believes that Bertha Pappenheim herself destroyed the records when the Nazis invaded the family home.

---

[1] In the throes of her severest periods of disintegration she was beset by hallucinatory fragmentation products. Magid (this volume) suggests that these images symbolized her ambivalent relationship with her father. For example, the images of her fingers becoming snakes' heads and the appearance of the death's head in the mirror possibly reflected the unmanageable anger she felt toward her beloved father, who was also her oppressor. In my view, the images may also symbolize intolerable thoughts, such as the needed father's impending death, which were warded off and returned as "fragmentation products." There is no doubt that she was enraged at her mother and brother (see, for example Hirschmuller, 1989, p. 285); and that anger at her father when she felt *slighted* by him led to her mutism, for example.

COMPENSATORY STRUCTURE AND CURE—THE ESTABLISHMENT OF AN INDEPENDENT SELF

After reassessing Breuer's case histories, it does not come as a complete surprise that the eventual strengthening of his former patient's fragmentation-prone self took place in a world of people with accessible selfobject functions with whom she established rich and varied bonds. During the next 40 years of her life, she formed self-selfobject ties with members of her mother's large, extended family, some of whom became very close friends as well as supporters; homeless Eastern European Jews; two idealizable women; her grown "daughters" (orphans she raised who became her students and coworkers); Orthodox rabbis who sided with her; educational and spiritual leaders like Martin Buber; and, finally, Orthodox rabbis and businessmen who opposed her. The experiences she had with them resonated with the deepest layers of her psyche, with her injured self, as well as with her still-remaining healthy needs for recognition and ideals. The emotional burdens of an undiscovered transference, on both the patient and the therapist, did not disrupt the bonds she formed. There was time for Bertha Pappenheim to make the functions of the bonds into inner supports of her own.

The Self in the World of Selfobjects

In November 1888, when she was 29 years old, Bertha Pappenheim and her mother resettled in Frankfurt on Main, the city where Recha Goldschmidt Pappenheim had been born and raised. As far as is known, Bertha had recovered from her addiction and was reconciled with her mother. There were no overt manifestations of her dissociative disorder or the conversion symptoms, nor would there be for the rest of the long and meaningful life she lived in and near Frankfurt until her death in 1936. (While Bertha was hospitalized at Bellevue her mother recognized that her daughter's life would have to change; see Hirschmuller, 1989). The two women lived together until Recha's death in 1905. The possessions they brought with them and trips back for the opera and theater linked them to their former life in Vienna (Bertha supported a musically gifted child so that he could pursue an artistic career). In Frankfurt they lived a gracious life, close to Recha's very large, extended family.

The Goldschmidts were wealthy German Jews, proud of their cultural achievements, who traced their roots in Frankfurt to the 17th century.[2] The women were highly developed in exactly the areas where their Viennese relative was stunted: they had strong values and a strong sense of purpose. They accepted Bertha as one of them—they appreciated her typical Viennese charm, wit, and gaiety, although some thought her "spoiled." Bertha, for her part, became involved in their interests and activities, especially in the German feminist movement of the time, which promoted education as the path to women's liberation; and in social welfare work, especially with the steady stream of displaced European Jews who flooded Frankfurt before the first world war. In the feminist literature she exposed her to she found guides she could look up to and emulate. In the refugees she found alter egos, people like herself; she made empathic contact with them by speaking Yiddish (a language many of her assimilated relatives did not know) and became more and more interested in their plight. Forming an alter ego bond with an injured self in need of restoration, she began to expand herself and her horizons. In effect she was on a compensatory pathway for self-restoration.

In their mirroring and alter ego aspects, then, the Goldschmidt women, as well as the refugees, were the spark for the education of Bertha Pappenheim. The manifest contents of her education—reading, writing, and social work—were accompanied by gradual, inner changes in the self of the young woman who had been at once indulged and pampered and deprived of what she actually needed. In a world with enough nutriment, the capacities Breuer described—her penetrating intellect, quick grasp and intuition, her imaginative and poetic gifts, her language skills, her common sense, energy, will power, obstinacy, and oppositionalism—were liberated and "bubbled-up."

To put what "bubbled-up" means in theoretical terms: With authentic responsiveness to girlhood needs, the stunted poles of the unmirrored self (the pole of ambitions expressed in the "private theater" and the pole of ideals expressed in directionless goals to help the poor and sick) were first revitalized, then joined to unused skills and talents, and finally transformed.

Reading, Writing, and Social Work—Revitalization of Ambitions and Ideals

In the first decade in Frankfurt, Bertha Pappenheim volunteered in soup kitchens, worked in an orphanage, began organizing construc-

---

[2]Unless otherwise noted the following is based on Edinger's (1968) biographical sketch and some published letters, writings, and essays of Bertha Pappenheim's.

tive social programs like those she saw in Karlsruhe, and read feminist literature. She also took the advice of her writer-cousin who liked her fairy stories (like those she told Breuer) and passed through a sort of belated adolescent spell of creativity: she used her "poetic and imaginative gifts" to write fiction. She published the little stories for children she had read to her cousin after her discharge from Kreutzlingen (Hirschmuller, 1989), another series of sad stories for children, *In the Rummage Store* (1890), and a play called *Women's Rights,* (published in 1899 when she was 40 years old), part melodrama, part feminist tract. The stereotypic plot concerns women victimized by men and their attempt at mastery.

I believe that Bertha's fiction was a continuation of, and successor to, Anna O's "private theater" where the unmirrored self tried to embellish itself. That is, her fiction, like her fantasy life, was a part of the split off, unresponded-to self that passed over into a dissociative illness when her father became ill and she had no purposes of her own. For Bertha, writing fiction was in a developmental line of mirroring needs that did not undergo extensive transformation. Fantasy was used "defensively," in Kohut's (1977) sense, to stimulate and revive her failing (unmirrored) self. Perhaps the mirroring needs could not be revived in depth; perhaps her talents lay elsewhere. In any event, her poetic and imaginative gifts did not lead to structure formation. Rather, it seems likely that she did not experience either her fantasies or her fiction as fully her (self) and, hence, that neither became part of the strengthened and restored sector of the self that became an unrolling path. Unable to reestablish herself through fiction, she changed direction: "A self that had been threatened in one sector . . . managed to survive by shifting its psychological point of gravity toward another one" (Kohut, 1977, p. 83).

In fact, the self and its energies changed direction: she herself and her writings began to undergo an inner transformation as she went from her stage in the private theater to the stage of life in pre-World War 1 Germany. The shift was effected with the help of two idealizable women she found in a past she shared with the feminists. She could idealize, emulate, and metabolize those women into her own self protein, so to speak. Through her extensive reading of the feminist literature, Bertha became acquainted with Mary Godwin Wollstonecraft's *A Vindication of the Rights of Women* (1792), and through Wollstonecraft she came to a 17th-century ancestor of the Goldschmidts, a woman from the ghetto who left memoirs (Memoirs of Gluckel von Hameln 1689–1719; see Pollock, 1971) intended for generations of her family to come. Gluckel von Hameln's memoirs were compelling to Wollstonecraft and other feminists. She was the rare person of her times who overcame the restrictions that ghetto life imposed on women: she was educated, capable, the equal of her husband and his partner in business. The caring mother of 12 children, she carried on successfully, as mother and businesswoman, after her husband's death. In short, through Mary Wollstonecraft, the woman who founded feminism on the ideal of equality and mutuality between men and women, Bertha Pappenheim made empathic contact with a relative of hers who was an idealizable, independent self. Although Gluckel was "liberated," she was also a pious Orthodox Jew. The father ideal, which could not be made into a viable self, was exchanged for another.

The inner work that transformed Anna O's unformed goals into the idealized goals that gave direction and meaning to Bertha Pappenheim's subsequent life course went on in this way. First, she immersed herself in the lives of Mary Wollstonecraft, Gluckel, and other ghetto women of the Jewish past. Second, she placed her unused linguistic skills in the service of consolidating her emerging ideals (recall that Anna O spoke four or five languages, in jargon, during her illness). She translated Wollstonecraft, Gluckel, and the old documents about women's life in the ghetto into German. Hers was the first German translation of Wollstonecraft, published in 1899; and the first German translation, in 1910, from Gluckel's Judisch-Deutsch Middle High German, the precursor of modern Yiddish (Pollock, 1971). Third, she made a study of the old documents on ghetto life (she had been led to them by the *Memoirs*) and made the stunning discovery that the status of Jewish women and the prejudices against them were remnants of Jewish polygamy and the laws governing it (Edinger, 1968).

In particular, Bertha Pappenheim found that three groups of the refugees were unprotected and vulnerable because of still-existing Jewish law. Homeless, stateless teenage girls, pregnant teenagers and their babies, and unmarried women were protected neither by state authorities nor the Jewish community (in Russia and Turkey) and were thus fair game for sale to procurers for the flourishing prostitution industry in Europe and South America. The *Augunah,* Jewish women abandoned by their husbands, could not obtain a Jewish divorce and remarry unless they could present proof to the rabbis of their husband's death; unable to remarry and with no work they were also especially vulnerable to recruitment as prostitutes.

Finally, Bertha strengthened herself by playing dress up, so to speak: enacting a gross identification, she commissioned a portrait of herself, dressed as Gluckel, entitled "Bertha Pappenheim as Gluckel." She was in the process of laying down compensatory structure, becoming the independent, educated, caring, enterprising, Orthodox womanly self she wanted to be (like). In 1899, the year the feminist play was published, Bertha Pappenheim published the first translation in German of *On The Vindication of the Rights of Women,* the next year she published her first essay on *The Jewish Problem in Galicia,* a subject that would take her farther away from her parents and their values and goals than they could ever have imagined (see Pappenheim in Edinger, 1968). These publications are markers of the inner changes leading to a narcissistic transformation not mentioned per se by Kohut: a gradually deepening sense of justice.

An Independent Self

Both of the women she idealized were a powerful influence on the growth and reshaping of Bertha Pappenheim's lived-out goals. From Mary Wollstonecraft came the vision of mutuality and of men and women sharing equal responsibility to establish a just society (Edinger, 1968, pp. 16–17), and Bertha forged a National Association of Jewish Women, to work side by side with Catholic and Protestant women's organizations. (As its president she could be difficult, dictatorial, and impetuous when slighted.) From Gluckel came an intensification of Bertha's investment of herself in the orphaned children she initially worked with, the teenagers and their babies, and women who were deprived of rights and ignored by Jewish civil law. She established a residential home for delinquent and disturbed teenagers at Isenburg (a small town near Frankfurt), the first of its kind in Germany, and later expanded it to include pregnant teenagers, in spite of opposition from reactionary rabbis. However, by no means was she simply an adversary of the Orthodox rabbis. There were rabbis who supported her and with whom she allied herself, and she idealized Rabbi Gershon, who ended Jewish polygamy in 1000 A.D.. Spurred by her recognition of the need the refugees had for restoration of pride and self sufficiency, she nurtured programs that provided educational opportunities, social and recreational activities, and vocational rehabilitation. She organized training programs in modern social worker methods. Later, as the Nazi threat grew, she taught social work ethics in the school founded by Buber and Rosenszweig.

The twinship ties with teenagers deepened. (She lived near the Isenburg home and actively participated in the young women's development there for the rest of her life; a lecture series commemorates her work at Isenburg [Hirschmuller, 1989].) As the refugees continued to pour into Frankfurt, she grew more and more concerned with the conditions that had uprooted young people and their families. Through empathic contact with the uprooted young women who were another version of herself, she expanded herself and her work further. She began her investigations in Russia and Poland and eventually traveled farther, at times alone, to Palestine, Turkey, and Egypt. Her writings now concerned her investigations and social concerns: from all the countries mentioned she sent letters to her world, her audience of "daughters" and subscribers who supported her work. Eventually her investigations brought her face to face with social evils she had seen only from afar: she confronted wealthy Jews with financial interests in obtaining young women for brothels and eventually played a role in international conferences with colleagues who were trying to deal with the selling of women into prostitution (see Bristow, 1983).

Nowhere are the limitations of Freud's view of the Anna O case and his theories about girls' development (and the reductionistic application of these theories) more evident than in the most frequent explanations of Bertha Pappenheim's growing sense of justice, the direction of her work, and her capacity to live in opposition. These limited views are exemplified in Karpe (1961), who concludes that she lived out her life rescuing women who did what she dared not do—who became whores, flaunted their sexual desires, and got pregnant. While it is impossible here to review the volumes written on this case, it is an embarrassment for psychoanalysis that Freud's reconstruction of the pregnancy fantasy and Karpe's reduction of Bertha Pappenheim's values and ideals to her presumed repressed sexuality have remained so generally and uncritically accepted. More than anything else, Bertha Pappenheim's feminism and social work was the expression of an independent self, which she belatedly established in a world with enough psychological oxygen to revitalize her girlhood needs.

Bertha Pappenheim's stubborn opposition to both parents' restricting goals for her preserved the tendrils of independence that were finally validated and strengthened by her ties to idealizable women of the past and by her mirroring and twinship bonds. Her essential character traits—obstinacy, perseverance, tenacious will power, kindness, and regard for others—formed an amalgam that consolidated the self in one sector: she thrived now by fighting for what she believed in, by opposing the defenders of a status quo that consigned women to the fate she knew well from her own experience: the unrecognized women with no rights were extensions of her own unmirrored self. The Orthodox rabbis who stigmatized children born out of wedlock, who turned their backs on teenagers and abandoned women, and the Jewish financial backers of prostitution who callously exploited them were her adversarial selfobjects. (There were other Orthodox rabbis who were her allies and she idealized Rabbi Gershom, "who, in 1000 A.D., began to end Jewish polygamy and its evil effects" [Wolf, A. in Edinger, 1968]). She was well aware that her adversaries had an energizing, strengthening function for her. "I think contact with adversaries gives more strength and energy than contact with congenial people" (quoted in Freeman, 1972, p. 19); and she was well aware of another of their functions, "I have often thought that if one has nothing to love, to hate something is a good substitute" (letter from Warsaw, May 10, 1912, quoted in Edinger, 1968, p. 47). The wrath of the "frail girl" Breuer (Breuer and Freud, 1895) described, the young woman who rescued a helpless cat from a powerful Newfoundland dog at Inzersdorf (p. 31), was joined to her sense of justice and rechanneled: she was the "splendid" rescuer Breuer saw, now with a much larger purpose.

Psychoanalysis Without Utopia

The restoration of Bertha Pappenheim's self took place gradually through the establishment of selfobject bonds that anchored and strengthened her and catalyzed a transformation of stunted ambitions and ideals into adult values and goals and a sense of justice. The transformations do not satisfy analytic theories of cure, which, soaked with hidden value judgments, require linear progression, for example, from pregenitality to postambivalent genitality and heterosexual object love; from oneness with others to wholeness through resolution of ambivalence and separation. In fact, Bertha Pappenheim's recovery, in the course of her long life, did not entirely satisfy her either—she was both heartened and saddened when she reflected on how far she had gone from her parents' outlook (Edinger, 1968); and she lamented the lack of a personal love in her life and that she had no children of her own. The main point about the restoration of the self by the laying down of compensatory structure is that we do not want to formulate an ideal goal, a psychoanalytic utopia (Erikson, 1950, originally discussed genitality as psychoanalytic utopia).

> We do not formulate a norm for (analytic) cure derived from (Freudian, Kleinian, Mahlerian, Kohutian) theory. There are many good lives that cannot be defined by such norms. There are many good lives, and some great and most fulfilled, not lived by individuals who (for example) were heterosexual [Kohut, 1984, p. 7].

The Unmirrored Self

All the original aspects of the nuclear self are not re-mobilized—"cure" is no more and no less than the establishment of at least one durable sector of the self in depth, at least one channel for a life lived with meaning.

In a fascinating act of ironic self-contemplation, Breuer's former patient wrote five obituaries for herself in 1934 when she learned she was dying of stomach cancer, one each for an Orthodox publication, *Family News,* a German-Jewish paper, a Zionist review, and the Women's Federation she founded. The one for the Orthodox paper went like this: "She was by descent and training an Orthodox woman, she believed herself separated from her roots—obviously under revolutionary feminist influence—She was often hostile—but did not defy her origins. With her descent she should have done more for Orthodoxy—let us remember that her father was a co-founder of the Schiffschul at Vienna. What a pity!" The essence of her self-recognition was that she did not please any group enough: the members of each group wanted her to be more like them! "Yet," she wrote, "she remained consciously outside our ranks because she sternly rejected ideas she did not like." And so each obituary ended with the same refrain, half-defiant, half-resigned: "What a pity!" (Edinger, 1968, p. 99). Clearly by this time in her life course, like it or not, Bertha Pappenheim was an independent self.

In my view, some of the causes Bertha stubbornly fought for were guided by mistaken views—she held views that are not enough like mine! For example, worried that the personal dimension in care for others would be lost, she fought for volunteer social workers instead of professional; she fought against efforts to resettle teenagers in Israel and against Zionism, in a mistaken assessment of the danger Hitler presented, which she shared with most other German and Austrian Jews. (She believed that families needed to be kept together, and that German culture should not be exchanged for Zionist hardships.) In the end she had the grace to recognize that she had been tragically wrong about the Nazis. She overexalted motherhood to the point that, although she fought against stigmatization of unwed mothers and their children, she opposed abortion. In response to my admixture of admiration for her inner psychological achievements and my disappointment in some of her stands, she would probably say, "What a pity!"

One of Bertha Pappenheim's last acts was a personally courageous encounter with the Gestapo. A worker in the Isenburg home reported her because one of the mentally retarded girls said that Hitler looked like a criminal. The Gestapo accepted her calm explanation that no one could be held responsible for the words of a mentally deficient child and let her go (Edinger, 1968, p. 21). An example of Kohut's Tragic Woman, as well as an "uncommonly instructive and scientifically important" (Breuer, quoted in Cranefield, 1958, p. 319) example of the unmirrored self and compensatory structure and cure, Bertha Pappenheim died on May 28, 1936, before all she had built, and many of the young women she had loved and trained, were destroyed in the Holocaust.

REFERENCES

Breuer, J. & Freud, S. (1893–1895), *Studies on Hysteria. Standard Edition*, 2:21–47. London: Hogarth Press, 1955.
Bristow, E. J. (1983), *Prostitution and Prejudice.* New York: Oxford University Press.
Cranefield, P. F. (1958), Josef Breuer's evaluation of his contribution to psychoanalysis. *Internat. J. Psycho-Anal.,* 39:319–32.
Edinger, D. (1968), *Bertha Pappenheim.* Highland Park, IL: Congregation Solel.
Ellenberger, H. F. (1970), *The Discovery of the Unconscious.* New York: Basic Books.
_____ (1972), The story of "Anna O": A critical review with new data. *J. Hist. Behav. Sci.,* 8:267–279.
Erikson, E. (1950), *Childhood and Society.* New York: Norton, 1963.
Freeman, L. (1972), *The Story of Anna O.* New York: Walker.
Freud, S. (1914), On the history of the psycho-analytic movement. *Standard Edition,* 14:3–66. London: Hogarth Press, 1957.
_____ (1920), The psychogenesis of a case of homosexuality in a woman. *Standard Edition,* 18:145–174. London: Hogarth Press, 1955.
_____ (1924), An autobiographical study. *Standard Edition,* 20:3–74. London: Hogarth Press, 1959.
_____ (1932), In: *The Letters of Sigmund Freud, 1873–1939,* ed. E. Freud. New York: Basic Books, 1960.
Greenson, R. R. (1950), The mother tongue and the mother. *Internat. J. Psycho-Anal.,* 31:18–23.
Gedo, J. E., Sabshin, M., Sadow, L. & Schlesinger, N. (1964), "Studies on hysteria": A methodological evaluation. *J. Amer. Psychoanal. Assn.,* 12:734–751.
Hirschmuller, A. (1989), *The Life and Work of Josef Breuer.* New York: New York University Press.
Jensen, E. M. (1970), Anna O—A study of her later life. *J. Amer. Psychoanal. Assn.,* 39:269–293.
Jones, E. (1953), *The Life and Work of Sigmund Freud,* Vol. 1. New York: Basic Books, pp. 245–248.
Karpe, R. (1961), The rescue complex in Anna O's final identity. *Psychoanal. Quart.,* 30:1–27.
Kluft, R. P. (1985), *Childhood Antecedents of Multiple Personality.* Washington, DC: American Psychiatric Association Press.
Kohut, H. (1977), *The Restoration of the Self.* New York: International Universities Press.
_____ (1979), The two analyses of Mr. Z. *Internat. J. Psycho-Anal.,* 60:3–27.
_____ (1984), *How Does Analysis Cure?* ed. A. Goldberg & P. Stepansky. Chicago: University of Chicago Press.

Miller, J. P. (1985), How Kohut actually worked. *Progress in Self Psychology*, Vol. 1, ed. R. Goldberg. New York: Guilford Press.

Pollock, G. H. (1971), Gluckel von Hameln: Bertha Pappenheim's idealized ancestor. *Amer. Imago,* 8:216–227.

Reeves, C. (1982), Breuer, Freud, and the case of Anna O.: A re-examination. *J. Child Psychotherapy,* 8:203–214.

Schonbar, R. & Beatus, H. R. (1990), The mysterious metamorphoses of Bertha Pappenheim: Anna O revisited. *Psychoanal. Psychol.,* 7:59–78.

Paul H. Ornstein
DID FREUD UNDERSTAND DORA?
Fragment of an Analysis of a Case of Hysteria (1905)

WHY DORA AGAIN?

Freud's (1900) magnum opus, *The Interpretation of Dreams*, has become an indispensable source for all who are interested in the inner workings of the human psyche. The subsequent clinical and experimental research and published works it has engendered, and continues to engender, fill libraries; and there is no end in sight to its continued heuristic value. Freud's (1905a) essay on "Fragment of an Analysis of a Case of Hysteria" was meant to be a sequel to that work, to demonstrate the practical-clinical application of dream analysis within a psychoanalytic process. It was an ambitious undertaking, and Freud was enormously invested in it—his work with Dora also coincided with his self-analysis. Dora's abruptly ending her treatment after only 11 weeks thwarted Freud's ambition, since he had hoped for a "complete" solution to the enigma of hysteria. Nevertheless, "fragment" as it is, written between the Dream Book and the *Three Essays on the Theory of Sexuality* (Freud, 1905b), it is the centerpiece of the three works that present the very core of Freud's original contributions. This centerpiece was to offer the clinical underpinnings to these core ideas: "Dora was meant to provide *the ground* for Freud's theoretical flights in *The Interpretation of Dreams* (Kahane, 1985, p. 22; italics added). For this historical-conceptual position alone, the *"Fragment"* commands renewed and ongoing interest (see also Jennings, 1986, and Buckley, 1989).

Reading Freud's Dora we soon realize that,

> despite a tendentious quality, Freud does not restrict his clinical observations. He repeatedly broadens his vistas, critically allowing himself to reach new and surprising conclusions, tempting the reader to join him in *independent discovery* . . . vivid descriptions of clinical data . . . permit us to continue his work, to reevaluate and reconstruct. *As he did, so can we benefit from his errors* [and] confirm, correct and elaborate on [Freud's] brilliant revolutionary insights [Glenn, 1980a, p. 17; italics added].

This "independent discovery" and our "benefit from [Freud's] errors" characterize the accumulated body of literature on Dora.

Freud's five major case histories—Dora, Little Hans, the Rat Man, the Schreber Case and the Wolf Man—are the most significant relics of the early history of psychoanalysis. Because they are so masterfully composed, are so rich in descriptive and historical detail, and read like short stories or detective stories, they permit the contemporary reader to transcend the conceptual-theoretical limitations of the time period in which they were written. In other words, remarkably, the empirical data Freud assembled come through to us in these case histories in spite of the treatment techniques and theoretical framework that guided their collection; that is, in spite of each story's being, of necessity, the dated product of Freud's method and theories.

Yet, we should also recognize an important *caveat* when we undertake a reexamination of any of these (or other) case histories: psychoanalytic understanding (guided by the analyst's theories) emerges most compellingly in the immediate context of a unique psychoanalytic situation—the overall analytic climate and the relationship of the two participants. It is in this setting that the patient's formative and life-long experiences within the family, and in the larger social context, come alive and make sense. If this is indeed the case, as most analysts believe it is, any later effort to reinterpret the original analytic experience would be a hazardous undertaking.[1] One of the hazards is that we might *impose* our own current theories and their correlated treatment techniques on assessing the stories that emerged in very different contexts under the impact of a very different dyadic experience. In this view there are no data separable from the method with which we collect them and from the meaning we give to them. Thus "Freud's case histories are obviously not 'raw material'" (Sand, 1983, p. 334). While these reservations need not

---

[1] Erikson (1962) remarked that "Freud selected and disguised the clinical data he published, thus rendering reinterpretations hazardous" (p. 47).

deter us from a reassessment, they require of us to spell out as clearly as we can the goals, methods, and guiding principles of our approach.

When a case report vividly portrays the patient's as well as the analyst's participation in the treatment process—as all of Freud's case histories do—(even without the preferable inclusion of process notes or some samples of the interpretive sequences, which would more directly reveal Freud's actual analytic technique) we are enabled to "transport" ourselves back into the original context, put ourselves imaginatively in the position of patient and analyst, and thus have an immediate[2] sense of their respective experiences. We have to form an image of how analyst and patient related to each other and "let" the meaning of their experiences emerge from that dyadic relationship.[3] Only when we are able to conjure up from the available narrative the necessary dyadic context in which the analyst's interventions co-determined the emergence of the data and their meaning, can we offer a revision (or a new version) of the understandings and explanations under scrutiny (see also Ornstein, 1990b).

Two guiding principles should guard us against unduly *imposing* our own perspective on Freud's data. (1) A close reading of the text, and documenting each of our perceptions and their elaborations from the text itself, will curb any speculation beyond the available data and protect us against unwarranted inferences from the perspective of our own theories.[4] (2) We may now also expand the context Freud gave us in his texts, on the basis of data made available about him and his patients since then, and we can thereby buttress our current, text-based, revised understandings.[5]

---

[2] The quotation marks around the word "immediate" are to acknowledge that all our experiences are mediated—yet the empathic perception of another's inner world is considered by many as the only and most "direct" route available to enter that world. Empathy is thus an observational vantage point that is different from the usual process of inference, even if we cannot as yet satisfactorily articulate that difference. There is, however, no consensus on this issue among psychoanalysts.

[3] This approach is very different from one in which the exploration focuses, predominantly or exclusively, on the patient's utterances, experience, and history, (bypassing the transference) and where the interpretation (or reinterpretation) of their meaning occurs on the basis of inferences dictated by the explorer's own theory, as was the case in Dora's analysis.

[4] Here is where the "data" will have to be separated (to the extent this is at all possible) from the meaning given to them in Freud's theoretical framework and will have to be reinterpreted from the vantage point of our own theories, with due regard to the dyadic context in which they originated.

[5] Such expansions of the original contexts are now at our disposal regarding all of Freud's cases, including the case of Dora (e. g., Rogow, 1978, Bernheimer and Kahane, 1985; and especially Decker, 1991). These expansions do indeed serve us well as underpinnings for our revised formulations.

What makes Freud's case histories today relics of the past are, of course, the outdated treatment techniques, some of the outdated underlying theories, and certain basic assumptions—Freud's *Weltanschaaung*—that inevitably pervade them all. To the extent that these case studies are relics of the past, it makes no sense to fault Freud or his work—our task is to understand them both as rooted in their time. To the extent that aspects of the old theory and technique are still adhered to by contemporary psychoanalysts, they are legitimately subject to critical scrutiny from our current vantage point.

But aside from their historic value, what draws the contemporary reader to revisit Freud's case histories are the opportunities they provide for identifying the empirical data by separating them from their interpretations. This separation of the empirical data[6] from their interpretations allows us to retrace Freud's own mode of operation, thinking, and theory formation, as well as the way in which these were affected by his countertransference. In conjunction with this effort, we can also study the explanatory power of our own current theories: Do they help us see more than we had seen before? Do they help us see more clearly?

It is enormously instructive to reread Dora, then to wade through carefully and chronologically each subsequent critique and reinterpretation, and then to return once more—now armed with all the new and critical ideas—and reread Freud's Dora again.

Having done that, one cannot help but gain renewed respect and admiration for Freud's brilliance as a master story teller, a superlative Sherlock Holmes, a compelling theory builder, and an innovative therapist. No matter how thoroughly and how justifiably one might now criticize Freud's approach to Dora and the theories that guided his investigations or those that he derived from this "fragment of an analysis," these do not alter the fact that he opened for us all the currently available new paths to a more comprehensive (and perhaps even more accurate) grasp of Dora as a person, the pathogenesis and nature of her problems as well as the requirements for her treatment.

---

[6]As an aside—because I shall not be able to deal with this issue in the present context—I am well aware that what constitutes "empirical data" in psychoanalysis is debatable. Contemporary philosophers of science view all data of science as thoroughly imbricated with and dependent upon the methods and theories applied to their study—hence as inseparable from what we may consider to be the **data** themselves. We psychoanalysts often speak—mistakenly, they say—as if such data could exist apart from our method and theory. On this view, then, there are no "**pure**" empirical data. Without doing violence to this well-established tenet, I nevertheless hold that the *effort* at delineating the empirical-observational components of psychoanalytic formulations has considerable heuristic value. (See in this connection especially Sand, 1983).

It is in the spirit of testing the explanatory power of the old as well as alternative theories (and sharply criticizing Freud's technique, theories, and basic assumptions in the course of it) that Dora's has undoubtedly become the most frequently reexamined and reinterpreted case study (see, for example, Muslin and Gill, 1978, Kanzer and Glenn, 1980, Bernheimer and Kahane, 1985, Jennings, 1986,[7] Buckley, 1989, Decker, 1991).

FREUD'S PRESENTATION AND THE CRITICS

> "If it is admitted that art and science have the power to do good, then it must also be admitted that they have the power to do harm" (Rieff, 1963, p. 7).

Dora in Freud's View[8]

Let me first offer a thumbnail sketch of Freud's presentation. Dora, at age 18, suffered from a variety of emotional and somatic symptoms (e. g., dyspnea, periodic coughing spells, intermittent aphonia for years, chronic fatigue; recently also depression, irritability, suicidal ideas—culminating in a recent suicide note and a fainting spell). Wanting her father to terminate his affair with Frau K, she gave her father considerable grief over it. Dora felt particularly enraged that her father had almost literally handed her over to Herr K, in the hope that this *quid pro quo* would silence her and permit him to continue his affair with Frau K undisturbed. Dora's father denied the affair and brought Dora to Freud, asking that he "try to bring her to reason."

Both Frau K and Herr K were close friends of Dora's family. Dora was particularly close to and intimate with Frau K. She was in awe of her and expressed a great deal of admiration for her in many ways; she spoke of her "adorable white body." She was drawn to, and visibly caring about, the K's two young children. Freud (1905a) remarked, "A common interest in the children had from the first been a bond between Herr K and Dora. Her preoccupation with his

---

[7]Jennings (1986) credits the "Dora revival" in the 60s and 70s with "the revolutionary change in attitude among psychoanalysts toward the phenomenon of countertransference" and with "the development of a more comprehensive psychoanalytic theory of adolescent psychology and its treatment" (p. 621).

[8]Both this resume and that of the critics' comments later are inevitably highly selective. They focus on those elements of this vast literature that are of significance for my own reading of Dora. Hence, they are also inevitably tendentious, in spite of my efforts to minimize this in the service of objectivity.

children was evidently a cloak for something else that Dora was anxious to hide from herself and from other people" (p. 37). Her relation to Herr K himself was also a close one in many ways. He showed her many favors, gave her presents and flowers, and the like. But their relationship was marred by two incidents during which he appears to have overstepped the bounds of friendship. He became inappropriately physical with her—inappropriately, as she experienced it. In one instance, he surprised her with a sudden passionate kiss—she was only 14 years old then—evoking in her a reaction of disgust. In another, during a stroll around a lake, about two years later, he proposed to her or propositioned her. It is unclear whether this incident was a simple seduction (as she perceived it) or whether it also contained a proposal for marriage (which Freud assumed), since Dora instantly slapped Herr K on the face and ran away without allowing him to finish what he wanted to say.

Later that afternoon (Dora was staying with the K's at their vacation home), she had good reason to believe that Herr K had not given up his designs on her. He intruded into her bedroom while she was taking a nap. She awoke, startled, and ordered him out of the room. She had planned to stay with the K's alone for a while, but after this incident she abruptly decided to leave with her father.

Several days later, Dora told her family about the earlier incident at the lake, but when her father and uncle confronted Herr K with this story, both he and Frau K accused Dora of having fabricated it in her vivid imagination. This accusation infuriated her, especially since her father agreed with the K's and did not seem to accept her version of the incident. This pained Dora immensely, and her own persistent agenda with Freud was to set this record straight: she wanted her father, Herr K and Freud to acknowledge the wrong done her. Freud, on the other hand, had his own agenda to demonstrate the unconscious driving power of the Oedipus complex, and he pursued this relentlessly, brushing Dora's painful concerns aside with his interpretations.

In this pursuit Freud painstakingly reconstructed the sources and meanings of Dora's symptoms and behavior—especially around the two major dreams she reported in the middle and near the end of her interrupted analysis—and ultimately linked them all to his basic conception that Dora was in love with Herr K, frightened of the implications of her love and defended herself against it by remobilizing her old oedipal attachments to her father and thereby camouflaging her love for Herr K. Thus it was impossible for her to respond to Herr K's advances "properly," that is, positively, Freud argued, as a healthy young girl should have been able to do. Freud assumed that

Dora resented that Herr K had not approached her in a straightforward, above-board manner and that therefore she could not be certain of his true intentions. Freud saw Dora's vehement objection to her father's affair as a mark of her oedipal jealousy of Frau K. Freud later recognized Dora's relation to Frau K, however, as a manifestation of her deeper, pathogenetically more significant, homosexual love for Frau K—her negative Oedipus complex, as psychoanalysts would later describe it.

The details of Freud's interpretations and reconstructions—the data on which they were based (or which they had overlooked) and which Dora could not confirm—are fascinating and worthy of step-by-step microscopic tracking. Here, only Freud's procedure of arriving at his conclusions (Freud's truth versus Dora's truth) commands our interest in order to arrive at a self-psychological reading of the text. How did Freud decide to press his interpretations in the face of Dora's sustained rejection of them? What evidence did he use for holding on so firmly to the validity of his own explanations as pitted against Dora's?

Before turning to the focus of my own reading with these questions in the background, I shall consider previous readings of Freud's presentation.

Previous Readings of the Dora Case

Severe criticisms[9] pervade the literature side by side with genuine admiration for Freud's genius in formulating the nature of Dora's psychopathology on the basis of a mere "fragment of an analysis." Almost without exception, these critics add to our fund of knowledge as well as to our speculations about the many issues involved in the case of Dora. The critics' clinical acumen, applied in the context of a much advanced and more complex set of theories since 1905, permit all of them to stand on Freud's shoulders and see much farther. With their enhanced vision, these critics see more clearly what Dora brought to her analysis (her adolescent struggle for fidelity; her wish to consolidate her femininity; and her effort to throw off the oppressive, pathogenic influence of her family and her culturally assigned, limited and limiting, position in life as a woman) and what she wanted from Freud (the affirmation of the validity of her perceptions and

---

[9]These criticisms are directed especially at Freud's many-faceted countertransference reactions—the effects they had on his method of data gathering and on his emotional responses to Dora as well as on his view of her sexuality. They are also directed at Freud's aim for a general theory of hysteria and of sexuality.

experiences; and the legitimization of her struggle to free herself from the impact of her noxious milieu). Since Freud could not hear these concerns as primary and central but only as secondary and defensive, he could not "join" Dora analytically in her struggle. The critics can also see much more clearly what Freud brought to this analysis (an enormous gift for observation and theorizing as well as his own personal and culture-bound biases about women and their sexuality) and what he wanted from Dora. What he wanted was nothing less than a confirmation of his sweeping theories of instinctual infantile sexuality, the Oedipus complex, and female sexuality, both in the pathogenesis of hysteria and, even more broadly, in health. Freud could not see or acknowledge how his assumptions and countertransference reactions had adversely intruded on Dora's analysis. He insisted that he was reading Dora, when in fact he was often only reading his own mind.[10]

Critics reexamining and reinterpretating Dora's analysis largely fall into the following overlapping categories: (1) those who find Freud's approach to Dora as an *adolescent* faulty on account of accumulated new knowledge of that developmental phase, which requires a different understanding of the nature of Dora's problems, leading to a different set of treatment principles (Erikson, 1962, 1964; Schlesinger, 1969; Blos, 1972a,b; Marcus, 1976; Rogow, 1978; Glenn, 1980b; Jennings, 1986); (2) those who up-date Freud's approach from the perspective of modern *ego psychology* (structural theory, the tripartite model), replacing Freud's id psychology (and its correlated direct search for the hidden secret) and the topographic theory prevalent at that time (Kanzer and Glenn, 1980; Glenn, 1980a); (3) those, especially French feminist psychoanalysts who consider Freud's views on *femininity* and *female desire* to have been highly skewed in the direction of a Victorian, patriarchal, male-chauvinist bias that prevented him from understanding Dora's *sexu-*

---

[10]It ought to be acknowledged that the proper psychoanalytic reading of the patient's mind (his or her subjective experiences) is always accomplished through the reading of one's own as a method or procedure—vicarious introspection (empathy). This is a necessary step in the process of comprehending the subjectivity of the other. Elaborate safeguards are necessary to insure that we shift over to a consideration of the patient's experiences and not remain focused on our own. Hence, the danger of the manner in which Freud read Dora is ubiquitous. Freud's failure to make this shift consistently—as I shall indicate later—contributed to his failure with Dora. Rieff (1963) made a cogent remark in this connection, while speaking of "the tessellated quality of Freud's mind." "That tessellation," he said, "is inseparable, of course, from the fusion of his own mind as it confronts the experience of Dora, with his own inner experience. *Freud's scientific knowledge is highly personal, an achievement first won with himself as patient*" (p 13; italics added).

ality and from developing the requisite therapeutic approach to her problems. They consider Freud's failure in this regard to have been most damaging to Dora (Bernheimer and Kahane, 1985; Decker, 1991); (4) others who follow Freud in elaborating in greater detail his own later discovery that he failed to recognize and interpret the *transference* in time; and that he failed to stress sufficiently Dora's homosexual attraction to Frau K (which he claimed later to have been even more fundamental than his missing the focus on the transference) as key contributing factors to Dora's breaking off her analysis (Muslin and Gill, 1978; Bernstein, 1980; Glenn, 1980b; Langs, 1976, 1980; Scharfman, 1980; Bernheimer and Kahane, 1985); (5) critics—most of them—who identify various layers of Freud's *countertransference* and consider it (along the lines of the objections of some of the feminist readers) to be the most important factor causing Dora to flee from her analysis (Muslin and Gill, 1978; Bernstein, 1980; Glenn, 1980b; Langs, 1980; Scharfman, 1980; Bernheimer and Kahane, 1985; Decker, 1991); (6) and, finally, those whose scattered references to epistemologic questions (mostly not labeled as such) pervade the literature. There are two noteworthy contributions, one questioning the existence of a masculine versus a feminine way of knowledge (Moi, 1985) and the other (Sand, 1983) entirely devoted to the question of verification of Freud's interpretive hypotheses in Dora's analysis.

Many of these criticisms are very much to the point, and the alternative formulations they offer are often well substantiated within their particular frames of reference. I find most of them germane and significantly advancing our understanding of Freud's approach to Dora (and why his analysis of her failed) and perhaps even of Dora herself (and why she had to leave the analysis when she did). A detailed and systematic appraisal, however, would reveal some of the new formulations as clinically more relevant and theoretically sounder than others, some as highly imaginative and disclosing the impact of many subtle and not so subtle elements of Freud's countertransference (including his *Weltanschauung*) on his analytic understanding and treatment, still others as more speculative—not reading the text as much as reading *into* the text their own, different, contemporary biases. A sampling of these contributions should suffice.

Dora as an adolescent. The series of reassessments of Dora's analysis began with the recognition that she, as well as two other of Freud's 18-year-old patients, Katharina and the (unnamed) "homosexual woman," were all adolescents (Erikson, 1962, 1964; Adatto, 1966; Schlesinger, 1969; Marcus, 1976; Rogow, 1978; Glenn, 1980b;

and later many others, e.g., Buckley, 1989).[11] The idea of adolescence as a distinct phase in the life cycle was a relatively late addition to psychoanalytic developmental theory (see e.g., Blos, 1962, for a comprehensive overview).

To distill from the voluminous literature on adolescence what is most pertinent for a better understanding of Dora, we should keep in mind the following. There is an overriding, central need in adolescents for the *consolidation* of (Blos, 1962), *commitment* to (Pumpian-Mindlin, 1965), and establishment of a firm sense of adult *identity* (Erikson, 1959). The adolescent struggle to achieve this occurs against great odds. According to the libido theory, the adolescent struggle, related to increase of drive pressure, renews libidinal and aggressive ties to both parents, on one hand, and then necessitates fighting off the resurgence of libidinal ties, on the other. This fighting off occurs by turning aggression (hostility) against the parents both to control drive-tension by increasing the emotional and physical distance from the parents and to overcome dependence and achieve independence. In this process, it is of enormous importance for the adolescent to find "nonincestuous objects," (mentors) with fidelity, trustworthiness, and ideals worthy of admiration and emulation.

Adolescent ambivalence and expressions of innate bisexuality are ubiquitous, as is the relentless and uncompromising search for the truth that is the expression of their idealism (Erikson, 1962, 1964; Schlesinger, 1969). Erikson (1962, 1964) spoke here of "historical truth," "the actuality of events," "reality and actuality" and "truth in action." This is in contrast to "psychic truth" or the "genetic truth," which is what Freud was searching for in his analysis of Dora. Erikson's (1962, 1964) reading is compelling in that he recognized that Dora doggedly sought her "historical truth," whereas Freud was interested only in the "genetic truth," which he held as analytically the only important one—and she would have none of it. This is how Glenn (1980b) put it: "Dora seemed to be trying to prove that the internal determinants of her behavior were less important than the external events—or [that they were] not significant at all" (p. 35).

These ideas have far-reaching technical implications, which Glenn (1980b), Scharfman (1980), and Bernstein (1980) spell out in detail. All of them consider respect for the adolescent's demand for fidelity

---

[11]Glenn (1980a) compares Freud's three 18-year-old patients, and pinpoints the similarities in their dynamics and in Freud's reactions to them. He notes that Freud was much friendlier toward the Rat Man and the Wolf Man and accepted from them what he could not tolerate either in Dora or the "homosexual woman," both of whom he essentially dismissed when they no longer pleased him (p. 14).

a sine qua non; and they recognize that the typical, but unrecognized, transference and countertransference configurations of adolescents require special attention. In this connection they refer to the fact that Dora's psychic structure was still "in a state of flux" (Glenn, 1980b, p. 24; Bernstein, 1980, p. 87), but they do not explicitly link this observation of an unconsolidated (in certain ways not adequately "structuralized") psyche to the nature of Dora's transference to Freud, namely, that hers might not have been a bona fide oedipal transference, which does require prior consolidation. The implication is that Dora's transference had more profoundly archaic (preoedipal) features, an idea stressed by a number of feminist readers (e. g., Ramas, 1985; Sprengnether, 1985; Van Den Berg, 1987) and other critics (e.g., Meissner, 1984–1985; Slipp, 1977), and forcefully contradicted by others, who emphasize its phallic-oedipal roots (Krohn and Krohn, 1982).

The evolution of ego psychology and increasing knowledge about adolescence certainly advanced our ideas about the nature of Dora's difficulties in life as a teenager as well as in her brief analytic experience. This evolution undoubtedly contributed to our better understanding of Freud's difficulties with Dora as well. It is more than a historical curiosity, therefore, that as late as 1972(a) Blos still had to remind us that "if there is one thing adolescent analysis has taught us, it is that ill-timed id interpretations are unconsciously experienced by the adolescent as parental—that is, incestuous—seduction" (p. 130). Freud's approach to Dora is seen by many commentators as having evoked just that—it contributed to the sexualization of the transference (e.g., Muslin and Gill, 1978, p. 320; Glenn, 1980b, p. 32).

Dora in the light of ego psychology. Erikson (1962, 1964) focused on Dora's (adolescent) ego development and adaptive ego needs. He also remarked in this context that Freud's analytic approach to Dora inevitably bore the marks of id psychology: a relentless, direct search for Dora's hidden secret, without prior attention to her "adaptive ego needs" or resistances. But a fuller up-dating of all of Freud's major case histories from the perspective of ego psychology was most impressively accomplished by Kanzer and Glenn (1980). Glenn (1980a) introduces the project by saying that

> all of [Freud's] case histories were written during the dominance of the topographic model, prior to the establishment of the structural point of view (Freud, 1923). The modern reader may [therefore] become confused by Freud's terminology since he used words that continued to acquire different meanings. It is often necessary to "translate" Freud's pre-1923 language into that of today" [p. 5].

There follows an exemplary, condensed survey of the changed concepts (as well as of Freud's style of writing in these case histories) to permit an easier comprehension of Freud's early work, including its inevitable, but highly instructive, flaws, which the contributors clearly recognized and admirably detailed.

But in addition to the appropriate revision of the language of psychoanalysis from the early 1900s, the contribution to the Kanzer and Glenn book also demonstrate how the new idiom allows a grasp of new dynamic configurations: for example, Dora, "fearing betrayal and desertion" by Freud, "became the deserter and perhaps betrayed Freud by ending treatment;" and thereby (via her "ego-defense") turned passively endured traumata into an active attack against the whole string of perpetrators, her father, Herr K, Frau K, and Freud (Glenn, 1980b, p. 32).

Another area in which the new language wrought decisive changes is through the subsequently introduced dual drive theory, where aggression is considered on a par with the libido. Its ubiquitous pathogenic impact, many critics hold, requires early interpretation, even before focusing on libidinal conflicts. This focus is what Freud could not yet carry through systematically with Dora (Bernstein, 1980 p. 84–85).

Dora's femininity, her female desire and sexuality. It is in relation to these core issues that feminist literary critics persistently, with great alacrity, challenged the foundational concepts underlying Dora's analysis. Although most psychoanalytic critics were willing to question Freud's technique, his then-limited conception of the transference, his manifold, unrecognized countertransferences and their impact on Dora, his culture-bound prejudices and their influence on various aspects of his theories, they did not, as the feminist critics had done, reopen Dora's analysis for a radical revision. Whatever the animus behind the feminists' fervor, their project was a sophisticated and in many ways valid and successful entry into a territory (human sexuality, especially its female variety) that was not yet satisfactorily conquered even in contemporary psychoanalysis, let alone when Freud analyzed Dora. Perhaps what the literary critics and feminist psychoanalysts achieved could have been done only by them because they were not burdened by an oppressive orthodoxy.

What, then, is our image of Dora's femininity, her unconscious desire and sexuality, in the light of the feminist reinterpretations?

Freud used his prior template of hysteria—"the case has smoothly opened to my collection of picklocks" (Bonaparte, Freud, and Kris, 1954, p. 325)—to answer the question of what Dora's "secret" was, and he thereby hoped to solve a fundamental riddle of psychoanalysis: "What does woman want?"[12] That quest was quite a heavy burden on a pioneer who could not yet sufficiently overcome the Victorian prejudices of his time and place. This ultimately wrecked Dora's analysis. Freud constructed Dora's femininity and what he considered to be her "secret desire" on the foundation of her conversion symptoms; her "reversals"-dominated, seductive, oppositional and revengeful personality. But Freud both overgeneralized from this single case and imported the data from other experiences to buttress his interpretive strategy, when he could not have the confirmation for his assumptions from Dora herself.

As Kahane (1985) put it, "What contemporary readings of Dora suggest is that . . . in constructing a narrative of Dora's desire, [Freud] essentially represented his own" (p. 20). This idea justifiably pervades feminist readings and (among other insights) it led to the recognition of some fundamental flaws in Freud's theorizing about femininity as well as about sexuality. Freud was guided in conceptualizing Dora's sexuality by his early formulations of the Oedipus complex.

> Although he would later revise its structure, at the time of the Dora case Freud's Oedipus complex is a simple set of relations in which the child desires the parent of the opposite sex and feels hostility toward the same-sexed parent. In spite of his simultaneous belief in an innate bisexual disposition Freud assumed *a natural heterosexual attraction* [in Dora] and saw his task as the liberation into consciousness of that *natural desire*, which when repressed, resulted in hysterical symptoms" [pp. 21-22; italics added].

Hence Freud's translation of Dora's disgust into its opposite, a sexual attraction to Herr K that had to be denied and turned into its opposite.

It is in relation to defining woman's natural desire that most feminist critics (basing themselves, in part, on Lacan's reading of Dora and many others find the "flaw." Believing in innate bisexuality, Freud had no basis on which to privilege, they feel, heterosexuality over homosexuality in women, since the mother is the first love object of both girls and boys. (See also Lewin, 1973; Moscovitz, 1973.) On that account, love of a woman (mother) is as *"natural"* for the girl as it is for boys. "What Dora revealed was that sexual difference [in the choice of object] was a *psychological problematic*

---

[12]"Was will das Weib?" is frequently quoted incorrectly as "What does a woman want?" or "What do women want?"—neither of which conveys Freud's meaning as sharply, as does my quote of Strachey's translation, which captures Freud's concern with generic woman.

rather than a natural fact, that it existed within the individual psyche as well as between men and women in culture" (Kahane, 1985, p. 22; italics added).

It is the oedipal narrative (even in its later expanded and revised version), the feminists believe, that led Freud astray. He could not hear clearly (and when he did, he relegated those hints and allusions to the sidelines) Dora's *preoedipal* love for her mother (e.g., Ramas, 1985; Moi, 1985; Van Den Berg, 1987). Freud "occulted" the importance of Dora's longing for her mother as displaced to Frau K and then to himself (transference), although he retrospectively recognized this as one of the prime causes of the failure of the analysis (Collins et al., 1985). The emphasis on the preoedipal attachment to the mother as decisively shaping female sexuality is a main theme of many feminist re-interpretations. Kahane (1985) refers to this issue thus:

> Dora . . . is a paradigmatic text of patriarchal assumptions about female desire that still carry cultural authority and a vivid record of the construction of those assumptions as they emerge from the desire of the interpreter. Even more provocatively the traces of Dora's story that form the subtext to Freud's oedipal narrative and continually disrupt it suggest an *alternative preoedipal narrative that many feminists are reinscribing* [pp. 24–25; italics added].

In contrast to this preoedipal emphasis, Krohn and Krohn (1982) argue that Dora's homoerotic impulses stemmed from her phallic-oedipal conflicts and that these should have been the focus of Freud's interpretation (see also Kohon, 1984; Lewin, 1973).

Dora's transference to Freud. Recognition of the centrality of transference and countertransference to an up-dated view of the psychoanalytic process is, I believe, one of overriding methodologic, clinical, and theoretical significance. The up-dated views in the literature contain the crucial acknowledgement that the analyst, *volens nolens*, shapes the analytic process. Hence his or her participation cannot be encompassed by such terms as "neutrality" (unless neutrality is restricted to mean that he or she has no special ax to grind as far as *conscious* intentions are concerned; *unconscious* intentions are always present and are regularly a part of the analytic process). This view has allowed the critics to find new meanings in both Dora's and Freud's contributions to their analytic experience. Thus the critics appraise this "fragment of an analysis" afresh, leading to new, useful, and at times startling clinical and theoretical insights regarding Dora's transference to Freud (Gill and Muslin, 1976; Muslin and Gill, 1978; Bernstein, 1980; Glenn, 1980b, 1986; Langs,

1980; Scharfman, 1980; Bernheimer and Kahane, 1985; Decker, 1991).

At the time he treated Dora, Freud was not yet searching for transference manifestations and meanings in his patients' associations as assiduously as analysts of subsequent generations learned to do. Clearly, "Freud did not often include himself in the cast of characters to which his patient was reacting. Associations to and about another person—whether father, mother, or lover—were seldom recognized, or at least written of, as implicitly pertaining to him" (Muslin and Gill, 1978). Freud focused his attention on extratransference issues with Dora—with preference for establishing genetic connections in order to trace Dora's sexuality to their ultimate sources, in which he openly expressed special interest. In spite of Freud's claim that he did not yet recognize the transference, Muslin and Gill (1978) astutely detect throughout the text the constant presence of allusions to the transference and its avoidance by Freud. Two examples of many they carefully assembled will illustrate their findings and interpretations[13]:

> [A]t the beginning Dora was constantly comparing [Freud] with her father, anxiously trying to make sure whether he was being straightforward with her. It is clear, then, that Dora's talk about her father was the disguised transference material that required interpretation, and there were not slight clues but gross indications of the probable transference [p. 315].

> Another set of associations with a closely related implicit transference meaning is the material about the governess who *pretended an interest* in Dora, but was in fact only interested in her father (Freud, 1905a, pp. 36–37). Again Freud interpreted correctly that Dora's reproach against the governess concealed a reproach against herself, but he missed her implied transference reproach against Freud that *he pretended to be interested in her but was really working for her father* [p. 315; italics added].

The repetitive, forceful, explicit interpretations of Dora's manifold libidinal wishes toward Herr K according to many observers, sexualized the transference, a sexualization that is difficult to avoid under the best of circumstances with adolescents (e.g., Glenn; 1980b, Scharfman, 1980). Scharfman (1980) remarks that in Dora's brief analysis

---

[13]They properly caution us that "the test of the validity of a transference interpretation lies in the patient's response to the interpretation. If the interpretation has not been made, one cannot be sure of its validity" (Muslin and Gill, 1978, p. 320).

transference had indeed developed [into] an intense, erotized and ambivalent one . . . [in which] . . . the analyst was . . . reacted to as if he were indeed [Dora's] father or Herr K. Such a reaction is more likely to occur where there have been early repetitive transference interpretations of feelings toward the original parental object" [p. 50].

Dora had attempted to defend against her attachment to her "oedipal objects" by turning to "new objects," "nonincestuous objects"— from her father to Herr K (and also from her mother to Frau K) and in analysis from both of them to Freud. It is here that Freud's focus on the "genetic truth" and his brushing aside Dora's "historical truth" and missing both the heterosexual and the homosexual transference to himself contributed to the failure of this analysis. Dora's analysis

> might have been a chance at having a different kind of relationship with a man. She needed to go through the intermediate phase of development of the younger girl in which she has a relationship with a man that is not immediately sexualized, but rather one in which she feels *accepted as a person*, while still looking for derivatives of oedipal wishes in terms of the wish to feel *loved, admired, paid attention to*. Dora's attempt to find this in the relationship with Herr K had led to another disappointment and her symptoms had intensified" [Sharfman, 1980, p. 55; italics added].

Her original traumatic disappointment in her father was repeated in her relation to Herr K and was now traumatically inflicted on her by Freud in the "misalliance" between himself and Dora (in that he knew both her father and Herr K personally (Langs, 1976,1980). Thus, Freud and Dora were talking past each other or at cross purposes. Dora's even earlier disappointment in her mother was repeated in the relationship with Frau K, and this was again missed in the transference.

Kahane (1985) refers to one of the sharpest criticisms in this regard:

> [Freud] failed to acknowledge a more threatening transference with Frau K, a women who is the object of homosexual love as well as maternal object. If Frau K is a significant love object for Dora, she must also be part of the transference. . . . what Freud occults in Dora's history—the mother and her subsequent displacements—he also occults in the theory of the Oedipus complex, which exemplifies the repression of the mother . . . at the root of Western civilization itself" [Collins et al., p. 251].

Freud's countertransference to Dora. That transference is ubiquitous and that any aspect of the analyst's participation in the analytic process "could become plausible stimuli to transference elaboration" permit Muslin and Gill to reconstruct many of Freud's activities and attitudes as rather blatant countertransference reactions to Dora (Muslin and Gill, 1978, p. 323). Freud himself never questioned the validity of his interpretations, nor did he indicate any awareness of countertransference (Bernheimer and Kahane, 1985, p. 23). Critical readers who view transference and countertransference as inevitably reciprocal reactions, determining the emerging analytic process and substantively contributing to its success or failure, take Freud severely to task.

Decker (1991), for instance, catalogues the "vital areas" of Freud's countertransference (many of which have already been described by others): Freud's erotic arousal by the young, attractive, and intelligent Dora—and his failure to recognize his own seductiveness in his metaphors of penetration and violation, (which express themselves in his use of "picklocks," revealing his sexual and intrusive fantasies); his manifold identifications with her and with the whole cast of characters—Dora's father, Herr K as well as Frau K; his own discomfort with and embarrassment about sexuality—his defensiveness in talking about it so explicitly; his anger and retaliatory revenge that Dora left him abruptly—and his refusal to take her back into analysis when she returned on her own; he also appears to have envied her youth.[14]

Many readers see Freud as having unconsciously identified with Dora (Hertz, 1985, p. 225; and especially Glenn, 1986); with the virile Herr K "as an attractive lover" (Sprengnether, 1985, p. 259); as having "reacted to Dora as if she were a maid, complementing her self-image as a servant" (Glenn, 1980a, p. 14). In a later elaboration by Glenn (1986), Dora identified with one of her own governesses or maidservants (who was in love with her father) as well as with the governess or maidservant of the K children (who was in love with Herr K). She behaved like a maidservant toward Freud—he felt—in the manner in which she terminated her analysis. He, on the other hand, treated her

---

[14]Malcolm (1981) makes some penetrating remarks about Dora when she says that "Freud conveys the idea that it was the erotic importunities of his women patients that caused him to postulate the presence of the universal phenomenon [of transference] that would explain the behavior he was convinced he had not provoked. Yet from the evidence in the postscript one would gather that it was, rather, Freud's rage, frustration, and disappointment over Dora's defection that was the fulcrum of his momentous discovery" (p. 94). The literature reviewed in this chapter indicates to me that we have to place both sexuality and aggression in the same category. Both were provoked as I read the text and the critics.

as one in his behavior (by letting her leave without any effort to interpret its meaning because he was hurt and angry; and by giving her the pseudonym "Dora." Glenn shows that Freud had both positive and negative countertransference reactions to Dora. At their root, these reactions related to his early experiences with his nanny, the ambivalently beloved mother-substitute, Monika, who "abandoned" him at a very early age (see also Kanzer and Glenn, 1980).

Malcolm (1981) sees Freud as also reacting with fear to Dora as Pandora, evoking the negative side of the countertransference (p. 96). She also views Freud's conduct of Dora's analysis with sharp criticism. She says that the case history "reads like an account of an operation performed on a fully awake patient" (Malcolm, 1987, p. 197). Freud's countertransference is also revealed in giving his patient the pseudonym Dora. He claimed that he chose this name through an association with the nursemaid Rosa, who worked for Freud's sister, also named Rosa. To avoid confusion in the household, the nursemaid Rosa was called Dora. Decker (1991), however, has pointed to the likelihood that Freud was also influenced by the name of Dora Breuer, the daughter of Joseph Breuer, his mentor and collaborator in writing up the case of Anna O. Dora Breuer was of the same age as Freud's patient.

And then there is Freud's obsessive desire for complete knowledge as an obstacle to treatment (Moi, 1985, p. 194). A large number of cogent examples are presented of Freud's impeding behaviors (esp. by Langs, 1976, 1980; Glenn, 1980b; Scharfman, 1980; Begel, 1982; Possick, 1984; Glenn, 1986). But Freud did not

> fully appreciate the impact of his behavior on [Dora]. He noted that Dora responded to certain phrases of his, like 'Where there is smoke there is fire,' but he did not recognize how his providing a *reality basis* for certain of her reactions *rendered the transference difficult to analyze* [Glenn, 1980a, p. 13; italics added].

In the same vein, Glenn (1980b) also notes that "Freud failed to observe that his own behavior reinforced Dora's conviction that he was like her father and Herr K. Without being aware of this he could not make the interpretations necessary to allow Dora to continue her analysis" (p. 32; see also Glenn, 1986).

Freud's epistemology in Dora's analysis. Many of the readers surveyed, implicitly or explicitly raised questions about Freud's epistemology in Dora's analysis. For instance, Glenn (1980b), in connection with discussing one of Dora's potential transference configurations (from her father to Herr K and then to Freud) suggested that to establish the existence of such a transference "today we would have more stringent criteria for proof that the reconstruction [of oedipal wishes from childhood] was true [than what Freud actually presented] (p. 31). Moi (1985), in a powerful hermeneutic tour de force, argued successfully against Freud's division of epistemology into a masculine and feminine model based on the shape of male and female genitalia—Freud representing the masculine and Dora the feminine way of acquiring knowledge.

> There is absolutely no evidence for the actual existence of two such gender-determined sorts of knowledge, to be conceptualized as parallel to the shapes of human genitals . . . [t]o undermine this phallocentric epistemology means to expose its lack of "natural" foundation [p. 198].

To my knowledge only Sand (1983) subjected Freud's case report to a comprehensive, systematic, epistemologic analysis, thereby questioning the very foundations of Freud's approach to Dora. Because Sand's is a fundamental contribution not only to the literature on Dora, but also to psychoanalytic methodology as a whole, her approach and findings should be highlighted.

Sand properly sets the stage for her assessment of Dora's analysis by insisting that

> confirmation of the value of psychoanalysis, of its truth claims and its claims for efficacy . . . must start with the demonstration that the low-level homely clinical hypotheses of the practitioner are true. According to this view confirmation must originate at these grass roots; if it cannot be obtained there, further efforts to vindicate psychoanalysis would seem to be uninteresting in any case [p. 333].

It is at this clinical level that Freud violated certain basic requirements of validating his hypotheses and where Sand finds "flaws in the confirmation process" (p. 334). She demonstrates these flaws by first clearly distinguishing between the "usual blurring of two categories in psychoanalysis: hypothesis formation and hypothesis confirmation" (p. 335) and by requiring "low-level, particular clinical hypotheses, i.e., the patient is competing with the analyst" to be the subject of the clinician's efforts at confirmation (p. 335). For Sand "[t]he confirmation process rules out unsupported hunches and depends upon evidence" (p. 336). She spells out the evidence she requires:

> In general, the patient's behavior constitutes evidence. His free associations, his self reports, his reactions to interpretations, his conduct, manifest and subtle, his circumstances and their alterations comprise

the material which can be used as proof. This is to say that confirmation, one way or another, lies with the patient [p. 335].

In her further exposition of the nature of evidence (as she is to look for it in her study of the "Fragment"), she adds:

> The products of the analyst's mind do not constitute evidence. No hunch, fantasy, empathy or even strong belief of the analyst's establishes anything. A minimal requirement for evidence—whatever else it may be—is that *it must originate independently outside of the analyst*. It is here that a sharp distinction must be made between hypothesis formation and confirmation. A psychoanalyst may use his imagination to formulate a hypothesis about what is going on in his patient's mind; he cannot use his imagination to corroborate his hypothesis. *He cannot create a hypothesis by thinking and then, by thinking some more, to prove it*. The analyst's thinking about the patient's thoughts and the patient's actual thoughts must be clearly distinguished" [p. 336; italics added].

It is truly amazing that as late as 1983 all of this still had to be spelled out as a prelude to the epistemologic exploration of Dora's analysis and that

> although technique and theory have been scrutinized, the method of proof has gone without examination and Freud's contentions have been generally accepted without epistemological inspection. As a result many analysts, in spite of their technical and theoretical reservations about the case, accept without question such things as that Freud uncovered Dora's unconscious fantasies, that he explained the connection between these fantasies and her symptoms, that he traced the symptoms back to her childhood and that he showed how dream analysis facilitated these disclosures [pp. 338–339].

Quoting chapter and verse, Sand convincingly shows in great detail that Freud had done none of the above. She establishes this fact by first identifying Freud's main goal and his several subgoals and their component parts in his analysis of Dora and then examining how far he reached them or failed to reach them. Sand accomplishes this task by making explicit ten of Freud's central hypotheses and combing the text for evidence of their verifications.

Freud's main goal was to demonstrate the psychosexual aetiology of hysteria and simultaneously to illustrate the use of dreams in elucidating the meaning of symptoms and in filling in gaps in memory—removing amnesias. His subgoals involve discovering the two kinds of determinants for hysteria: psychological and somatic. To identify the psychological determinants requires the recognition of a recent psychic trauma (leading to repression of an affect); and a childhood impression (with an effect "analogous to trauma"). To identify the obligatory "somatic compliance" requires the recognition of the somatic determinant(s) to have originated in childhood (p. 339). Sand then carefully cites Freud's ten claims in order to learn which ones were confirmed and which ones were not. Here are Freud's ten claims:

> 1. Dora's current neurotic difficulties were occasioned by a recent sexual trauma. 2. The trauma had brought about the repression of a powerful affect. 3. Her symptoms were caused by this affect. 4. Her symptoms represented this affect. 5. The earlier appearance of these symptoms was to be explained by childhood experiences which had an effect 'analogous' to that of a trauma. 6. There existed a "somatic compliance" occasioned by either a normal or a pathological process in or connected with the bodily organs. 7. Dream interpretation fills in amnesias and elucidates symptoms. 8. Dream interpretation shows that dreams refer to the current psychic trauma. 9. Dreams also refer to an event in childhood. 10. The dream represents an associative link between #8 and #9" [p. 339].

Sand's findings and verdict are startling. She ends up stating that Freud's epistemology was deeply flawed (in all of his case histories). Hence his claims about Dora should be viewed only as interesting, often brilliant, hypotheses—but only as hypotheses, since they have essentially remained clinically unconfirmed (p. 338).

The procedure that enables Sand to make her discoveries is of considerable interest. To begin with she tentatively accepts, unexamined, Freud's explanatory framework as well as his first and second claims (i.e., that Dora loved Herr K, and that she repressed her love) as corroborated (p. 341). If she had also subjected these to her stringent scrutiny, she might have found less justification for examining the remaining eight claims, since the latter depend on the validity of the former. Sand then takes Freud's analysis of Dora's three major symptoms (her loss of voice, her cough, and her shortness of breath—all present intermittently ever since age 8) and her two dreams to study the fate of hypotheses three through ten. Sand offers a precise description of the evidence she will look for:

> If his demonstration of his theses is to be successful, Freud must explain the origin and meaning of Dora's symptoms in a fashion which is quite stringently predetermined. He must show that each of them is occa-

sioned by her repressed passion for K, that it symbolically represents this passion, that it was preceded in childhood both by a psychological impression "analogous to a trauma" and by a somatic impression leading to a "somatic compliance" [p. 341].

Sand's sensitivity and logic as she selects her data and shares with the reader her careful assessment of whether they confirm each of Freud's claims or not cannot be adequately appreciated in this abbreviated description. Here some of the findings and final results will have to suffice.

Regarding the first symptom, Dora's loss of voice, its cooccurrence with Herr K's absences for three to six weeks at a time was to establish the necessary linkage to her passionate love for Herr K; it would have to be shown that it was this repressed love and not some other repressed affect that caused the symptom, and that the loss of voice represented this repressed passionate love. The regularity of the cooccurrence would at least have been suggestive, but such regularity could not be firmly established.

> Nevertheless, Freud regarded the explanation [he proposed] as conclusive; he believed that a "psychoanalytic interpretation" of the attacks of voice loss had been furnished. In his further discussion of the case he assumed that the symptom "enabled [Dora] to express her love for a man who was periodically absent." However, I submit that the evidence does not warrant this conclusion. He had not shown that the symptom was caused by her repressed passion for K or that it represented this passion, let alone that it was a piece of "sexual activity." [p. 343]

Regarding the second symptom, Dora's cough, Freud was searching for a "fantasy with sexual content." It was he, however, who proposed the unconscious fellatio fantasy to explain the cough; it was not Dora's independent, spontaneous association. Furthermore, she rejected it. Thus, again, Freud produced no evidence.

Regarding the third symptom, Dora's shortness of breath, its sexual etiology based on an assumed primal scene is pure conjecture, without evidence, and therefore merits no further examination.

Based on her findings, Sand concludes that Freud did not substantiate claims three and four—"[h]e did not demonstrate that Dora's symptoms were caused by a repressed affect nor that they represented this affect" (p. 345). Neither did he provide any link between Dora's thumb sucking in childhood and her supposed fellatio fantasy causing her cough "but was too ready to content himself with mere sequence as ground for causal claim" (p. 345). Thus he did not substantiate claim five (pertaining to childhood events "analogous to trauma"); nor claim six (pertaining to the necessity for "somatic compliance").

Sand next puts her epistemologic high-power lens on Freud's analysis of Dora's two dreams, which are the centerpiece of Dora's analysis and around which the case report is organized. Freud's last four claims, seven through ten, are then subjected to close scrutiny. Again Sand first makes Freud's goals explicit:

> Freud wanted to illustrate that [the dreams] referred to the "current exciting cause," the attempted seduction by the lake, that they referred also to some "momentous event" in [Dora's] childhood and that they set up an associative connection between these events, that is, that in the dream, past and present were linked. Further, he hoped to show how Dora's free associating to a dream resulted in the uncovering of repressed memory [p. 347].

To make a long and exciting examination short, regarding claims seven through ten Freud could only demonstrate that a part of claim eight, the connection to a current psychic trauma (the scene at the lake—one of the two legs of the dream) was confirmed; the connection to the past—the second leg of the dream, was not.[15] Claim seven (that dreams fill in amnesias and elucidate symptoms), claim nine (that dreams also refer to an event in childhood, and finally claim ten (that the dream provides an associative link between claims eight and nine) were not substantiated in Dora's dreams (p. 351).

Among the many findings that led Sand to her conclusions, an outstanding and pervasive one ought to be stressed again in closing: Freud's failure to distinguish between his own and Dora's associations; mixing the two, and treating them all as if they were hers, created an epistemologic mare's nest, from which we have not yet sufficiently extricated ourselves.[16]

Expansions of Dora's and Freud's Sociocultural Contexts

Dora's hysteria, viewed from the perspective of Freud's own presentation and that of subsequent critical readers, reflects three interre-

---

[15]Muslin and Gill (1978) added to Freud's idea of the two legs on which the dream stands a third one; the leg of the transference, which was left unrecognized in these dreams.

[16]It ought to be acknowledged, however, that Freud learned a great deal from his mistakes with Dora, and his writings prior to WWI review extensively each and every one of them and he offers his new ideas about analytic technique (Decker, 1991, pp. 160–162).

lated layers of her life's struggle. (1) Her individual, innately determined (drive-based) internal (oedipal and/or preoedipal) struggle; (2) her struggle with her family and immediate milieu in asserting her age-specific developmental (adolescent) needs; and (3) her struggle against the oppressive sociocultural and political climate of her time and place.

Dora's persistent and recurring symptoms and behavior patterns reflect various aspects and stages of these struggles and her failure to ever having mastered them.

Since Dora's analysis (which occurred shortly after Freud abandoned the seduction theory) psychoanalysts have continuously grappled with the problem of how to conceptualize the precise relationship between these three layers of experience as contributing factors to the etiology and pathogenesis of the neuroses. Although he opted for a near-exclusive emphasis on the first layer—the (drive-based) intrapsychic layer—Freud always included in his narratives some aspects of the other two, albeit without their adequate *theoretical* integration. In fact, the various psychoanalytic schools reflect differing attempts to deal with the relative pathogenetic significance of the three interrelated layers of experience.

Modern psychoanalysts claim to be all-inclusive—and in their clinical reports they often appear to be—but in their interpretive work and theoretical discourse generally fail to find the appropriate position for each of the three possible sets of contributing factors to their patients' psychopathology.

Examining this issue more closely in Dora's case is greatly facilitated by the spate of contributions (reviewed earlier) that began with the first and only direct follow-up with Dora in 1922 and reported 35 years later (Deutsch, 1957). The first follow-up serendipitously added important details about Dora's postanalytic circumstances and her ultimate fate to what we had already learned from Jones (1953, 1955, 1957). Rogow (1978) further extended our knowledge with the disclosure of Dora's identity as Ida Bauer and thus provided hitherto unavailable material about the life of Dora, her prominent brother, Otto, and the entire Bauer family and thus opened the way for further historical research. This research culminated (after two preliminary papers, in 1981 and 1982) in the recent monograph on "Freud, Dora and Vienna 1900" by Hanna S. Decker (1991), who, with outstanding historiographic skills and a matching grasp of the relevant psychoanalytic issues, offers us a compelling portrait of Freud, Dora, and their encounter within the wider context of their time and place.

From Deutsch's (1957) "Footnote" perhaps only a few bare facts are trustworthy since his entire statement (reflecting only two consultative sessions) is suffused with a depreciatory, contemptuous tone toward Dora and an uncritical acceptance of Freud's view of her, as Thompson's (1990) amazing "deconstruction" of the report demonstrates. In addition, Deutsch recorded quite a bit of factual information inaccurately. But the data in the follow-up that we may rely on is that most of Dora's earlier symptoms and personality features continued essentially unabated up to the time of the consultation (Dora was 40 then and not 42; this is just one of those inaccuracies Rogow, 1978, corrects).

"When I ventured to connect [Dora's] Ménière's syndrome with her relationship to her son," wrote Deutsch (1957), "and with her continual listening for his return from his nightly excursions, she appeared ready to accept it, and asked for another consultation with me" (pp. 162–163). Interestingly, Dora's dizziness and tinnitus disappeared between the first and second session, and Deutsch felt that "[m]y familiarity with Freud's writings evidently created a very favorable transference situation" (p. 162), a circumstance to which we may assign greater significance than to the specific content of a single, hastily given, interpretation of what might have been at the root of the conversion symptom. Dora then apparently became more communicative and expressed a great deal of hostility toward her husband; his indifference to her suffering, and his unfaithfulness and voiced disgust with marital life. Her complaints also included her son's beginning estrangement from her because of his growing interest in girls. According to Deutsch, Dora resembled her mother at that point, both physically and in her obsessive cleanliness and hypochondriacal attitude.

Learning of Dora's death in New York, Deutsch was able to obtain further information about her and her family. Dora had spent the rest of her life after her consultation suffering from the same array of symptoms for which she originally saw Freud. She had been able to get out of Vienna to France (just before she would certainly have been deported to a concentration camp), whence her successful musician son, who was already in this country, brought her to the United States. She died in New York of cancer of the colon, which was inoperable by the time it was detected. Deutsch (1957) concluded his report by saying that Dora's death "seemed a blessing to those who were close to her. She had been, as my informant phrased it, 'one of the most repulsive hysterics' he had ever met" (p. 167)— a remark for which many readers have severely criticized Deutsch, assuming that it had also been his own view.

Rogow (1978) in a "further footnote" adds to our knowledge of the Bauer family, their origin and background in Bohemia prior to their move to Vienna. He draws his information primarily from historical and biographical writings about Dora's famous brother, Otto, who was an extremely gifted, leading socialist thinker and political activist as well as a one time foreign minister of Austria. A significant aspect of the Bauers' background, about which Freud was completely silent, is mentioned here for the first time—the Bauers' Jewishness. Although conversion was frequently a self-protective motive in their social circle, "Philipp Bauer never converted to Chistianity, but the Bauers were assimilated Jews who identified with German culture. They did not, however, formally disaffiliate themselves from membership in the Austrian Jewish community" (p. 353)—except for Dora and her husband, who left their Jewish faith and converted a few months after the birth of their son (Decker, 1991 p. 127). The Bauers were thus fully "exposed to the virulent anti-Semitism that had deep roots in both [German and Czech] national groups," which rapidly escalated at the turn of the century, culminating in the Nazi invasion of Austria, heralding World War II. As a result, "both Otto and Dora were forced into exile" (p. 355)—to put it mildly.

The intimately personal, as well as the broad, historical-cultural and political, context in which Freud lived and developed psychoanalysis and continued his work has long been appreciated and has been the object of countless, extensive studies. His life and work have drawn (and continue to draw) ongoing research and scholarly attention (e.g., Jones, 1953, 1955, 1957; Ellenberger, 1970; Schur, 1972; Sulloway, 1979; Clark, 1980; Gay, 1988). In recent years, the lives of Freud's patients have also been subjected to more extensive biographical studies (e.g., Gardner, 1971; Oberholzer, 1982; Mahoney, 1984, 1986).

What Decker (1991) does, which has not been done to the same degree and depth before, is to offer us a unique portrayal of both Freud and Dora in their brief encounter by putting the lives of the Freud and Bauer families under her historical-political and cultural microscope. She explores the origins and parallel lives of Sigmund Freud and Philipp Bauer in Bohemia (and their parents' prior existence in what later became Poland) as well as their move into the Austrian capital at the dawn of the emancipation of the Jews from their second-class citizenship and repeated brutal persecutions in the Austro-Hungarian Empire. She depicts the lives of the two families as in many ways prototypical of the Jewish experience of turn-of-the-century Vienna (and of the whole Austro-Hungarian Empire). At first the Jews showed a staggering, unprecedented, rapid rise in their various sociocultural and economic accomplishments (within just a few decades after their emancipation) and were soon inexorably driven toward their next and most horrendous, well nigh complete, destruction.

Decker uses pertinent details of this historical background to put Freud and Dora as Jews into the larger context of Jewish and middle-European history of that period. With clarity and deep appreciation for the protagonists of her story, she paints a multidimensional picture of the immediate as well as the wider milieu into which Dora was born and in which she grew up to be sick; nearly the same world into which Freud was born earlier, became who he was, and developed psychoanalysis. Decker masterfully (almost seamlessly) integrates these "external" worlds with the "internal" worlds of Freud and Dora. She shows what their individual, private concerns were on the threshold of their meeting and how these concerns were in part created by what was occurring around them. In an exemplary fashion, Decker brings the cultural, the familial, and the intrapsychic into a coherent narrative of who these two people were; what their respective vulnerabilities were at the very time of their meeting; what they strove for in life and then in their analytic encounter—as these were undoubtedly determined by all three layers of their prior and ongoing life experiences.

The necessity of knowing as much as possible of this wider context for a proper analytic appraisal of the patient was clearly acknowledged by Freud (1905a) when he said that psychoanalysts were "obliged to pay as much attention in [their] case histories to the purely human and social circumstances of [their] patients as to the somatic data and the symptoms of the disorder" (p. 18). But he deliberately chose a somewhat narrower, clinical-theoretical focus for his presentation of Dora's analysis to make his major, revolutionary, points subsequent to his recent abandonment of his seduction theory. Decker greatly expanded the context (sketchily given by Freud) by depicting the social, cultural and political climate in *fin de siècle* Vienna.[17] She focused largely on three significant elements: the state of the art and science of psychoanalysis, on the status of the Jews, and on the status of women as these inevitably impinged on both Freud and Dora. These influences codetermined the nature of Dora's problems as well as her analytic encounter with Freud. Decker's vivid and lively historiography is here coupled with her knowledge of the development of psychoanalysis and an unusual grasp of the crucial conceptual issues involved.[18]

---

[17] For another highly relevant and interesting depiction of *fin de siècle* Vienna, see also Schorske (1980).

[18] My admiration for this well-researched and well-documented monograph, written with the necessary empathy for both Dora and Freud, is marred by the fact that Decker, in spite of her impeccable scholarship, did not include Kohut's (1977) reformulation of the Oedipus complex in her assessment of Freud's work with Dora. This omission is

I shall sample Decker's findings in order to capture her view of the analytic atmosphere Freud created and her view of how the various influences codetermined the nature of Dora's hysteria; how her illness, although known throughout recorded history, became emblematic (it was the leading psychopathology) of Victorian Vienna. I shall also refer to the immediate emotional issues Dora and Freud brought to their analytic encounter.

On historical and socio-cultural influences. In the portrayal of Dora's and Freud's political heritage, anti-Semitism and antifeminism had become thoroughly intertwined. This is how Decker states the issue:

> Frequent expulsions [from cities and certain regions of the empire] were usually followed by some limited permission to resettle, and life would once more resume, but never with ordinary surety. The legacy bequeathed to Philipp and Katharina Bauer and their two children by centuries of state-decreed inferiority, familial upheaval, and spasms of dubious quiet was the trauma of hopes raised only to be brutally dashed. This pattern appeared yet again once the Jews were formally emancipated, and it colored the background of Freud and Dora's encounter" [p. 15].

Thus Freud and Dora must have lived—in fact, we know they did live—with an "inherent sense of vulnerability." Dora's must have been even more burdensome as she was both a Jew and a woman. Decker goes on to say that

> [i]t is a convergent conclusion of modern psychological, sociological and historical literature that ethnic discrimination and the stresses of acculturation are sources of mental ill-health, and experimental studies have buttressed this view. . . . the worst psychological damage did not result from inevitable restrictions and special taxes but from the physical attacks and repeated expulsions, often capricious or sudden, that violated the continuity of family life and the pursuit of livelihood [p. 16].

---

regrettable, since Kohut's work on the Oedipus complex had been available since 1977, and the issue is central to the monograph. Knowledge of this reformulation might have enabled Decker to free herself (and her talent) even further from prevailing orthodoxy, to write an even more pathbreaking monograph, in my view. I put the blame on her psychoanalytic consultants (and the *Zeitgeist*), who might have shielded her against a more drastic revision of Freud's theories. But even as the monograph stands, Decker is on the verge of discovering the overriding importance of lived experience as against the primacy of drive-based unconscious fantasy, since she properly emphasizes Dora's experiences as a Jew (in an increasingly dangerous anti-Semitic and antifeminist milieu) as significantly contributing to Dora's psychopathology.

The relevance of all of this to our main theme has to do with the fact that just as Freud and Dora met at the turn of the century, another eclipse in the fate of the Jews began, culminating in the Nazi Holocaust. Decker depicts this well:

> Historical accounts of the era refer to the feelings of approaching doom that underlay the superficial air of gaiety and insouciance in *fin-de-siècle* Vienna. But usually these histories do not state clearly enough the extent to which pessimism about the future reflected the despair of the Jews and the liberals, as they saw the disintegration of their deeply held aspirations [p. 33].

Freud (1900) himself reacted to the appointment of the notorious anti-Semite Lueger as mayor of Vienna by writing "of the increasing importance of the effects of the anti-Semitic movement upon our emotional life" (p. 196)—and yet no word of it appears in his work with Dora in spite of the fact that "Jews of both Freud's and Dora's generation found their self-concept warped by the all pervasive anti-Semitism (Decker, 1991, pp. 37–38). Decker (1991) amply documents that reports of the vulgar diatribes of the Viennese anti-Semites, the repeated blood-libels all around the empire, the Dreyfus affair, and the various responses of the Jews (e.g. Zionism, socialism, conversions to Christianity, and the like), were in the daily press—neither Freud, nor Dora could have avoided reacting to them and suffering from them. Equally open were the repugnant antifeminist invectives in the press and at large political gatherings. Anti-Semitic attacks were coupled with openly demeaning references to women and with restrictions in their educational and career pursuits. Dora suffered greatly from a lack of opportunity to pursue, on a serious educational level—as her brother Otto was able to do—her interests and ambitions commensurate with her intelligence. With great sensitivity and passion Decker characterizes what Dora's experience must have been like:

> Consider then Dora's mind at eighteen. She belonged to the very first generation of Jews to be born to equal legal status after hundreds of years of officially decreed inferiority and familial disruption. But neither the state nor the populace was reconciled to emancipation, and as the years went by Dora encountered more, not less, anti-Jewish sentiment. As a woman she heard the faint beginnings of cries for female equality, but the hard fact is that the confident voices that preached women's inherent inadequacy drowned out any contradiction. It was the general consensus that women were inferior and the anti-Semites insistently proclaimed that the proof of the Jews' defi-

ciency lay in their exhibition of traits commonly associated with women. Thus did antifeminism and anti-Semitism unite at the turn of the century. A young Jewish woman like Dora could be filled with more self-doubt, and even self-loathing, than a Jewish man [p.40].

Thus "the inferiority she felt as a Jew cannot be separated from what she experienced as a women in her culture and as a human being who had been used and betrayed by her parents and the Ks" (p. 156). Here, and at many such points in her narrative, is where Decker shows how the cultural and the family influences became intimately intertwined and how both pushed Dora in the same direction: toward her particular emotional and somatic response, hysteria, rather then toward an open rebellion.

On the influence of family and friends Decker depicts Dora's experiences within the circle of her deceitful family and friends and encapsulates her findings as follows:

Dora's psychopathology was constructed on a foundation laid by a willful [and deceitful] father and an angry [depressed and self-absorbed] mother and buttressed by a patriarchal society and an anti-Semitic world. Although this base was malignant, it was not enough by itself to entrench the physical symptoms that engulfed Dora nor to induce the depression that caused her spiraling despair. The extent and chronicity of her illness also derived their power from the very special friendship of her family with another family in Meran, the Ks[19] . . . . Although Freud overlooked the roots of Dora's sickness in the larger world, he was quite correct to hypothesize links connecting Dora's symptoms with both the Ks as well as her father" [p. 62.].

Here Decker alerts us to the fact that the familial and the intrapsychic influences are intimately intertwined (to the point of being inseparable) and reinforce each other in propelling Dora toward her neurotic solution.

Among the many factors contributing to Dora's illness was the fact that by the time she was 10 or 12, she knew a lot about her father's "loose life" prior to his marriage and that he had contracted syphilis. This knowledge greatly added to her massive disillusionment with him, on top of an earlier one with her mother (p. 64). In addition, a particularly close and intimate relationship developed between the very young Dora and her father, in which she took her mother's place

---

[19] In this section of this chapter I shall follow Decker's usage of Mrs. K, Mr.K, or just K as she does. Elsewhere in the chapter, as customary in the literature, I retain the appellations Frau K and Herr K.

in caring for him during his long illness in Meran. This special relationship ended abruptly when Mrs. K. took over the role of nursing, which later developed into an affair with Dora's father. In the meantime "Dora turned for friendship and vicarious mothering to Mrs. K" (p. 68) and in her emotions also replaced her father with Mr. K. Decker recognizes why Dora's relations with the K family were so special to her: "These connections were *the main emotional sustenance* as she began to mature into a young women" (p. 69; italics added). She also appreciates that "Dora's idealization of her beloved father crumbled" for multiple reasons, the last straw having been "[h]er parents' refusal to believe her [version of the incident at the lake], Mr. K's lie and Mrs. K's betrayal," which plunged her into a deep despair for 2 years (p. 78).

On intrapsychic influences and the analytic encounter. Decker makes the bold claim that "[t]o understand Freud's psychoanalysis of Dora . . . it is necessary to know as much about Freud and his world when he was forty-four, as it is about Dora and hers when she was eighteen" (p. 87). This is in keeping with the modern psychoanalytic notion of the necessary and inevitable mutual impact of transference and countertransference.

Here, in a nutshell, is what Freud came to the encounter with: He was in the midst of his self-analysis. He had discovered the Oedipus complex and recently abandoned the seduction theory. He had just published the interpretation of dreams and was feeling his way toward a theory of sexuality. In September 1900, just before he started Dora's analysis, he was once again denied promotion to professorship and became quite despondent about it. He believed he had beens passed over because he was a Jew, that he was a victim of anti-Semitism (p. 90). This personal insult, as well as the increasingly rabid public anti-Jewish agitations, unsettled him to the point of worrying about his own and his children's future (p. 91). (Thus it seems to have been impossible for him to overlook such concerns in his Jewish patients, although he never mentions them.) Decker cogently elaborates how all of this bore on the way in which Freud conducted Dora's analysis.

Dora, on the other hand, symptomatic as she was upon returning to Vienna (somewhat ahead of her family's move), was preoccupied with her educational and career aspirations. The gymnasium, offering a full classical education as a prerequisite for entry into a university, was not open to her as a women. She pursued what was available: she attended lectures for women, studied on her own, and frequented art galleries to satisfy her thirst for knowledge. She was greatly impaired in pursuing all of this regularly, though, on account of her depression, her social withdrawal, her physical symptoms, and her unhappiness with her family in the aftermath of the K affair. She now felt increasingly powerless overall, especially vis-à-vis her father, whom she could not move to acknowledge the validity of her side of the story about Ks sexual advances at the lake. She was determined to have her father stop his affair with Mrs. K's at all cost. It was under these circumstances that her symptoms escalated; her depression intensified and she left a suicide note that her parents found. Also, she had recently fainted and convulsed after one of her latest arguments to get her father to stop the affair. This is when he became gravely concerned and brought her to Freud. In Decker's words this is what led up to the analysis:

> But the crucial moment for Dora's mental health came when she was fifteen and told her parents about Mr. K's sexual proposal, and her father declared—with her mother's tacit agreement—that she must have imagined the entire episode. Until this point Dora herself had been a willing member of the family conspiracy and an exemplary pupil of late Victorian middle-class morality as well. After this she would not tolerate the affair and begged her father to end it. The longer Philipp proclaimed his innocence, the more distraught Dora became, ending by writing a suicide note and sustaining a loss of consciousness, accompanied by convulsions and delirium. These dramatic events . . . finally moved Philipp to take her to Freud, with the hope that the talented middle-aged physician would bring her to reason" [p. 199].

Again, Decker cogently elaborates how all this came to bear on the way in which Dora presented herself to Freud, responded to his interventions and ultimately found it necessary to interrupt the analysis abruptly.

Only Decker's perception and characterization of the ensuing analytic atmosphere, rather then her extensive and detailed portrayal of the entire analytic experience, can be illustrated here with a few random quotations. To begin with, Decker states that

> [i]n spite of its short duration, Freud's psychoanalysis of Dora was a most complex affair *involving strongly held beliefs*. As Freud learned Dora's story and sought to evaluate the determinants of her illness, he was heavily influenced by contemporary medical views about women, and by late Victorian middle-class customs and conventions [p. 110, italics added].

Thus "Freud appears to have shared fully his culture's misogyny" (p. 204). The impact of these views is reflected in Freud's reaction to Dora's aspirations:

A conventional girl of Dora's background was expected to marry and to run a household. Although Dora presented Freud with a great deal of evidence that this was precisely what she did *not* want to do, *Freud was unable to respond empathically to any of it* [p. 107; italics added].[20]

At another point she emphatically states that "Freud lacked a natural sensitivity and empathy with Dora" (p. 125). This lack of empathy for Dora's predicament pervaded the analytic climate. Decker offers many telling examples. Here is one:

When Dora once insisted that "[t]he most important adults in [her] life had not only used her for their own ends, but then denied using her . . . [and] protested such treatment to Freud, he interpreted it as a resistance by which she could avoid admitting the truth about her feelings for Mr. K. and for her father [p. 112].

Dora's reality did not matter; it was brushed aside with Freud's interpretation. Decker goes on to say: "Freud was technically right in this; Dora had loved her father and had spun many romantic fantasies about K" (p. 113). But this sounds like a nonsequitur, since it was neither Dora's love for her father, nor her romantic fantasies about K that made her ill, but the way they treated her and the massive disappointment they both evoked. Decker is shifting attention here to the intrapsychic elements of Dora's Oedipus complex and does not make it explicit whether in her view it was the parental treatment or the (assumed) repressed oedipal desires that carried the greater pathogenetic weight. The decision is important because it influences both the analytic climate and the analyst's interpretive strategy decisively, as it undoubtedly influenced Freud's. Decker's overall presentation—like that of so many other readers—does give the impression that the weight rests on the former. But none of the authors reviewed can quite capture this view theoretically within the framework of classical theory, and the answer therefore remains blurred. Decker's awareness of this problem finds expression in such statements as this:

[it] . . . seems likely that Freud's abandonment of the seduction theory made him attach less significance to the familial and the environmental malignancies in Dora's life: [to] her parents' unhappy marriage, their blind eye to K's courtship, K's prolonged seduction behavior toward Dora, and K's eventual sexual harassment of her, including his sadistic intrusion into the room where she was napping [p. 125].

---

[20]See also footnote #10 regarding empathy in this connection.

This does sound as if "lived experience" carried more weight in creating Dora's psychopathology than did "drive-based" oedipal or preoedipal fantasy.

Here, I believe—after having surveyed the literature—is the clinical and theoretical crux of the problem, which does not yield to any fundamental solution by altering the analytic climate or technique alone. Those alterations were indeed (in part) already suggested by Freud himself in his technical papers between 1910 and 1914. But neither those nor subsequent further alterations in technique and theory presented in the literature would have been enough in Dora's case if the analyst would still relentlessly (or even gently) have pursued Dora's oedipal fantasies and bypassed her own immediate concerns as merely defensive. In this connection it is instructive to look at another of Decker's critiques of Freud's technique:

> Freud's efforts in the treatment to gather theoretical evidence on the role of childhood sexuality in neurosis led him to announce to Dora all his findings, proudly and inexorably, as he deduced them. This bold, intrusive approach frightened her and prompted her to flee from her psychoanalysis *before it could do her any good* [p. 125; italics added].

This idea of "before it could do her any good" is quite peculiar when juxtaposed with one of Decker's later statements:

> Nevertheless the *psychoanalysis did Dora permanent harm*. Freud compounded her father's betrayal by his unconscious exploitation of her . . . Freud's sexual intrusion, although again unconscious, mimicked only too well Mr. K's and her father's. To whatever extent Dora came to believe that the adult world was manipulative and scheming before she got onto Freud's couch, the analysis helped to solidify her view [p. 199; italics added].

Precisely. If 11 weeks of Freud's approach was harmful, more of it, I believe, would have been more, not less, harmful, unless he could have changed course drastically and could have begun to listen to Dora'a subjective experiences.

There is one theme common to the critics I have just discussed—they all found hitherto unnoticed, unexplored, or inadequately understood facets of the case regarding both theory and treatment approach and selected issues on which they saw Freud as having been either mistaken or theoretically and technically not yet far enough advanced, and in either case obviously biased. There are, as would be expected in our field, many contradictory notions about the exact nature of Dora's psychopathology, the nature of her transference to Freud (or her potential transference, which he thwarted actively or by not recognizing its presence). Disagreements and often contradictory ideas among the critics not withstanding, it is remarkable how much global agreement there still is regarding many facets of the case. This is especially so concerning the various manifestations of Freud's negative countertransference, which hindered the analysis and ultimately led to its abrupt ending. These countertransference reactions were detected and described by those who studied them with great ingenuity and persuasiveness. If a conference could be convened of all those who have written about Dora, after some discussion and after listening to Decker's exposition, most participants would agree with her conclusion that "psychoanalysis did Dora permanent harm" (Decker, 1991, p. 199), although it moved psychoanalysis further along on its developmental trajectory. The conference would also strongly represent the view that this kind of harm would not be inflicted on Dora by psychoanalysis today. But the question of why not, of how such an outcome could be prevented, would stir enough heated controversy that another conference would have to be convened to discuss it once passions had cooled.

In what follows I shall make the case for one particular view, that of self psychology and its correlated treatment approach, as a further corrective for what went wrong with Dora's analysis.

A SELF-PSYCHOLOGICAL READING

> "An investigation of error logically depends upon trust that veridicality can be ascertained. The effort to show that something has gone wrong must be based upon the conviction that, at least in principle, things can go right" (Sand, 1983, p. 334).

The Focus of this Reading

For our immediate purpose I need not engage in an extensive dialogue with Freud's critics. I give credence to them in the overall sense in which I just summarized them. Here I restrict myself to reading Freud's text primarily from a methodologic-epistemologic perspective—left largely untouched by the critics, except for Moi (1985) and Sand (1983). In this endeavor I shall avail myself of the aid of the clinical and theoretical contributions of psychoanalytic self psychology.

Freud's text and the extensive discussion of it in the literature still leave us with a number of unresolved questions regarding the core issues to be explored from the view point of self psychology. The questions are these: (1) What was it in Freud's approach and theory that led to Dora's breaking off her analysis that might be even more fundamental—if such is possible to contemplate—than Freud's failure to focus explicitly either on both the positive and negative aspects of the transference or on Dora's homosexual attraction to Frau K? (2) If Dora did not "love" Herr K—as she persistently claimed she did not—then what did she feel for him that was so traumatically disrupted at the scene at the lake? (3) Why was this incident so traumatic that Dora could, essentially, never recover from the consequences of it? (4) Once we find some answers to these questions, how would the knowledge gained guide us in her treatment? Behind these questions lurk our persistent methodologic-epistemologic questions: How do we know what we think we know about Dora from Freud's report and all the other currently available additional sources and discussions? In other words, what are the criteria (within an analytic process) that may turn our observational data into systematic "knowledge?" How can we ever know, even if only with a moderate degree of certainty, that we, the critics and reinterpreters, know Dora better than Freud did?

I hope that some answers to these questions will emerge from what follows. I shall focus only on the core issues of Dora's analysis by making Freud's own entry point into Dora's problems—the assumed pathogenic event (the scene at the lake)—my own entry point into Dora's inner life. But first to some general conclusions and to a further delineation of the subject matter to be explored and reinterpreted.

Some General Conclusions. In my view, Freud did *not* understand Dora. He merely explained her from his own theoretical perspective and from the vantage point of some of his sociocultural prejudices. Hence, Dora did not feel understood by Freud. Furthermore, he insisted on the validity of his explanations in the fashion of an infallibly clever detective who had already solved the puzzle of who committed the crime and now simply had to prove it and had to have the "suspect" accept his conclusions. Brilliant and foolproof as Freud's explanations appeared to be—especially the thorough and exemplary systematic interpretation of Dora's two dreams—they trapped Dora, forced her to admit her secrets, and left her with no alternative but to "confess" to her oedipal crime. Freud's explanations were offered in an ambience characterized more by Freud's investigative stance—his impeccable logic and attention to detail and their *assumed* unconscious meaning—along with his overriding need to prove his theory right, rather than by an ambience characteristic of a necessary therapeutic stance: a joint venture and an effort to get hold of and grasp the meaning of Dora's *subjective experiences*. Another way of expressing this is to state that the entire analysis was conducted with an eye toward elucidating the dynamics and genetics of Dora's symptoms and behavior on the basis of the *content* of what she brought to the analysis. Thus Freud essentially bypassed the dynamics and genetics of Dora's relation to himself, thereby almost entirely bypassing her subjective experiences. In fact, Freud practically fought Dora's subjective experiences in order to establish the validity of his own (more experience-distant) dynamic-genetic explanations. He recognized many of his errors later on and offered his own corrective ideas in his papers on technique between 1910 and 1914.

Having said all this, I no longer need to dwell on the discrepancy between Dora's psychoanalysis conducted at the turn of the century and one that would be conducted within the framework of the most advanced contemporary ego psychology or object relations theory that the critics brought to bear on their study of Freud's case report. From a general consensus about this in the pertinent literature I assume therefore that Dora's transference and the underlying positive and negative Oedipus complex—if their centrality could be substantiated in a second analysis—would now be properly in focus and her second analyst would also attend to the manifestations of countertransference and monitor its direct impact on the analytic process. It would now also be a matter of general agreement that the isolated pursuit of symptoms and behavior and the content of Dora's verbalizations would have to give way to a systematic focus on her transference (along with the ubiquitous defenses against it). Everything Dora brought to her analytic sessions would now be viewed within the context of the specific features of her transference. The analysis of the transference would—in this second analysis—have become the preferred route toward meaningful, affect-laden insight and structural change. Hence, I shall not direct my attention to these issues. These are thoroughly discussed and essentially settled in those prior studies that focused on up-dating Dora's analysis in the light of current knowledge from a variety of perspectives.

But what if Dora's problems could not be adequately encompassed within the oedipal paradigm of contemporary ego psychology or object relations theory? What if not even recognition and interpretation of preoedipal conflicts would substantially alter the analytic impasse in Dora's case? It is on account of these possibilities (clearly pointed to by many of the previous discussants of Dora's analysis, especially some of the French feminists) that I shall turn to some methodologic-epistemologic questions related to our mode of acquiring analytic knowledge. These matters would still have to be considered even with the availability of up-dated ego psychology- or object relations theory-based approaches to Dora's analysis (P.H. Ornstein, 1978, 1990a)..

The subject matter to be explored and reinterpreted. To delineate the areas of Dora's experiences to be understood and explained, the point of entry is clearly marked for us. On one hand, by Dora's incessantly repetitious complaints and demands (in the painful aftermath of the scene at the lake) that her father stop his affair with Frau K; on the other, by Freud's hypotheses about the origin and meaning of these complaints and demands. Dora reacted with disgust to Herr K's effort to make their relationship a sexual one. Freud insisted that Dora loved Herr K nevertheless, and he was puzzled by the fact that she could not react in a "normal" fashion to Herr K's honestly and seriously amorous approach. So, tersely put, Freud was convinced that Dora was in love with Herr K and that she repressed that love. Nothing Dora said could shake his conviction. Referring to the scene at the lake, Sand (1983) identified two of Freud's key hypotheses regarding its significance: "Dora's current neurotic difficulties were occasioned by a recent sexual trauma" and "the trauma had brought about the repression of a powerful affect" (p. 339)—these were at the root of Dora's hysteria. Freud thus found the obligatory "sexual trauma" in the incident at the lake and the obligatory "repressed affect"—here "love"—behind the disgust (reflecting a "reversal of affect"); these clinch the key elements of Dora's hysteria. Sand, as already noted, tacitly accepted these two fundamental hypotheses, without subjecting them to closer scrutiny, in order to focus her exploration on the question of the validity of Freud's remaining eight hypotheses—all but part of one she essentially found unsubstantiated. Having disposed of all other hypotheses, she left us only these first two crucial hypotheses to consider, I shall place them at the center of my considerations.

From my own perspective, and for the purpose of this exploration, the origin and meaning of the scene at the lake and its far-reaching, many-faceted, consequences will therefore have to be reexamined. Although Freud's two hypotheses and the explanations to which these led him—if one accepts the Oedipus complex as being at the root of Dora's symptoms and behavior—appear quite plausible (even ingenious), without further evidence from Dora herself the hypotheses could not be sustained. Dora never offered the evidence. There is no question, however, that the scene at the lake was a powerful precipitant for Dora's mounting difficulties. It is our main task, therefore, to search for the dominant meaning of this episode that may help us explain its consequences and trace the trauma to its source and origin. This effort will lead us to discover what Dora wanted from Freud, that is, the nature of her transferences or potential transferences, which would have required the fertile soil of an accepting ambience to emerge more fully and to flourish. The search for the meaning of the incident of the lake will also enable us to introduce Kohut's reformulation of Freud's theory of the positive and negative Oedipus complex (Kohut, 1977, 1984; A. Ornstein, 1983), which guides our current understanding of Dora's transference to Freud.

METHOD, DATA AND THEORY— A SELF-PSYCHOLOGICAL PERSPECTIVE

With his focus on symptoms, behavior and dreams,[21] Freud firmly drew an ever tightening concentric circle around Dora, closing off all her escape routes from his compelling interpretations. He thus practically tried to force her to accept the logic of his reconstructions. Dora herself, while consistently denying the validity of most of Freud's claims, nevertheless, appears to have supplied Freud with associations on the basis of which he could maintain his definitive line of reasoning without difficulty (especially, as we have seen, since he supplied his own associations whenever Dora was not forthcoming with what he expected on the basis of his biases and theoretical preconceptions). To do this, Freud did not have to enter Dora's inner world. He did not have to, and, in fact, did not, take up the empathic vantage point of observation within Dora's inner world. He could remain outside, make his observations of the sequence of the themes in Dora's free associations, and make those inferences from them which supported his theories. No matter what Dora claimed, no matter how vehemently she claimed it, what she then revealed in her associations only further confirmed for Freud the validity of his own reconstructions.

We face here a pivotal methodologic-epistemologic challenge that is as problematic today as it was at the time of Dora's analysis. Can the analyst, as Freud did, bypass Dora's subjective experiences, insist on the validity of *his* reading of Dora's unconscious, based on *his own* assessment that her associations were confirmatory, and still obtain reliable psychoanalytic data? Or would it be necessary, even mandatory, to accept, explore, and understand the meaning of Dora's

---

[21]In connection with Dora's dreams, see McCaffrey (1984).

subjective experiences as a way to get to their dynamic and genetic meanings, before rushing in with explanations that apparently interfered with, often disrupted, and ultimately wrecked the analytic process?

Freud viewed Dora's reaction of disgust when Herr K kissed her when she was 14, as well as her abrupt rejection of Herr K's advances when she was 16 as abnormal—a hysterical reaction. This view has been repudiated by all who have since then discussed it as untenable, and it is considered a basic flaw in Freud's clinical approach to Dora. Freud's preconception made it impossible for him to listen to Dora's own subjective view, entertain its possible merits, and then search for a deeper understanding of her experiences. Freud did not understand Dora because he omitted the systematic use of "understanding" (the *first* step in the interpretive process) and proceeded to a systematic use of "explaining" her symptoms and behavior (the *second* step in the interpretive process). Whenever step one is omitted, the likelihood of arriving at faulty explanations, and their unacceptability to the patient, increases.

Understanding requires an observational vantage point of seeing the patient's experiences from his or her own perspective as an avenue toward insight, rather than brushing them aside in favor of one's own external observer's perspective, as an avenue toward supposedly more reliable *explanations*. Freud appears to have eschewed empathic entry into Dora's experiences in favor of remaining an external observer of the sequence and contiguity of her free associations.[22] And it was this fundamental methodologic decision that inevitably led to all other contributing factors that best explain the failure of Dora's analysis.

Freud's theory and technique not withstanding—and in this regard we are all in the same position—Dora's rage, and her relentless quest for righting the wrong done to her, prevailed. Her rage appears to have been fully justified. But whether it is justified or not, we cannot effectively silence a patient's subjective complaints. The empirical data, that is, what Dora brought to her analysis, come through to us loud and clear once we assume the stance of the empathic observer and consider her subjective experiences as the legitimate starting point for an analytic exploration. When we are able to consider

---

[22]It is important to note in this connection that Kohut (1959) offered a significant clarification when he suggested that the analyst's method was his systematic use of empathy (vicarious introspection). Free association and defence analysis were auxiliary methods which made subjective experience available for scientific study by psychoanalysis.

Dora's reaction of disgust at Herr K's unexpected and surreptitiously inflicted kiss as reasonable and justified from *her* vantage point, we have entered her inner world and can begin to inquire about the possible unconscious determinants of that disgust. Dora's reaction to the incident at the lake two years later might then also be viewed as reasonable and justified, that is, as not a priori "hysterical." This approach would not preclude further analytic investigation by way of the analysis of the transference and countertransference.

Thus, considering Dora's reactions to both incidents as justified and reasonable does not remove them from further analytic exploration. In fact, whether they are justified and reasonable is not our analytic task to judge. Dora's reaction of disgust was her subjective experience in any case and therefore merits exploration. Accepting her subjective experience, we may still ask: Why were these incidents so painful and enraging to Dora, in view of the nature of her intense and close relationship to Herr K as depicted by Freud and to a small extent, begrudgingly agreed to by Dora? This question has undoubtedly a great deal to do with what Dora expected and wanted from Herr K in their relationship and now from Freud in the analysis.

We should turn to a sample in the text to pursue this question and note the emotional atmosphere of the analysis Freud's words clearly convey. This incident concerns the moment when, after another comprehensive restatement of his view that Dora was in love with Herr K (meticulously demonstrated to Dora by Freud by a great number of her own statements—he nailed her to the wall!), again Dora could not confirm it. This is what Freud (1905a) then says: "Later on, when the quantity of material that had come up had made it difficult for her to persist in her denial, she admitted that she might have been in love with Herr K at B _____ , but declared that *since the scene at the lake it had all been over*" (pp. 37–38; italics added). Thus, whatever feelings Dora harbored for Herr K, had been shattered as a consequence of the incident at the lake. Freud appended a footnote to the following statement by Dora, which is of particular interest to us:

> The question then arises: If Dora loved Herr K., what was the reason for her refusing him in the scene by the lake? Or at any rate, why did her refusal take such a brutal form, as though she were embittered against him? And how could a girl who was in love feel insulted by a proposal that was made in a manner neither tactless nor offensive? [p. 38].

We are asking the same question without Freud's a priori assumption that what Dora felt for Herr K was ordinary "love." Here, of course, Freud is the external observer and social judge par excellence; it is from his vantage point that Herr K's behavior appears neither tactless nor offensive. But Dora decidedly felt otherwise! Can we explain why?

We are searching for a parsimonious understanding and explanation to this question without violating Dora's subjective experiences and also trying to stay as close as possible to the empirical data Freud presents. We are aided here in our quest by Freud's own interpretations and reconstructions.

Freud is convincing in his depiction of an intense and sustained emotional involvement between Dora, Frau K, Herr K, and their two children. This Dora does not deny. What, then, is the nature of these relationships? Why does Dora object to calling her feelings and involvement with Herr K "love?" And why did she become so infuriated when Herr K attempted to turn it into an overtly sexual relation? Freud even insists on seeing Dora's relation to Frau K ultimately as a (homo)sexual one. He views Dora's relation to the K's children as in the service of her sexual attachment (on a more surface level) to Herr K, and (on a deeper level) to Frau K, both of which relationships are denied and hidden behind Dora's reawakened oedipal love for her father, which is what Freud retrospectively considers to be the content of Dora's transference that he missed.

Once we take up the empathic listening position, however—which Freud did not do—we can hear the predominant, sustained, and cohesive theme in Dora's relation to Freud: her insistent demand to be heard regarding her version of the scene at the lake and to be affirmed and validated in her view of her father's affair with Frau K, and have him stop it.[23] Nothing less than that seemed to satisfy her. It appears from this element in Dora's reaction that there were two separate aspect to the traumatic incident at the lake. One was Herr K's attempt to *sexualize* his relationship to Dora—rather than remaining

---

[23] Freud made an intriguing remark in this connection. He assumed that if Dora could get her way with her father and make him stop his affair, she would be able to relinquish her neurosis. Freud also stated that he was opposed to such a move by Dora's father, because Dora would then gain such power from her neurosis that she would use this at any time to coerce her environment to do what she wanted from it. He thought her relinquishing her demand would lead to a more fundamental cure. Why was Freud so concerned with the negative impact of "empowering" Dora?

What also interests us here is the implicit notion of pathogenesis in Freud's mind, the question of the function of lived experience in the genesis of neurosis, which this idea hints at. The question extends from the impact of her immediate to her wider milieu—i. e., the impact of anti-Semitism and antifeminism—which Dora is viewed by many as having fought off with her hysteria. Freud's distinction of primary and secondary gain appears now as an inadequate solution to this fundamental dilemma in the etiology and pathogenesis of the neuroses.

for her the much-needed idealized stand-in for her father; continuing to be her nonincestuous object, her mentor—or, in the present context, more appropriately defined as a *selfobject*.[24]

The other was her father's disbelief in her story, compounded by the fact that Herr K denied it and defamed Dora instead; and Frau K supported him against Dora. This profound betrayal by her own father and by her idealized father- and mother-substitutes constitutes the essence of the lakeside trauma, a replica of even earlier traumatic experiences sustained at the hands of her parents. Evidence is found in the fact that, it was only *after* the incident at the lake, and *after* everyone denied that it happened, that Dora began to object so violently to her father's affair with Frau K. This also helps us understand why, she might have "loved" him before, but "since the scene at the lake it had all been over." Had Freud been able to hear Dora's story without immediately brushing aside her assertions and demands in favor of his own agenda and setting out to prove her wrong in her denial that she loved Herr K,[25] she might well have developed an *idealizing transference*[26] to Freud. The vicissitudes of the working through of this idealizing transference would then have undoubtedly revealed Dora's deep and painful disappointment in her father as well as her search for an idealizable substitute for him in Herr K. It would then also have become clear that not only did she direct her idealizing needs toward Herr K who rewarded her amply by affirming her unfolding feminine self (e.g. the presents, the flowers, and the like); but she also idealized Frau K, as a more worthy and admirable stand-in for her own mother, from whom she also ex-

---

[24] Kohut (1971) defined the "archaic selfobject" (he spoke of the mirroring, idealized and alter-ego selfobject) as an "other" who is needed and used for his or her functions in the formative years of the self to enable the process of "structure building" through "transmuting internalization." He later (1980) introduced the concept of the "mature selfobject"—an "other" who is needed for maintaining (and occasionally restoring) the cohesiveness and vitality of the self.

[25] Although Freud notes that he accepted Dora'a story of the kiss and the lakeside incident as accurate in all details, there is no evidence in his text that he ever expressed this to Dora directly. His overall interpretive strategy does not seem to have conveyed this attitude to her.

[26] Freud's case history as given does not permit a clear-cut recognition of whether Dora's idealizations were archaic, oedipal, or adolescent in nature. The authors (e.g., Glenn, 1980; Scharfman, 1980) who have discussed Dora as an adolescent have not yet absorbed this significant differentiation possible on the basis of the well established cohesive selfobject transferences in a well conducted analysis. I shall assume (and try to document) that Dora's psychopathology had very early roots and that under proper circumstance she would have remobilized an archaic mirror transference as well as an archaic idealizing transference to Freud, indicating an early disturbance in her relation with both her mother and her father.

pected support, affirmation, and approval of her unfolding feminine self, and apparently never received it. Dora was traumatically disappointed by both Herr K and Frau K. Thus deeply hurt and undermined in her effort to find in these relationships a remedy for her deficiencies in development (inadequate mirroring by her mother and the mother's unavailability as an idealized selfobject; massive, traumatic de-idealization of her father and wanting him to make up for what she did not receive from her mother), she turned to Freud with expectations to make up for the consequences of these failures in parental empathy. However, in the treatment she was again brutally disappointed by Freud and after a relatively brief respite she essentially remained an emotional cripple for the rest of her life (Deutsch, 1957, Rogow, 1978, and especially Decker, 1991).[27]

The successful mobilization and working through of Dora's idealizing transference might well have enabled her to remobilize later an even more profoundly disturbing and earlier traumatic relationship to her mother in an archaic mirror transference.

But Freud offered her no such opportunities because he could not take temporary leave from his oedipal paradigm and his culture-bound prejudices and listen to Dora afresh. It is worthy of note that, if Dora's Oedipus complex did in fact represent the core of her

---

[27] Decker offers us a more detailed follow up on Dora's life after her last visit to Freud until her consultation with Deutsch in 1922 and from that time on until her death in 1945.

While Dora could not really escape Viennese antifeminism, she did try to escape anti-Semitism and its consequences shortly after her son was born, by converting to Christianity. Two historical events conspired to defeat her efforts. Her parents died before WWI; its aftermath and the ensuing peace treaties deprived her of much of her inherited fortune, since her father's textile factories were now situated in a foreign country, Czechoslovakia, without her access to them. The security of her social life as a convert was progressively less and less secure. It appears from Decker's research that Dora managed her external life against all odds fairly, but emotionally only marginally and never symptom free for long. With mounting anti-Semitism and progressively more stringent anti-Jewish laws Dora was ultimately considered a Jew according to the Nuremberg racial laws. This brought her back legally to the group whose fate she hoped to escape rather than share. Further impoverished, and now a widow, she obtained work as a bridge teacher (ironically worked with Frau K in this capacity) doing fairly well at it but now doing marginally both socially, economically and emotionally. Yet, after prolonged persecution and facing deportation and (now we know) certain death, she managed to immigrate almost miraculously in the last minute. It appears from Decker's narrative that under these circumstances Dora was able to mobilize whatever it took to survive and elude what the Nazis had in store for her—perhaps this, too, reflects a hidden strength she could never fully recover in her analysis or later in life. The distinct impression Decker leaves us with is—as she also stated explicitly—that Dora remained an emotional cripple for life. But it is also evident from Decker's narrative account of her life that she had the potential for something much better.

neurosis, it would have emerged in the transference more convincingly (without the need for him to force it!) had Freud been able to give a hearing to her desperate effort to find validation for her actions vis-à-vis Herr K and her painful disappointment in Frau K.

The severity and intractability of Dora's reaction to Herr K's dual betrayal (the attempted sexualization of the relationship and its subsequent denial) and Frau K's abandonment of her at a crucial moment (when she sided with her husband against Dora), require further explanation. Of course, Freud knew (and the critics agreed, each in his or her own fashion) that it was Dora's relation with her own mother and father (for Freud primarily or exclusively the father) that was the source of her later vulnerability to the specific traumatic events. Freud, as we saw, focused almost exclusively on the innate, drive-related origins of Dora's vulnerabilty, while he simultaneously told us in his narrative of the role of her early and later experiences with her mother and father and seemed to ascribe predisposing (but not causative) significance to them in relation to Dora's hysteria.[28]

The question of severity and intractability, therefore, takes us back to the nature of Dora's transference to Freud. It is in the working through and reconstruction in the transference of Dora's earlier experiences, in conjunction with the additional data available, that we would have to search for the answers. But it is here that we are handicapped since a "regressive" transference did not develop, on account of the brevity of the contact but even more so because of Freud's attitudes and interventions which blocked Dora's idealization of him and certainly interfered with her feeling mirrored. She often felt just the opposite, attacked. We shall have to exrapolate from the available data.

Is it not plausible that Dora left the analysis abruptly because she felt powerless to change the atmosphere in the analysis? She was already suffering from her inability to bring her parents around to her view of the scene at the lake, to move the Ks to recant their accusations against her, and, certainly, to change the anti-Semitic and antifeminist climate of Vienna. The only place where she could act to throw off what she must have felt as an oppression (replicating and reinforcing what she had already experienced with her family, with her friends the Ks, and in her wider milieu of Vienna) was in the analysis. Here, she must have felt, she did not have to endure the repetition of the sexualization of the relationship with Freud, which

---

[28]Freud did not yet have his later notion of the "complementary series" to include both under the rubric of causation, indicating relative strength in it for the innate and the environmental and their relation to each other.

his explicit probing for details on sexual matters and his explicit interpretations of them unintentionally fostered. Here she could stop it and exercise some power.

Focusing on the revenge motive—while perhaps accurate from an external observer's perspective (it did reflect the way Freud experienced it but that does not by itself prove that that was Dora's motive)—Freud thereby deflected attention from and did not explore how Dora experienced from the inside what he called her revengefulness. Freud considered Dora's revenge an inevitable (drive-based) phenomenon rather than her response to what he actually did and stood for. From Dora's perspective, her revenge might have been that she reached the limit of her tolerance for being misunderstood, disregarded, used, or exploited again, for Freud's purposes. If so, her abrupt departure might actually have revealed some hidden strength in self-assertiveness that she could not exercise in her life outside of the analysis except through the covert manner of her symptoms and behavior. She refused to accept Freud's reality as her own. Since he could not offer her the needed appreciation of her own reality, we would now read and interpret Dora's "hysteria" as a profound self-disorder and understand it as reflecting her inner struggle to resume her derailed and thwarted development as well as her failed attempts to throw off all that was oppressive to her (within her family, her immediate and wider milieu and then in the analysis) in order to achieve her recovery. A second analysis today would recognize this reemerging capacity (interpretively) and would not undermine (let alone punish) Dora's strivings for independent, even if to an outside observer "willful," action.

The depth, persistence, and pervasiveness of Dora's illness and our knowledge of the confluence of intrafamilial "toxicity" and environmental reinforcements as causes indicate early and ongoing traumatization. The portrayal of Dora's mother and their earliest and later relationship makes the assumption of inadequate or unreliable mirroring experiences with her plausible. Dora's efforts to obtain these experiences belatedly from her aunt, from Frau K, and later from Freud in the transference offer us more than just speculative evidence (based only on the anamnesis) that Dora remained "mirror hungry" all her life. Having turned to her father had some tangible benefits. He admired her budding intellect, made her (all too early) his confidant and gave her a role in nursing him when he was ill in Meran. That made Dora feel important, useful, needed—but seduced and prematurely sexually stimulated. Thus, her idealization of her father and his response of mirroring her early intellectual gifts and other talents, as well as her budding femininty, carried the extra burden of having to compensate her for what she had missed in her relations with her mother. This is what made her massive disillusionment so traumatic rather than a phase-appropriate, slow process, one with ensuing internalization of values and ideals during her development. She then turned to Herr K and Frau K to fill in her "missing psychic structures"—on one hand: assertiveness, reliable self-esteem, capacity for enjoyment and the free pursuit of her goals and ambitions; on the other hand: the internalization of ideals and values leading to an ability for self-soothing, self-calming, and general internal regulation. In all of these areas Dora remained deficient, but was searching for a way to acquire these abilities belatedly elsewhere. It is idle to speculate whether or not she would have succeeded had Herr K and Frau K been able to live up to their assigned roles. Perhaps she would not even have needed an analysis then and could have lived a full life, her "compensatory structures" (Kohut, 1977) providing her with a cohesive self. But this thought is no more idle than Freud's notion that if Dora's father had given in to her demand that he stop his affair she would have recovered. It all depends on how we view the nature of Dora's psychopathology. (Freud's suggestion that Dora marry Herr K and that her father marry Frau K, falls essentially under the same rubric.).

Freud (and some of the readers) took many of the manifest elements of Dora's story (the triangle with her father and his mistress; the love of an older man and the assumption that she loved him and deep down wanted his sexual advances, but could not accept them on account of their incestuous nature, and so on) as indicating an oedipal pathology. They failed to explore the psychic functions these behaviors served, which would have revealed a much earlier disturbance. Some other readers did recognize a more basic, earlier developmental disturbance beneath the symptoms and behavior, again without explicitly exploring the functions they served. For instance, Dora's "flirtatiousness," or any other manifestations of her effort to get attention in the service of bolstering her shaky and enfeebled self, was either seen in oedipal or preodipal terms, without reference to the function her symptoms and behavior with the Ks served and without recognition that these were efforts at recovery, efforts at reopening a thwarted and interrupted emotional development. This recognition raises the possibility that what appeared as "oedipal" and "sexual" were attempts at self-stimulation to relieve loneliness, depression, powerlessness and despair. Dora tried to "cure" herself through her relationship to Herr K and Frau K and then through the transference to Freud.

Kohut's (1977, 1984) reformulation of the Oedipus complex sheds light on the nature of Dora's developmental deficits. First of all, Kohut differentiated the normal oedipal phase or period from the already disordered Oedipus complex. The oedipal period itself may be full of conflicts, transient and less frightening than usually portrayed; but mainly it represents a more joyous developmental achievement, a consolidation of the self and its basic functions as a prelude to healthy adolescence and adulthood, although further traumata at any later time along the way may still have pathogenic impact. By the time the child reaches the oedipal phase in a favorable milieu, he or she has acquired a reasonably cohesive self. Successfully traversing this phase means that one's gender-specific attributes, one's maleness and or femaleness, has been appropriately mirrored (affirmed, validated, admired, and valued). It is these experiences that facilitate the resolution of normal oedipal conflicts. For the girl, it is important that her mother admire and accept her budding femininty without undue competitiveness for her affection for her father and that the mother allow its unfolding in relation to a preference for paternal, non-seductive, approving responses. For the boy, it is equally important that he receive his father's pride in his budding masculinity without undue competitiveness for his affection for his mother.

This is the milieu in which the normal oedipal conflicts of both boys and girls find their proper resolution. If the child arrives at this phase with an already traumatically enfeebled, fragmentation-prone self (as Dora undoubtedly did), the oedipal phase will become the battleground for attaining a compensatory cohesiveness belatedly. This phase will under such circumstances, not permit the attainment of a gender-specific sexual maturation. It will still be a battle to gain or regain the cohesiveness and vitality of the self. This was the struggle that Dora was involved in. Her so called "oedipal" issues appeared so paramount and unresolvable, in part because they were reinforced socioculturally and in part because their function and purpose in Dora's life and in her analysis were misunderstood. It is this aspect of Dora's psychopathology that none of the previous critics recognized in the corrective measures they recommended.[29]

The idea of Freud's belatedly strong emphasis on Dora's "love" of Frau K (what he called her negative Oedipus complex) as an even more fundamental problem than her positive Oedipus complex was is again of both clinical and theoretical interest and should be looked at

---

[29]There are some notable exceptions. See especially Scharfman (1980) on Dora's need for a mentor and a nonincestuous new object and Decker (1991) for the needed emotional sustenance Dora sought from the K's

from the perspective of self psychology. A recent discussion of "An Idealizing Transference of the Oedipal Phase" (A. Ornstein, 1983) sheds light on the meaning and significance of Dora's "homosexual love" for Frau K. Ornstein writes:

> It could be argued that the appearance of idealizing needs that are coupled with sexualization represent the negative Oedipus complex in the transference, a retreat from the infantile sexual longings for the mother and competition and murderous toward the father. The negative Oedipus complex has been viewed traditionally as a pathological constellation when it becomes manifest in the transference. In contrast in the course of normal development, this phenomenon has been linked to the fate of archaic narcissism. (Blos 1979 says: "The negative oedipal attachment is a narcissistic object tie.") I believe that this contradiction between the interpretation of the meaning of the transference phenomenon in which idealization and erotization are combined can now be understood as an *intense (therefore sexualized) need to be merged with and to be admired by the parent of the same sex*. I am suggesting that what has traditionally been described as 'the negative Oedipus complex' in the transference, can now be recognized *as an effort to resume [arrested] psychological development* at that phase when the child through phase-appropriate mirroring by an idealized homogenital parent acquires pride and pleasure in his own masculine strength or her own feminine beauty and nurturance. Therefore, when, in the transference, the experiential content is either longing for the sexual closeness with the homogenital parent or, when the longing appears as "latent homosexuality" in dreams and free associations or, when these affects are defended against with an exaggerated emphasis of the positive oedipal affects, the erotization under these circumstances [e.g., what Freud incorrectly called Dora's "love" for Frau K.] represents the intensity of longing to be united with and to be mirrored by the idealized homogenital parent" (A. Ornstein, 1983; p. 140; italics added; see also Blos, 1979).

Freud tied the gender-specific attainment of normal sexuality to the overcoming of the positive as well as the negative Oedipus complex. It is therefore pertinent to close with a statement by Kohut (which may well serve as a foundation for a further elaboration of the nature of sexuality, male and female, from a self-psychological perspective, which has not yet attained common currency and has been missed by the feminist critics of Freud's views on female sexuality). Kohut said:

> The healthy self-esteem of the female baby—whose nuclear self had been mirrored empathically by an adult, experienced by the baby as a selfobject, who is proud of her—will in other words, lead to the healthy

self-esteem and to the healthy self-expression wishes of the older girl, and will, ultimately, enter into the joyful wish of the grown women to have babies (if hormonal stimulation and the cultural milieu support this wish) or will prompt her to seek self-expression via different routes (if hormonal stimulation is lacking and the cultural milieu directs her toward the joyful pursuits of other goals). And in the obverse, the not-empathically-responded-to, the depressed female baby, older girl, and, ultimately, woman—lacking a firmly established self which proudly wants to exhibit and express itself—will hypercathect the experience of isolated drives, and isolated body pats and body products, in order to stimulate herself, in order to feel alive and will then, secondarily, experience the failures in the supraordinated area of the self, (the depressed self, the loss of self-expressive joyfulness, the disconnectedness from sustaining idealized goals) as shortcomings of body parts and the frustration of circumscribed drives . . . the self—the basic experience of being a center of independent initiative and of being the recipient of impressions and of having cohesiveness in space and continuity in time—with its nuclear ambitions and and ideals and its creativeness cannot be adequately conceptualized within a framework of drives . . . [pp. 787–788].

Dora's psychology is more accurately assessed by these considerations. Clearly pointing to the fact that her suface "oedipality" was an expression of a more profound pre-existing self disorder. Thus, oddly, contrary claims in the Dora literature notwithstanding hysteria does not provide us with an accurate prototype of femininity—a formulation of health based on pathology, as promulgated by Freud.

CONCLUDING COMMENTS AND AN EPILOGUE

From a self-psychological perspective, Dora's "love" for Herr K reflected an archaic idealization, at times in oedipal garb, of him and her need to be valued and affirmed by him. Her need to maintain a close relation to a (nonincestuous) paternal selfobject was traumatically rebuffed when Herr K attempted to sexualize his relationship with Dora and defamed her afterwards. Dora's "love" for Frau K also expressed her archaic needs for mirroring and idealization (again at times in oedipal garb), in her search for acceptance and validation of her budding femininity and sexuality, and in her attempt to make up for her mother's failed mirroring of her. What other meaning could be attributed to her unrelenting demand that Freud (as well as her father,

Herr K, and Frau K) validate her perceptions? That this validation was so crucial (and without which the analysis could not successfully proceed) is attested to by the fact that once Dora confronted Herr K and Frau K with her accusations and they accepted them (Frau K verified her knowledge of the affair and Herr K validated her version of the scene at the lake), Dora calmed down considerably and was even able to return to Freud and ask for a continuation of her analysis. She was ready to pursue, I believe, "a more fundamental cure" for which Freud, in fact, had held out to her some hope before. I read this as evidence that Dora's demand for validation of her perceptions (an aspect of her need for mirroring) required first priority in the analysis, which Freud could not give it on theoretical grounds. Yes, she did want to confront him too with her newly won evidence that she was right all along, but why did Freud (and some other readers) see this as a pathologically intense revenge? Freud placed such emphasis on Dora's inevitable revengefulness that he doubted the therapeutic benefit of a continued analysis at that time and painted a bleak prognosis of what analysis could accomplish with such an enraged and revengeful person. This may be one of the reasons why he did not understand what Dora wanted from him on her return. The fact is that Freud disappointed Dora deeply in her efforts to remobilize in the transference her mirroring and idealizing needs toward both her father (and Herr K) as well as toward her mother (and Frau K). Had this been made possible for her by Freud then, or in a second analysis in our time, Dora would have been found eminently analyzable. She would now be seen as someone whose shaky, fragile, and enfeebled self could be analytically consolidated. This consolidation would then allow further work on strengthening her traumatically weakened feminine self.[30]

---

[30]It is my perception that although Dora was "courted" by Herr K (the flowers, the presents, the long walks and the time spent together), this positive and at first not overtly sexual response strengthened Dora's fragile, enfeebled self. For Dora these responses of Herr K were necessary "nutrients" for the consolidation of her nuclear self. The discussions of Dora's femininity in the literature assume a much more advanced level of emotional maturity than she was ever capable of attaining. Yes, her femininity was an issue—but it still served earlier, more archaic needs, while she was also striving to attain higher levels of maturity. This is what made the scene at the lake so traumatic. It is interesting in this regard that, while the kiss at 14 disturbed her, she could forgive and forget; and she could continue her relations with Herr K—she knew what she needed from him and wanted to get it. Dora's need and the K's response to it was crucial even at 18, when the scene at the lake was a more blatant transgression of the necessary nonsexual frame and Herr K's subsequent denial made it all the more painfully traumatic.

EPILOGUE

The case of Dora is not yet finished. No case ever is, since the process of interpretation is an endless one, with only temporary (often quite satisfying) resting places along the way. Each generation of psychoanalysts and psychotherapists, with their advancing knowledge, will see more and different aspects both of Freud's and of Dora's contributions to this earliest of analytic case reports. They will then inevitably consider their own vision of Dora, Freud, and psychoanalysis as being the most compelling one, just as we do now.

A new psychoanalytic paradigm, such as that of self psychology (Kohut, 1971, 1977, 1984), allows us to see what we could not see, or what we could not see and articulate as clearly, before. And what we do see only vaguely cannot yet be assigned the proper theoretical weight or be fitted into a comprehensive new view. However, in the end, this new outlook will also limit our horizon. When that happens, it will be time to break out of the confines of a limited and limiting set of theories. The difficulty is that those of us "inside" our preferred theoretical framework discover its limitations only gradually and against great reluctance. If and when we do so, we may not be able to find the necessary remedy, a new and equally compelling paradigm, right away. This needed step can be taken only by the rare, creative innovators in psychoanalysis. Until such a moment as that, we generally cling to an already outdated paradigm, oblivious of its shortcomings, in order to conserve our energies so that we may continue their investment in our clinical work unencumbered by serious doubts.

REFERENCES

Adatto, C. P. (1966), On the metamorphosis from adolescence into adulthood. *J. Amer. Psychoanal. Assn.*, 14:485–509.

Begel, D. (1982), Three examples of countertransference in Freud's case of Dora. *Amer. J. Psychoanal.*, 42:163–169.

Bernheimer, C. & Kahane, C. ed. (1985), *In Dora's Case*. New York: Columbia University Press.

Bernstein, I. (1980), Integrative summary: On the re-viewings of the Dora case. In: *Freud and His Patients,* ed. M. Kanzer & J. Glenn. New York: Aronson, pp. 83–91.

Blos, P. (1962), *On Adolescence*. New York: Free Press.

———— (1972a), The function of the ego ideal in late adolescence. *The Psychoanalytic Study of the Child*, 23:93–97. New York: Quadrangle Books.

———— (1972b), The epigenesis of the adult neurosis. *The Psychoanalytic Study of the Child*, 23:106–135. New York: Quadrangle Books.

———— (1979), Modifications in the classical psychoanalytic model of adolescence. In: *Adolescent Psychiatry*, ed. S. Sherman & P. Giovacchini. Chicago: University of Chicago Press, pp. 6–25.

Bonaparte, M., Freud, A. & Kris, E. ed. (1954), *The Origins of Psychoanalysis*, New York: Basic Books.
Buckley, P. (1989), Fifty years after Freud: Dora, the Rat Man and the Wolf Man. *Amer. J. Psychiat.*, 146:1394–1403.
Clark. R. W. (1980), *Freud: The Man and the Cause*. New York: Random House.
Collins, J. et al. (1985), Questioning the unconscious: The Dora archive. In: *In Dora's Case*, ed. C. Bernheimer & C. Kahane. New York: Columbia University Press, pp. 243–253.
Decker, H. S. (1981), Freud and Dora: Constraints on medical progress. *J. Soc. Hist.*, 14:445–464.
──── (1982): The choice of a name: "Dora" and Freud's relationship with Breuer. *J. Amer. Psychoanal. Assn.*, 30:113–136.
──── (1991), *Freud, Dora, and Vienna 1900*. New York: Free Press.
Deutsch, F. (1957), A footnote to Freud's "Fragment of an Analysis of a Case of Hysteria." *Psychoanal. Quart.*, 26:159–167.
Ellenberger, H. (1970), *The Discovery of the Unconscious*. New York: Basic Books.
Erikson, E. H. (1959), *Identity and the Life Cycle*. Psychological Issues, Monogr. 1. New York: International Universities Press.
──── (1962), Reality and actuality: An address. *J. Amer. Psychoanal. Assn.*, 10:451–474.
──── (1964), *Insight and Responsibility*. New York: Norton.
Freud, S. (1900), *The Interpretation of Dreams. Standard Edition*, 4 & 5. London: Hogarth Press, 1953.
──── (1905a), Fragment of an analysis of a case of hysteria. *Standard Edition*, 7:3–122. London: Hogarth Press, 1953.
──── (1905b), *Three Essays on the Theory of Sexuality. Standard Edition*, 7:133–243. London: Hogarth Press, 1953.
──── (1911–1915), Papers on technique. *Standard Edition*, 12:85–173. London: Hogarth Press, 1958.
──── (1923), *The Ego and the Id. Standard Edition*, 19:3–66. London: Hogarth Press, 1961.
Gardiner, M. ed. (1971), *The Wolf Man by the Wolf Man*. New York: Basic Books.
Gay, P. (1988), *Freud: A Life for Our Time*. New York: Norton.
Gill, M. M. & Muslin, H. L. (1976), Early interpretation of transference. *J. Amer. Psychoanal. Assn.*, 24:779–794.
Glenn, J. (1980a), Notes on psychoanalytic concepts and style in Freud's case histories. In: *Freud and His Patients*, ed. M. Kanzer & J. Glenn. New York: Aronson, pp. 3–19.
──── (1980b), Freud's adolescent patients: Dora, Katharine and the "homosexual" woman. In: *Freud and His Patients*, ed. M. Kanzer & J. Glenn. New York: Aronson.
──── (1986), Freud, Dora and the maid: A study of countertransference. *J. Amer. Psychoanal. Assn.*, 34:591–606.
Hertz, N. (1985), Dora's secrets, Freud's techniques. In: *In Dora's case*, ed. C. Bernheimer & C. Kahane. New York: Columbia University Press.
Jennings, J. L (1986), The revival of Dora. *J. Amer. Psychoanal. Assn.*, 34:607–635.
Jones, E. (1953), *The Life and Work of Sigmund Freud*, Vol. 1. New York: Basic Books.
──── (1955), *The Life and Work of Sigmund Freud*, Vol. 2. New York: Basic Books.
──── (1957), *The Life and Work of Sigmund Freud*, Vol. 3. New York: Basic Books.
Kahane, C. (1985), Why Dora now? (Introduction, part 2.) In: *In Dora's case*, ed. C. Bernheimer & C. Kahane. New York: Columbia University Press, pp. 19–32.
Kanzer, M. (1980), Dora's imagery: The flight from a burning house. In: *Freud and His Patients*, ed. M. Kanzer & J. Glenn. New York: Aronson, pp. 72–82.

———— & Glenn, J., ed. (1980), *Freud and His Patients,* Vol. 2. New York: Aronson.
Kohon, G. (1984), Reflections on Dora: The case of hysteria. *Internat. J. Psycho-Anal.,* 65:73–84.
Kohut, H. (1959), Introspection, empathy and psychoanalysis: An examination of the relation between mode of observation and theory. In: *The Search for the Self,* Vol. 1, ed. P. H. Ornstein. New York: International Universities Press, 1978, pp. 205–232.
———— (1971), *The Analysis of the Self.* New York: International Universities Press.
———— (1975), A note on female sexuality. In: *The Search for the Self,* Vol. 2, ed. P. H. Ornstein, New York: International Universities Press, 1978, pp. 783–792.
———— (1977), *The Restoration of the Self.* New York: International Universities Press.
————(1980), Reflections of advances in self psychology. In: *Advances in Self Psychology,* ed. A. Goldberg. New York: International Universities Press, pp. 473–554.
———— (1984), *How Does Analysis Cure?* ed. A. Goldberg & P. Stepansky. Chicago: University of Chicago Press.
Krohn, A. & Krohn, J. (1982), The nature of the Oedipus complex in the Dora case. *J. Amer. Psychoanal. Assn.,* 30:555–578.
Lacan, J. (1985), Intervention on transference. In: *In Dora's Case,* ed. C. Bernheimer & C Kahane. New York: Columbia University Press, pp. 92–104.
Langs, R. (1976), The misalliance in Freud's case histories. I. The case of Dora. *Internat. J. Psychoanal. Psychother.,* 2:411–431.
———— (1980). The misalliance dimension in the case of Dora. In: *Freud and His Patients,* ed. M. Kanzer & J. Glenn. New York: Aronson, pp. 58–71.
Lewin, K. K. (1973–74), Dora revisited. *Psychoanal. Rev.,* 60:519–532.
Mahony, P. J. (1984), *Cries of the Wolf Man.* New York: International Universities Press.
———— (1986), *Freud and the Rat Man.* New Haven, CT: Yale University Press.
Malcolm, J. (1981), *Psychoanalysis: The Impossible Profession.* New York: Vintage Books.
———— (1987), Reflections: J'appelle un chat un chat. *The New Yorker,* April 20, pp. 84–102.
Marcus, S. (1976), Freud and Dora: Story, history, case history. In: *Representations.* New York: Random House, pp. 389–442.
McCaffrey, P. (1984), *Freud and Dora:* New Brunswick, NJ: Rutgers University Press.
Meissner, W. W. (1984–1985), Studies on hysteria: Dora. *Internat. J. Psycho-Anal.,* 10:567–598.
Moi, T. (1975), Representation and patriarchy: Sexuality and epistemology. In: *In Dora's Case,* ed. C. Bernheimer & C. Kahane. New York: Columbia University Press, pp. 181–199.
Moscovitz, J. (1973), Aspects of homosexuality in "Dora." *Revue Française de Psychanalyse,* 37:359–372.
Muslin, H. & Gill, M. (1978), Transference in the Dora case. *J. Amer. Psychoanal. Assn.,* 26:311–328.
Oberholzer, K. (1982), *The Wolf Man Sixty Years Later.* New York: Continuum.
Ornstein, A. (1983), An idealizing transference of the oedipal phase. In: *Reflections on Self Psychology,* ed. J. Lichtenberg & S. Kaplan. Hillsdale, NJ: The Analytic Press, pp. 135–148.
Ornstein, P. H. (1978), Introduction: The evolution of Heinz Kohut's psychoanalytic psychology of the self. In: *The Search for the Self,* Vol. 1, ed. P. H. Ornstein. New York: International Universities Press, pp. 1–106.
———— (1990a), Introduction: The unfolding and completion of Heinz Kohut's paradigm of psychoanalysis. In: *The Search for the Self,* Vol. 3, ed. P. H. Ornstein.

Madison, CT: International Universities Press, pp. 1–82.
―――― (1990), How to enter a psychoanalytic process conducted by another analyst: A self psychology view. *Psychoanal. Inq.*, 10:478–497.
Possick, S. (1984), Termination in the Dora case. *J. Amer. Acad. Psychoanal.*, 12:1–11.
Pumpian-Mindlin, E. (1965), Omnipotentiality, youth and commitment. *J. Amer. Acad. Child Psychiat.*, 4:1–18.
Ramas, M. (1980), Freud's Dora, Dora's hysteria. In: *In Dora's Case,* ed. C. Bernheimer & C. Kahane. New York: Columbia University Press, pp. 149–180.
Rieff, P. (1963), *Freud: Dora—An Analysis of a Case of Hysteria.* New York: Collier Books.
Rogow, A. A. (1978), A further footnote on Freud's "Fragment of an Analysis of a Case of Hysteria." *J. Amer. Psychoanal. Assn.*, 26:331–356.
Sand, R. (1983), Confirmation in the Dora case. *Internat. Rev. Psycho-Anal.*, 10:333–357.
Scharfman, M. A. (1980), Further reflections on Dora. In: *Freud and His Patients,* ed. M. Kanzer & J. Glenn. New York: Aronson, pp. 48–57.
Schlesinger, H. (1969), Family: A study of family member interactions. In: *Psychoanalytic Forum,* Vol. 3, ed. J. A. Lindon. New York: Science House, pp. 13–65.
Schorske, C. E (1980), *Fin-de-Siècle Vienna.* New York: Knopf.
Schur, M. (1972), *Freud: Living and Dying.* New York: International Universities Press.
Slipp, S. (1977), Interpersonal factors in hysteria: Freud's seduction theory and the case of Dora. *J. Amer. Acad. Psychoanal.*, 5:359–376.
Sprengnether, M. (1985), Enforcing Oedipus: Freud and Dora. In: *In Dora's Case,* ed. C. Bernheimer & C. Kahane. New York: Columbia University Press, pp. 254–275.
Sulloway, F. J. (1979), *Freud: Biologist of the Mind.* New York: Basic Books.
Thompson, A. E. (1990), The ending to Dora's story: Deutsch's footnote as narrative. *Psychoanal. Contemp. Thought,* 13:509–534.
Van Den Berg, S. (1987), Reading and writing Dora. *Psychoanal. Contemp. Thought,* 10:45–67.

Anna Ornstein
LITTLE HANS
His Phobia and His Oedipus Complex
(The Analysis of a Phobia in a Five-Year-Old Boy, 1909)

A HISTORICAL PERSPECTIVE

The historical significance of the case of Little Hans can best be appreciated when the time of its publication is placed into the context of the evolution of Freud's theory of the neurosis. "The Analysis of a Phobia in a Five-Year-Old Boy" was published in 1909, before Freud postulated an aggressive drive, before the second theory of anxiety and the formulation of the structural theory. In 1905, Freud had finished "The Three Essays on the Theory of Sexuality," in which he suggested that "the motive force" of all neurotic symptoms of later life could be found in the vicissitudes of the sexual instinct and where he postulated that anxiety arose in relation to inadequately discharged libido.

As a researcher, Freud (1909) was eager to find proof for his theory and suggested that "surely there must be a possibility of observing in children at first hand and all the freshness of life the sexual impulses and wishes which we dig out so laboriously in adults from among their own debris . . ." (p. 6). It was important for Freud to find evidence of the existence of infantile sexuality and the affects associated with the Oedipus complex because, for him, solving the riddle of the psychoneuroses meant solving the riddle of the workings of the mind.

Placing the Oedipus complex into the center of the psychoneuroses had far-reaching consequences for the evolution of psychoanalytic theory, specifically, in relation to repression as a mental mechanism. Because the development of this crucial psychological mechanism, more than any other, is related to the resolution of the Oedipus complex, once the mechanism of repression was understood, other basic psychoanalytic concepts could be elaborated: infantile amnesia; the theory of psychic trauma and symptom formation; the evolution of primary process thinking into secondary process; and the transition from the pleasure principle to the reality principle.

In view of the centrality of the Oedipus complex to the neuroses, it is of particular importance that it was in relation to Little Hans, whose observation occurred directly, within the child's emotional milieu—a setting that Freud trusted not to interfere with the child's naturally emerging curiosity regarding sexual matters—that Freud asked the direction whence repression sets in: is it from the side of the libido or is it from the side of the environment? This question was the precursor to the one Freud raised later in relation to the superego; how are we to understand the harshness and punitiveness of the superego in cases where the parents are mild mannered and kind? In 1909, Freud answered these questions in terms of the vicissitudes of the sexual libido. Repression set in, he said "because of a somatic . . . constitutional incapacity of the masturbatory gratification. . . ." Since masturbation provided an unsatisfactory discharge of libido, the very persistence of sexual excitement "at a high intensity" made the establishment of a repression barrier, a psychological necessity. Characteristically for Freud, however, he added that "this question must be left open until fresh experience can come to our assistance" (p. 136).

Indeed, 17 years later, in "Inhibitions, Symptoms, and Anxiety" (Freud, 1926), after the ego has been delineated from the id and the superego recognized as a "gradient within the ego," Freud said that "an instinctual demand after all is not dangerous in itself; it only becomes so inasmuch as it entails a real external danger, the danger of castration" (p. 126).

SELF PSYCHOLOGY AND THE OEDIPUS COMPLEX

A reexamination of Little Hans's phobia cannot be undertaken without exploring the significance of the oedipal phase of development from a self-psychological perspective. The reexamination of the Oedipus complex represented a crucial turning point in the evolution of psychoanalytic self psychology. By including the psychoneuroses in the self-disorders in the broader sense, Kohut (1977) formulated the bipolar self as a supraordinate structure within the psyche.

In order to contrast the traditional view of the Oedipus complex with that in self psychology, it is helpful to consider these differences from the perspective of the three subphases of the oedipal period: (a) the child's readiness to enter the oedipal phase, (b) the actual experiencing of the oedipal passions, and (c) the resolution of the conflict.

The Child's Readiness to Enter the Oedipal Phase

We have to remember that Freud's intent with the case report of Little Hans was to trace the neuroses of adults to their genetic roots in childhood rather than to place the vicissitudes of the Oedipus complex into a developmental context. Freud was not at that time concerned with developmental experiences that preceded the oedipal period. Present-day analysts, regardless of their theoretical orientation, would have to take the developmental achievements prior to the oedipal experiences into consideration in order to assess the child's capacity to deal with the affects that are associated with this developmental event. For example, Silverman (1980), recognizing that Freud did not have available at that time the necessary theoretical tools, "completed" the case report by adding to it the "pregenital factors." Silverman pointed to Hans's "anal-sadistic resentment and jealousy of his mother's babies and baby-making capacity and his phallic wish to urinate into his mother to impregnate her"; and how the child's "submission over the years to frequent enemas contributed to a passive-feminine identification with his mother, and the wish to be impregnated and delivered of babies" (p. 109). And Kohut (1977), from a self-psychological perspective, stated that: "the presence of a firm self is a precondition for the experience of the Oedipus complex" (p. 227).

The Actual Experiencing of the Oedipal Passions

The affects associated with the oedipal phase—sexual stirrings and the desire to possess the parent of the opposite sex sexually, competition, jealousy and murderous wishes toward the parent of the same sex, and, most important, castration anxiety—are viewed very differently by traditionalists and self psychologists. In traditional theory, the inherently conflictual nature of the experience and the inevitability of castration anxiety makes repression mandatory, walling off the conflict and enabling the ego to turn to the next developmental phase, latency. Because of its incestuous and murderous content, the walled-off conflict remains burdened by guilt and therefore becomes forever the potential source of a neurosis. This essentially pathological view of a normal developmental phase can best be explained by the fact that Freud had conceptualized the Oedipus complex as this may occur developmentally on the basis of reconstructions from the analyses of adults; the case of Little Hans was to confirm what he already "knew."

Obviously, psychoanalysts have only reconstructed data available for postulating developmental experiences. Kohut too depended on such data for his constructions. His observations, however, led him to a conclusion very different from Freud's. He found that at the end of their analyses, some patients with primary self-disorders developed an oedipal constellation. This he considered to be the positive result of the consolidation of the self the patient had never achieved before. He observed that this "brief oedipal phase is accompanied by a warm glow of joy, a joy that has all the earmarks of an emotionality that accompanies a maturational or developmental achievement" (Kohut, 1977, p. 228). From such clinical observations, Kohut concluded that in normal development, where parents experience joy and pride in the child's developmental achievements, the oedipal phase, rather than being fraught with guilt and anxiety, is experienced joyfully.

In 1977 Kohut still retained the idea that the conflictual aspects of the Oedipus complex are the genetic focus of the development of Guilty Man and of the genesis of the psychoneuroses. His emphasis on parental responsiveness to the child's oedipal experiences, however, indicated a radical shift from the inevitable conflicts created by drive maturation to the potentially pathogenic impact of parental attitudes and responses to this forward move in development. He argued convincingly that the dramatic, conflict-ridden Oedipus complex of classical analysis, depicting the child's aspirations to be crumbling under the impact of castration fear, is not a primary maturational necessity but rather the result of frequently occurring failures of narcissistically disturbed parents to respond empathically to their oedipal-age children. He called into question the classical conception of the Oedipus complex as a ubiquitous, normal, human experience and posited it as a manifestation of an already pathological phenomenon. He distinguished between a relatively silent and joyful normal developmental phase during which, the child is able to integrate "his libidinal and aggressive strivings" and an Oedipus complex in which normal development becomes derailed, resulting in the formation of an infantile neurosis that may later give rise to a psychoneurosis:

> Subsequent to an oedipal phase that is marred by the failure of the parents to respond healthily to their child, a defect in the child's self is

set up. Instead of further development of a firmly cohesive self able to feel the glow of healthy pleasure in its affectionate and phase-appropriate sexual functioning and able to employ self-confident assertiveness in the pursuit of goals, we find throughout life a continuing propensity to experience the fragments of love (sexual fantasies) rather then love and the fragments of assertiveness (hostile fantasies) rather then assertiveness and to respond to these experiences—which always include revival of the unhealthy selfobject experiences of childhood—with anxiety [Kohut, 1984 pp. 24–25].

The Resolution of the Conflict

The resolution of the Oedipus complex, which results in the child's identification with the same-sex parent, has particular importance for classical theory. This is the developmental event that finalizes the construction of a repression barrier and the internalization of standards and values; the establishment of the superego as a relatively separate mental agency. Since self psychology views the psyche as an open system, no developmental experience is conceptualized with the same finality as is the resolution of the Oedipus complex in classical theory. The processes of idealization and the need to be mirrored by idealized others continue into adult life; they continue to make a contribution to the development of values and ideals and to the strengthening of the gender-related features of the personality. The ongoing developmental significance of these selfobject experiences can best be appreciated in the need of young adults to be approved and valued by their idealized superiors and in their need to be mirrored in their gender-characteristic attributes in order to feel sexually desirable.

COMMENTS ON THE ANALYSIS OF LITTLE HANS'S HORSE PHOBIA

Only after several readings can one appreciate the value of this detailed case report. The reader can trace the way in which the emergence of new material following interpretations, and the "overcoming of resistances," made the repeated revisions of Freud's understanding of the phobia necessary. We may not agree with his interpretations (and those that were made by the father, independent of Freud's recommendations) and how these may have been responsible for creating the "resistances." But we would still have to admire the consistency with which Freud employed the method of psychoanalysis to arrive at his particular conclusions.

Freud (1909) described Hans as a "cheerful, amiable, active-minded young fellow, whose sexual precocity is correlated to an intellectual precocity" (p. 142). At the time Freud introduced the child to the reader, the boy had already entered the oedipal phase and appeared to be well into the second subphase of his oedipal experiences; he was under the impact of strong affects and expressed a great deal of curiosity. Hans appears to have been a child with a lively intellect who was actively engaged in trying to solve the mysteries of life. He went about this as all children his age do, namely, by first observing his own body and its functions and then trying to make generalizations on the basis of his observations. In keeping with his cognitive development, Hans began to order his experiences and observations about himself and others into categories, such as noting that living things urinate while nonliving things do not. A lovely example of this occurred when Hans, at the age of three and three quarters, observed some water being let out of an engine and wanted to know where the engine's "widdler" was. After a while he added thoughtfully, "A dog and a horse have widdlers; a table and a chair haven't" (p. 9)[1]

Hans's father, however—in his eagerness to set Hans "straight" on matters sexual—appears to have interfered with this process of

---

[1] A reexamination of Little Hans has to include what we now know about the cognitive development of young children. The sexual curiosity that many parents observe in their children is part of young children's need "to make order" in their now rapidly expanding universe. Singling out sexual curiosity as if sexual matters were the only ones children are curious about may well be related to the fact that adults have more difficulty answering these questions then they do others. Questions related to the genitals and sexual differences appear to have special significance in the minds of adults, and the answers children receive may, at times, be more confusing then illuminating.

The oedipal phase (roughly between three and six or seven years) is the period in cognitive development that falls between the sensorimotor phase and "concrete" operations of thought and interpersonal relations. This is a transition from the sensorimotor phase (when children are dependent on action to orient themselves in their surround) to concrete operations, when they have the ability to build relatively accurate mental images of the world around them. This transition is a lengthy process primarily because to "achieve a systematic mental representation involves constructive processes analogous to those which take place during infancy; namely, the transition from the initial state in which everything is centered on the child's own body and actions to a "decentered" state in which his body and actions assume their objective relationships with reference to all other objects and events registered in the universe. This decentering, laborious enough on the level of action (where it takes at least eighteen months), is even more difficult on the level of representation, because the preschool child is involved in a much larger and more complex universe then the infant" (Piaget and Inhelder, 1969, p. 94).

intellectual and emotional mastery. There were a series of instances where the father contradicted Hans regarding the correctness of his observations and instead offered information that the little boy could not fully comprehend and that he experienced as confusing and challenging.

The first and most obvious misinformation related to whether or not women had widdlers. When he observed his mother urinating, Hans asked her if she had a widdler. The mother answered without hesitation that she indeed had a widdler. The father "corrected" the mother and informed Hans that women had *no* widdlers. Hans first resisted and wondered how little girls (his sister) could urinate; but since his father, in his idealized wisdom, knew "everything," Hans could not simply dismiss such information. This confusing state of affairs appears to have increased his urgency to ask more and more questions.

The father's information to Hans rested on his considering the widdler[2] only as a sexual organ and on his assumption that Hans's curiosity was spurred only by the sexual sensations he experienced in his widdler. Hence, he could not appreciate the child's logic and confirm the validity of his observation, which had established a connection between the act of urination and the need to have an organ to perform such an act. When the father eventually corrected his earlier "explanation" and told Hans that there was a *difference* between the widdlers of men and women—rather than that one group of people had one and the other did not—Hans's spirits lifted markedly. We have to leave the question open whether this clarification had alleviated the child's castration fears, as Freud assumed, or his spirits had lifted because this clarification coincided with his own observations and his logic was finally validated by his father.

Another remarkable misinformation occurred in relationship to childbirth. After Hans made the correct connection between his mother's moaning in pain, the bloody bath water, and the birth of his sister, he was informed by his father that the baby had been brought by a stork. Because of his very different agenda for the child, this was probably the father's most obvious failure to recognize Hans's extraordinary ability to make meaningful connections between disparate pieces of observations.

In another instance, the father, in his eagerness to "cure" Hans of

---

[2]In the original German, the word used is "wiwi-maker," which is more obviously connected to urination than is widdler, which is an ambiguous term and has more of a sexual connotation. (I am grateful to Dr. Barry Magid for drawing my attention to this distinction.)

his castration fear, made an interpretation that must have further thickened the fog in the child's mind. When Hans told his father that he did not want to touch a horse because it might turn around and bite his hand, the father corrected him by saying that he probably meant "widdler" when he said "horse." When the child protested and said that a "widdler doesn't bite," the father could not be convinced and replied: "Perhaps it does though" (p. 30).

Freud knew Hans's parents[3] and considered them to be people who could raise their children without coercion so that the manifestations of infantile sexuality would not suffer undue and premature repression and could therefore be more readily documented. To emphasize the central significance of infantile sexuality and castration anxiety in neurosogenesis and also to undo the influence of his earlier seduction theory, Freud appears not to have taken some obvious parental attitudes into consideration in the genesis of the phobia.[4] The most outstanding example of this omission was the way in which the various castration threats by both parents were not considered to be of pathogenic significance. Freud's argument was that these threats had been going on for about a year before the appearance of the phobia and by the time the child became ill he was "engaged in a struggle to break himself of the habit (of masturbation) that fits in much better with repression and the generation of anxiety" (p. 27). This statement indicates that Freud began to reformulate the theory of anxiety in the course of this analysis. (Indeed, in "Inhibitions, Symptoms and Anxiety," Freud (1926) returned to the discussion of the case for this very reason.) He, however, had not as yet made unconscious guilt

---

[3]Hans's father, Max Graf, was an enthusiastic friend of psychoanalysis at that time, and Hans's mother was briefly Freud's patient. The Grafs eventually divorced, and the father became disillusioned with psychoanalysis (Glenn, 1980).

[4]In traditional psychoanalytic theory, environmental factors in development and pathogenesis were incorporated into the concept of the complementary series; a term used by Freud to account for the etiology of the neuroses without having to make an either/or choice between endogenous factors (represented by the fixation of libido) and exogenous factors (represented by frustration or over-gratification of the instincts). The idea of the complemental series was not clearly articulated until the *Introductory Lectures* (Freud, 1917), and even afterwards there remained considerable ambiguity as to the role of the environment in relationship to development and pathogenesis. External factors have been recognized as pathogenic mainly in the form of relatively gross physical and mental or emotional deprivation and abuse. Such traumatic childhood experiences have been etiologically linked to severe borderline conditions and to the psychoses, that is, to the nonanalyzable psychological conditions. For these reasons, they have been conceptually carefully delineated from the psychoneuroses (A. Freud, 1968).

responsible for the appearance of the symptom. Rather, at this time it was in relation to masturbation "that the first piece of therapy was interposed" as he eventually concluded that "it was the child's sexual excitement that suddenly changed into anxiety" and agreed with the parents that Hans "was frightened of his own masturbatory indulgences." He advised the parents that in offering Hans this interpretation, they should lay great stress on his affection for his mother, "for that was what he was trying to replace by his fear of horses" (p. 119).

One of the most controversial (and contradictory) interpretations relates to the question why horses became the object of Hans's phobia? Answers can only be speculative, for the object of a phobia is overdetermined, and each "interpretation" may indeed touch on one or another aspect of this overdetermined choice. This is especially true when a child's shifting, and often contradictory, statements have to be fitted into a particular theoretical orientation. Slap (1961), for example, was impressed with the pathogenic significance of the tonsillectomy as a confirmation of the child's castration anxiety even though the onset of the phobia predated the tonsillectomy by a month. As evidence, Slap cites Hans's frequent references to this event in his fantasies and, most convincingly, for Slap—the fact that after the tonsillectomy, Hans's fear shifted to *white* horses. After the surgery, Hans feared lying down in the bathtub and became particularly distressed at seeing the black leather straps around the mouth and the eyes of horses.[5]

Freud interpreted the child's fear of horses (biting, falling down, "making a row") as a displacement from the hated and therefore feared father—a direct consequence of his wish to sexually possess his mother. Many of the child's associations, however, indicated that the horse most likely represented his mother, not his father. Freud briefly considered this possibility but then quickly dismissed it by asking, "What would be the meaning of his being afraid in the evening that a horse would come into his room?" (p. 27). Freud obviously maintained a deep conviction that a horse could only represent a male, and, if the child was afraid, he could only be afraid of his father, not his mother. Nothing could interfere with this conviction even when Hans called the coal-carts and furniture vans the horses were pulling the "stork-box carts," which were obvious references to his pregnant mother (p. 81); or when Hans related his fear of the horse making a

---

[5] Black surgical masks were apparently in vogue in Vienna at that time. Freud himself interpreted the black straps as representing the father's mustache—an additional support for the notion that the horse was a displacement from the father.

row and screaming to his sister's screaming "when Mommy whacks her on her bottom and she makes such a row with her screaming" (p. 72).

Along with the oedipal rivalry and hostility, Freud also recognized the child's deep attachment to and love for his father. These, however, had to remain in the background as Freud was pursuing his goal of proving the formulation of infantile neurosis, which he had arrived at from his reconstructions from the analyses of adults. For the same reason, Freud also had to discount the child's repeated assertions of anger at and fear of his mother—most likely responses to the mother's threats of castration[6] and abandonment.[7]

Hans was explicit about his feelings about both his parents. For example, he said to his father: "When you are away, I am afraid you are not coming home." Father: "And have I threatened you I shan't come home?" Hans: "Not you, but Mummy. Mummy told me she won't come back" (pp. 44–45). Or: after Hans came to his father's bed and told him that he was frightened, his father asked: "So you are fond of me and you feel anxious when you're in your bed in the morning? and that's why you come in to me?" Hans: "Yes. Why did you tell me I'm fond of mummy and that's why I am frightened, when I am fond of you?" (pp. 43–44). He also told his father that his fear of watching the men beating the horses with a whip had to do with his wish to beat his mother in retaliation for her threatening to beat him with a carpet beater.

In spite of the child's repeated disagreements with the oedipal interpretations and his continued protestations that he loved his father and feared his mother (which were understood to be resistances), his father continued to make these interpretations since he and Freud "knew better" what the child was supposed to feel. For example, in relation to Hans's reluctance to leave the house, the father said that Hans "sticks to the house from love of his mother, and he is afraid of my going away because of the hostile wishes he nourishes against me" (p. 45).

Hans was brought to Freud only once in the course of the analysis,

---

[6]When Hans was three and a half his mother found him with his hands on his penis and told him, "If you do that, I shall send for Dr. A. to cut off your widdler" (p. 8).

[7]One evening as he was being put to bed, Hans expressed a wish to sleep with his little friend Mariedl. When his mother told him the little girl would have to stay with her parents, Hans said that then he would go downstairs to sleep with her. Mother: "You really want to go away from Mummy and sleep downstairs?" Hans: "Oh, I'll come up again in the morning to have breakfast and do number one." Mother: "If you really want to go away from Daddy and Mummy, then take your coat and knickers and—good-by!" (p. 7).

at which time he told the child that his fear came from being afraid of his father because he was so fond of his mother. Hans disagreed and told Freud that he was not only fond of his mother but of his father as well and that when his father left, he worried that he would not come back.

A SELF-PSYCHOLOGICAL INTERPRETATION OF THE PHOBIA

In reexamining the case of Little Hans, we have to raise the following questions: Why did the experience and the resolution of the oedipal phase become problematic for Hans? Why did he develop a phobia in the course of it? From a self-psychological perspective, these questions cannot be answered without considering that the actual threats to the child's physical integrity and the mother's threatening him with abandonment had pathogenic significance.

Anthony (1970) commented on the one-sided view analysts have about the Oedipus complex. Drawing attention to Freud's description of the parents of Little Hans, Anthony wondered why, in spite of observations that child analysts had made on the behavior of parents of oedipal age children, "nevertheless, it is rare in any of these for the analyst's attention to be focused on the parent's reaction" (p. 279). As an example Anthony cites the case of seven-year-old Peter described by Rangell. The mother in this case was described as suffering from anxiety symptoms, "but little more is said about the reactions of the parents—the analysis of the oedipal conflict is confined to the boy" (Anthony, 1970 p. 280).

In his posthumously published book *How Does Analysis Cure?* Kohut (1984) devoted a section to the discussion of castration anxiety, and he returned once more to the developmental significance of the child's oedipal experiences. He did so because of the central role that castration anxiety is supposed to play in both healthy and pathological development. In classical theory, it is castration anxiety that either brings about adequate repression of the infantile conflicts or, when the anxiety is excessive, leaves the repression barrier permeable for the development of a later neurosis.

Kohut distinguished primary and secondary oedipal anxiety. The primary anxiety of the oedipal child, he said, was simply one special instance of the type of anxiety he had described earlier, as "disintegration anxiety" (Kohut, 1977), the experience of which is a profound dread of death and annihilation. This disintegration anxiety occurs when the environment, from an early age on, is fairly consistently unavailable and new challenges repeatedly overtax the child's immature psyche. The second form of anxiety is related specifically to the oedipal phase and "arises in the child when, after the disintegration of the healthy oedipal self, characterized by affectionate and assertive attitudes, the fragmented oedipal self, characterized by sexual and destructive fantasies and impulses, take over (Kohut, 1984, p. 16).

It could be debated, however, whether Hans's phobia was related to castration anxiety or, rather, was the symptomatic manifestation of separation anxiety. I build my case in favor of the latter possibility and suggest that Hans's separation anxiety was an expectable response to his mother's unpredictable attitude as she alternated between overstimulating the child and becoming verbally threatening and punitive with him. These attitudes may well have become accentuated during her pregnancy and after the birth of the new baby. Hans's reaction to his mother's attitude, her overt threats and Hans's murderous wishes toward his little sister, whom he was supposed to love,[8] generated a host of new feelings (anger, fear, and jealousy) in the child, which created conflicts that found a neurotic solution in the phobia.

When Hans first experienced anxiety while out on a walk with the maid, he asked to be taken home because he missed his mother; he did not want to be away from her. This appears to be a straightforward expression of separation anxiety similar to that which emerged when he woke up with anxiety, saying, "When I was asleep I thought you were gone and I had no Mummy to coax[9] with" (p. 23).

To consider that separation anxiety rather then castration anxiety was responsible for the phobia is not a uniquely self-psychological notion. Bowlby (1973), citing evidence similar to mine, considered the phobia to be related to the child's "anxious attachment" to his mother. More specifically, Bowlby related Hans's fear that a horse would bite him to an incident when Lizzi, a little girl who was staying in a neighboring house, went away and the luggage was taken to the station in a cart pulled by a white horse. Lizzi's father was there and had warned her not to put her finger to the white horse or it would bite her. "Thus," says Bowlby, "we find that Hans's fear of being

---

[8] At one point, Hans admitted to his father that he would prefer if Hanna weren't alive. Father: "If you'd rather she weren't alive, you can't be fond of her at all." Hans (assenting): "Hm, well." Father: "That's why you thought when Mummy was giving Hanna her bath, if only she'd let go, Hanna would fall into the water." Hans (taking the father up): ". . . and die." Father: "And then you would be alone with Mummy. A good boy doesn't wish that sort of thing, though." Hans: "But he may think it."

[9] Coax was Hans's expression for cuddle.

bitten by a horse is closely linked in his mind to someone's departure" (p. 286). Fromm (1968) and Garrison (1978) also considered the child's relationship with his mother to be the decisive factor in the development of the phobia. Lindon (1990) is most explicit in this regard. The mother, he says, rather then understanding the child's subjective experiences, was "mis-attuned, overstimulating, seductive, intrusive, and controlling."

It is interesting that in spite of the many questions raised about Freud's original formulation of the case, it remained the prototypical one for all later psychoanalytic theorizing related to the various forms of phobias. More important, it also remained convincing "evidence" that the oedipal phase of development is fraught with conflicts and inevitably becomes the source of neurosis either in childhood or later in life.

Addressing the question of parental participation in the psychopathology of the oedipal age child, I (Ornstein, 1983) concluded that it may be a historically determined theoretical bias in psychoanalysis that only what is instinctual is considered truly intrapsychic. There is a concern that the recognition of the neurosogenic impact of the environment means the abandonment of an intrapsychic position and a shift to an interpersonal, environmentalist one. The introduction of the concept of the selfobject, however, helped analysts maintain their intrapsychic focus without dismissing the potentially pathogenic impact of the environment not only in the early years of life but in the later phases of development as well.

The many sadistic and sexual features that have been interpreted by classical psychoanalysts as causative of Hans's difficulty in resolving the Oedipus complex would be interpreted in self psychology as secondary phenomena, as breakdown products, related to faulty parental responsiveness to the child's curiosity, his assertiveness, his anger at his mother, and his jealousy of his sister for replacing him in his special position in the family. As Kohut (1984) would say, this was an example where the healthy oedipal self (characterized by affectionate and assertive attitudes) fragmented and sexual and destructive impulses had taken over (p. 16).

Trying to cope with his jealousy and anger toward his mother and his new sibling, Hans looked to his father for closeness and understanding. Although Hans found him very interested in his dreams and fantasies, his father does not seem to have been very empathic to the child's state of mind; he repeatedly negated the child's subjective experiences and his observations of events around him. As a sensitive and bright youngster, Hans correctly perceived his father's interest and continued to "supply" him with information, which he, in turn, with equal eagerness, would take to "the professor." This arrangement appeared to suit both their selfobject needs: Hans needed his father's special investment in him at this time, and his father needed Freud's approval for bringing to him exciting and fresh material about Hans's interest in sexual matters.

What the consequences were for Hans for having to make internal compromises in order to retain a relatively optimal connection with his father and to be able to continue to idealize him is difficult to say. However, observations made on children who grow up with repeated breaches in parental empathy (which are experienced by the children as repeated narcissistic injuries) indicate that such breaches lead to the formation of masochistic and paranoid defenses, which become integrated into the growing psyche as permanent features of the personality (Ornstein, 1981; Ornstein and Ornstein, 1985).

As mentioned earlier in relation to the father's "misinformation," we also have to take into account the state of Hans's cognitive development. Even before the development of language, children begin to be aware of—and be responsive to—the subjectivity of the people around them (Stern, 1985). With the acquisition of language and symbolic play, their need to deal with, and to coordinate, differing views on their observations is greatly expanded. The universe that they are now constructing is subject to the responses they are receiving to their inquiries. "Unlike most actions, the operations always involve a possibility of exchange, of interpersonal and personal coordination, and this cooperative aspect constitute an indispensable condition for the objectivity, internal coherence and universality of these operative structures" (Piaget and Inhelder, 1969, p. 95).

Just as cognitive development, specifically logical thinking, is enhanced by validating children's observations of the world around them, in the same way, recognition and appreciation of their subjective experiences facilitate the thrust toward the development of self-coherence. Children can best achieve these forward moves when their caretakers are able to decenter from their own agendas and when their responses correspond to the child's ability to integrate the information offered. Oedipal-age children need such affirmative responses particularly since this is the age when relatively rapid intellectual, physical, and emotional growth demands an integration of contradictory and divergent affects, needs, and wishes. While being able to retreat safely—and without guilt—into the lap of mother, these children need their parents' delight and validation of their growing ability to perceive the world around them correctly in terms of causal connections between things and events. In this respect,

Hans's father failed him repeatedly, but the child's idealization of him never seemed to falter.

A SELF-PSYCHOLOGICAL PERSPECTIVE ON THE RESOLUTION OF THE PHOBIA AND FURTHER COMMENTS ON THE OEDIPAL PHASE OF DEVELOPMENT

In keeping with Freud's preformulated ideas regarding the Oedipus complex, Hans's father wanted to save him from the undue anxiety related to his son's sexual wishes for his mother and help him "face" his true feelings of hate and rivalry toward his father. Being concerned that premature repression of sexual wishes would leave Hans vulnerable to the later development of a neurosis, the father could not be available to the child as a validating and affirming selfobject.

But Hans's disappointment in his father was only temporary. The father's interpretations did not affect the child's idealization of him because the disappointment was related to what the father *did* rather than who he *was* (Kohut and Wolf, 1978, p. 417). The father's genuine interest in Hans and his careful attention to the details of his fantasies, in the end, outweighed the impact of the confusion Hans had experienced when his father failed to validate his inner experiences and his observations relative to events swirling inside and around him. His father made him feel that it was desirable to have questions and to ask them, that his son's curiosity pleased and delighted him: his observations may not have been "correct" in his father's opinion, but Hans was valued for making them.

The idealization of the father and the mirroring of the child by the idealized father are selfobject functions that at this phase of development still have important structure-building properties. To be mirrored by the idealized homogenital parent appear to be a special selfobject function that makes crucial contributions to the gender-specific features of the child's personality.

This view of the oedipal phase affects our current understanding of the major psychological experiences connected with it. Instead of assuming sexual identification to occur in response to the threat of castration, we have to consider that for a male child to develop a strong "masculine self" he has to be able to idealize his father as a strong and competent male and feel, in turn, affirmed and validated in his own masculine strivings by the idealized father. In other words, we have to distinguish between transmuting internalization of these optimal selfobject functions and identification as it is postulated by classical analysis. Transmuting internalization occurs when parental selfobject responsiveness is optimal during the oedipal phase of development. This mode of structure building has to be distinguished from identification. Identification, in the context of the Oedipus complex, would have to be considered to be identification with the aggressor, indicating that this is not "the normal" resolution of a normal developmental experience but, rather, that the child's self-assertive competitiveness and need to idealize the homogenital parent had gone awry.

Inasmuch as faulty parental selfobject functions[10] could have pathogenic significance, the Oedipus complex can no longer be considered as inherently neurosogenic because of the strength of the drives or because of the immaturity of the childish ego to deal with the instincts (A. Freud, 1968). Rather, when optimally failing parental selfobject responses are available, the oedipal phase would have to be considered to be that phase in development which makes crucial contributions to the ultimate consolidation of the adult self and provides it with its special features; a self that can "accommodate" needs and wishes that give rise to conflicts, sexual or otherwise and that not only can "tolerate" but welcome strong passions, be these strong sexual feelings or competitive ones. The Oedipus complex, then, instead of being viewed as a childhood illness that has to be "overcome" or "resolved," could be viewed as a period in development that significantly expands the child's growing self.

Just before the phobia disappeared Hans shared two fantasies with his father. Interestingly, both these fantasies were associated with the kind of joyful and triumphant affects that Kohut (1971) described in relation to the oedipal constellations he observed at the end of successfully completed analyses.

The first fantasy was that his father gave him a bigger widdler, one that "was not merely a repetition of the earlier fantasy concerning the plumber and the bath. The new one was a triumphant, wishful fantasy, and with it he overcame his fear of castration." In the second fantasy, he expressed the wish to marry his mother and to have many children by her. The father, instead of being killed, was "promoted"—to a marriage with Hans's grandmother. With this fantasy, both

---

[10]Kohut (1977) spelled out the various possible responses parents can give to the child's sexuality and competitive, self-assertive, behavior. He referred to "optimally failing" rather than "optimally responsive" parents in order to give recognition to the "average, expectable, failures" of parents when confronted with these particular developmental issues in their children (p. 237).

the illness and the analysis came to an appropriate end" (Freud, 1909 pp. 131 and 132).

THE FATHER AS THE THERAPIST

That the treatment was conducted by the father was considered by Silverman (1980) as having had "inevitable drawbacks." According to Silverman, it must have made it difficult for the father to deal with "Hans's negative oedipal, homosexual longings and . . . to provide Hans with information about the male's role in copulation and procreation" (pp. 113–114). Silverman also thought that in addition to Freud not having analyzed the preoedipal factors, the father's failure to include the sensation in the testicles as a source of sexual excitement made the analysis incomplete.

Glenn (1980) too considered the treatment by the father to have been unfortunate primarily because "accurate interpretations create the impression that the omniscient parents read the child's mind, thus interfering with his sense of mastery, his sense of reality and eventually, his sense of autonomy" (p. 123).

Freud himself was of a different opinion about the father's role in this treatment process. Freud (1909) felt that

> it was only because the authority of a father and of a physician were united in a single person, and because in him both affectionate care and scientific interest were combined, that it was possible in this one instance to apply the method to a use to which it would not otherwise have lent itself [p. 5].

I agree with Freud and would add that in this combination of "affectionate care" and "scientific interest," the affectionate care eventually gained the upper hand. This case history may be an example of treatment in which the content of inappropriate interpretations eventually wore off in the light of a more basic communication in the form of caring and respect for the child's emotional and intellectual growth. For the eventual outcome of "the analysis," it was of special significance that such attitudes were communicated to the son by the father himself.

ADDENDUM

Kohut (1984) recognized that the pivotal question related to the nature of the Oedipus complex could not be easily settled, and he suggested that "the gap in our knowledge here can only be filled by extensive clinical reports concerning analyses of cases suffering from structural neuroses treated by self psychologically informed analysts" (p. 23). Several analysts have taken up this challenge and reported on their findings (Terman, 1984/85; Ornstein, 1983, 1989). In the two case that I reported (one male and one female), the male patient's difficulties were related to the area of assertiveness and initiative, while the female patient suffered from an inability to experience her body as "truly feminine." Both patients developed transferences that reactivated the areas of their respective psychopathology. The male patient's yearning for an opportunity for idealization was most poignantly expressed in his regret for having chosen a female analyst—he felt that without experiencing me as a strong and competent male, who, in turn, could appreciate his own newly emerging assertiveness, he could not get well (Ornstein, 1983). The female patient developed an erotized transference and a deep desire to be able to bring a "rapture" on my face that she could experience as the ultimate expression of my pleasure in her beauty and attractiveness (Ornstein, 1989).

In both cases, I postulated that what was revived in these transferences was the "negative Oedipus complex," a constellation that, in classical analysis, has been viewed as a pathological constellation, which, Blos (1979), however, linked, in normal development, to the fate of archaic narcissism. In my view, the transference phenomenon in which idealization and erotization are combined can now be understood as an intense (therefore erotized) need to be merged with the gender attributes of the homogenital parent. These clinical instances lead me to the conclusion that

> what has traditionally been described as the negative Oedipus complex in the transference, can now be recognized as an effort to resume psychological development at that phase when the child, through phase-appropriate mirroring by the idealized homogenital parent, acquires pride and pleasure in his own "masculinity" or her "femininity" [Ornstein, 1983, p. 140].

SUMMARY

This chapter offers a self-psychological perspective on the Oedipus complex and on the origins of Hans's horse phobia. It asserts that the phobia erupted because of the child's separation anxiety, an increasingly insecure attachment to his mother. Although he received confusing and nonvalidating responses from his father, Hans was able to maintain the kind of idealization of his father that is a necessary selfobject experience for the oedipal-age child. From the case history, we know that the phobia disappeared, but we do not know what emotional price the child may have had to pay for remaining in relatively good contact with his father, which helped him become free of the anxiety related to his mother.

Herbert Graf (1972) appears to have retained his idealization of his father. He described him as a man who, in addition to having a doctorate in law,

> was a formidable scholar of literature and aesthetics . . . an astute political analyst . . . and equally at home in philosophy and science and quite capable of talking mathematics with Einstein. . . . He was a universal man but at the same time a true Viennese . . . [p. 25].

Though Herbert Graf created the position of a stage director at the Metropolitan Opera House, and he obviously enjoyed the creative aspects of the work, he considered his job to be in the "background" of an opera and himself to be an "invisible man."

REFERENCES

Anthony, E. J. (1970), The reaction of parents to the oedipal child. *Parenthood,* ed. E. J. Anthony & T. Benedek. Boston: Little, Brown, pp. 275–288.
Blos, P. (1979), Modifications in the classical psychoanalytic model of adolescence. *Adolescent Psychiatry,* ed. S. Sherman & P. Giovacchini. Chicago: University of Chicago Press, pp. 6–25.
Bowlby, J. (1973), *Attachment and Loss, Vol. 11.* New York: Basic Books.
Freud, A. (1968), Indications and contraindications for child analysis. *The Psychoanalytic Study of the Child,* 23:37–46. New York: International Universities Press.
Freud, S. (1905), *Three Essays on the Theory of Sexuality. Standard Edition,* 7:135–243. London: Hogarth Press, 1953.
_____ (1909), *Analysis of a Phobia in a Five-Year-Old Boy. Standard Edition,* 10:5:5–149. London: Hogarth Press, 1955.
_____ (1917), *Introductory Lectures in Psycho-Analysis. Standard Edition,* 16. London: Hogarth Press, 1963.
_____ (1926), Inhibitions, symptoms and anxiety. *Standard Edition,* 20:87–172. London: Hogarth Press, 1959.
Fromm, E. (1968): The Oedipus complex: Comments on the case of Little Hans. *Contemp. Psychoanal.,* 4:178–188.
Graf, H. (1972), Memoirs of an invisible man. *Opera News,* 36(1, 2, 3, 4).
Garrison, M. (1978), A new look at Little Hans. *Psychoanal. Rev.,* 65:523–532.
Glenn, J. (1980), Freud's advice to Hans' father: The first supervisory sessions. *Freud and His Patients.* New York: Aronson, pp. 121–143.
Kohut, H. (1971), *The Analysis of the Self.* New York: International Universities Press.

Kohut, H. (1977), *The Restoration of the Self.* New York: International Universities Press.
_____ (1984), *How Does Analysis Cure?* ed. A. Goldberg & P. Stepansky. Chicago: University of Chicago Press.
_____ & Wolf, E. (1978), The disorders of the self and their treatment, *The Search for the Self,* Vol. 3, ed. P. Ornstein. 3:359–385 Madison, CT: International Universities Press.
Lindon, J. (1990), Little Hans, his parents and his castration complex: A reassessment. Unpublished manuscript.
Ornstein, A. (1981), Self-pathology in childhood. Clinical and developmental consideration. *Psychiatr. Clin. N. Amer.,* 4:435–453.
_____ (1983), An idealizing transference of the oedipal phase. *Reflections in Self Psychology,* ed. J. Lichtenberg & S. Kaplan. Hillsdale, NJ: The Analytic Press, pp. 135–161.
_____ (1989), Klinische Darstellung. *Selbst Psychology.* Munchen: Verlag Internationale Psychoanalyse, pp. 43–72.
_____ & Ornstein, P. (1985), Parenting as a function of the adult self: A psychoanalytic developmental perspective. *Parental Influences,* ed. E. J. Anthony & G. Pollock. Boston: Little, Brown.
Piaget, J. & Inhelder, B. (1969), *The Psychology of the Child.* New York: Basic Books.
Silverman, M. (1980), A fresh look at Little Hans. *Freud and His Patients.* New York: Aronson, pp. 95–120.
Slap, J. (1961), Little Hans's tonsillectomy. *Psychoanal. Quart.,* 30:259–261.
Stern, D. (1985), *The Interpersonal World of the Infant.* New York: Basic Books.
Terman, D. (1984/85), The self and the Oedipus complex. *The Annual of Psychoanalysis,* 12/13:87–103. New York: International Universities Press.

Sandra Kiersky
James L. Fosshage
THE TWO ANALYSES OF DR. L:
A Self-Psychological Perspective on Freud's Treatment of the Rat Man
(Notes Upon a Case of Obsessional Neurosis, 1909)

"Notes Upon a Case of Obsessional Neurosis," which has come to be known as the case of the "Rat Man," is one of Freud's most taught and written about cases. Published in 1909, it is the clearest account of Freud's view of obsessional symptoms and compulsions; the most comprehensive narrative of what actually occurred between Freud and one of his patients; and the case that Freud felt was most clinically successful. While his claim (p. 249) that the patient's healthy personality was "completely restored" by the analysis seems exaggerated, there is no question that Dr. Lanzer entered treatment in an extremely painful state, with serious and disabling symptoms that were greatly reduced during the course of treatment. Given the many classical and ego-psychological critiques of Freud's handling of the case (see, e.g., Ellman, 1991; Mahony, 1986; and Zetzel, 1966), it is our purpose to explore what happened between these two men that was therapeutic and how we might understand the Rat Man today from a self-psychologically informed psychoanalytic perspective.

Ideally, to clarify how an analytic process has affected a patient requires access to the verbatim process between the patient and analyst and some sense of the analytic "atmosphere" and shifting emotional states of the participants. If process notes are not available, at least the significant interventions made by the analyst are needed: how they were framed, when they were delivered and, most important, how the patient reacted to them. The focus of analysis is the patient's subjective world, and therapeutic success can be measured only within each analytic process (Ornstein, 1990; Lichtenberg, Lachmann, and Fosshage, 1992). Ornstein suggests three criteria for assessing clinical process: First, does the treatment deepen the patient's exploration of his or her inner life? Second, does the analyst communicate to the patient, verbally or nonverbally, in a way that makes the patient feel understood? Finally, are the patient and the analyst on the same wave length?

Unfortunately, the actual treatment process is not available in the case of the famous Man with the Rats. Whatever questions we ask and answers we frame are speculative, even imaginative. What we do have is Freud's published account, which includes a description of the first seven sessions; Freud's dynamic formulation of the case; and notes taken on 34 days of the analysis between October 10, 1907 and January 20, 1908. These, published in the *Standard Edition* as "The Original Record of the Case" are surprising because Freud destroyed the original notes on all his other patients. The notes on the Rat Man contain highly condensed and selective summaries of sessions, some dreams, and a few of Freud's impressions of the patient and his progress. From this diverse and fragmentary material, we have tried to imagine what might have been the significant encounters between Freud and Dr. Lanzer, given our view of what is significant in psychoanalysis; to construct a somewhat more detailed understanding of the patient's early years; and to provide an alternative framework in which to understand the young Lanzer's illness and why his time with Freud was helpful. The limits of such an undertaking are, we believe, obvious and do not require extended discussion.

THE FIRST ENCOUNTER

In 1907, a 29-year-old lawyer named Ernst Lanzer visits Freud for the first time and reveals that since childhood he has suffered with obsessions that have intensified in the last four years. The chief features of his disorder are fears that something might happen to two people about whom he cares very much, his father and a "lady" he admires. He is also distressed by impulses to cut his throat with a razor, and he "produces prohibitions" often in connection with seemingly unimportant things. His only relief from these symptoms in recent years came during a course of hydrotherapy at a sanatorium where he met someone with whom he had regular intercourse. His sexual life, he feels, is stunted although his potency is normal. He had his first sexual experience at 26.

This is essentially the information presented to Freud on October 1, when he meets the Rat Man. What does Ernst Lanzer communicate about himself in this first encounter? From our point of view, he indicates that those close to him are not a source of security and comfort. Since childhood, he has feared losing those he loves. At times he is so distressed by these feelings that he wants to kill himself, but a period of calm was restored to him when he briefly felt connected to a woman who apparently made him feel welcome both physically and emotionally. Ernst's difficulties seem to center on extremely distressed self-states involving intense fear of attachment and loss, although he stresses sexuality over relatedness.

Freud immediately likes the young man. He finds him "clear headed and shrewd." Ernst explains that he came across something in one of Freud's books that made him feel that Freud might understand him. In fact, the ideas in the book reminded Ernst of his own attempts to understand his illness. For Freud, this must be an extraordinary moment, given his struggle to be accepted in scientific circles. Here before him is an educated, even like-minded young man who believes, on the basis of some knowledge of Freud's theory, that psychoanalysis may hold the key to his well-being. And so they begin. A young man who apparently hopes to be understood and helped, and an older man who hopes to understand him and further his work and reputation.

THE ANALYTIC DISCOURSE

What Freud does not include in his published account of this first meeting is that Lanzer has begun treatment only after obtaining permission from his mother to do so. Although he is an attorney and 29 years old, he has experienced considerable difficulty in establishing himself in the adult world. He remains economically and emotionally dependent on his mother and is unable to move forward personally or professionally. It seems to us that Ernst is a young man unable to consolidate a positive sense of himself as an effective male. He seeks, and finds in Freud a strong, affirming tie to a "father surrogate" who helps him to disengage from mother and to further needed self-delineation. Having experienced a series of traumas in childhood and subsequent parental failures to respond adequately, Ernst believes that his aggression is dangerous to others and that his sexuality is shameful. How have these particular fantasies come to organize Ernst's subjective experience? Freud believes that Ernst was an exceptionally sensual child who was appropriately punished by his father for sexual misbehavior. This punishment generated hate for the prohibiter of the child's sexual pleasure, hate that was repressed and that reemerged in Ernst's symptoms and behaviors. Freud decodes and interprets Ernst's death wishes for his father and believes that this lifting of repression is the mechanism for the observed improvement.

What we find significant in the record is that Heinrich, Ernst's father, was reportedly a likable, but unpredictably violent man who seemed literally to crush aggressive behavior in his son. Once, for example, when Ernst was three, he bit someone in the household. Heinrich's response was to beat the little boy until he was overwhelmed with rage and humiliation. This kind of parental retaliation, which treats the child's anger as potentially lethal, undoubtedly left Ernst convinced that his aggression was dangerously destructive and totally unacceptable to others. Parents who cannot tolerate a child's aggression and, "survive" it (Winnicott, 1971) create a feeling of destructiveness in the child, who never learns that his hate will not destroy those he loves. In addition, Heinrich was apparently unable to accept Ernst's sexual or autonomous strivings (Freud, 1909, p. 286) and thus created intense conflict in this arena, as well (Kohut, 1977).

With Freud, Ernst expresses, probably for the first time, his disappointment and rage at a parental figure, and the surrogate Freud survives. Freud's ability to survive the rage enables Ernst to experience his anger as less destructive and to modify his negative self-schema. Freud also welcomes and encourages Ernst's sexual initiatives and independence. He does not recoil from Ernst's incestuous and sadistic fantasies. In fact, his persistent decoding of Ernst's symptoms, feelings, and dreams must seem to Ernst the proof he needs that his inner experience is not shameful, disgusting, or destructive to others.

These, we feel, are the main therapeutic accomplishments of Freud's analysis of the Rat Man: furthered self-consolidation and the evocation and partial resolution of ambivalence in the transference. Interestingly, to accomplish these aims, the analysis seems to have proceeded on two quite different levels of discourse at the same time. The first level, which Freud understood and interpreted, addressed Ernst's conflict with the oedipal father who prohibited his sexual and aggressive feelings. The second level, however, consisted of transference and countertransference enactments during which Freud offered himself as the idealizable, mirroring father whose genuine interest, affection, and reliable understanding enabled the young man to identify himself with a capable and loving male and to self-delineate without fear of loss (Kohut, 1977). This idealization and identification furthered the process of self-consolidation and fostered a sense of security and safety in the adult world (Kohut, 1971; Blos, 1985). It may be that Freud sensed, rather than fully understood, this level of his analytic work. At times, he directly reassured the patient that he respected and cared for him. At other times, he clarified misinformation about himself and his family. Once, when Ernst was hungry, Freud fed him. Aspects of this dimension of the treatment are controversial and have been called by various analysts errors (Ellman, 1991), efforts to build the therapeutic alliance (Zetzel, 1966), or simply part of the "real relationship" as distinguished from the transference (Lipton, 1977). These critiques do not do justice to the clinical situation, however, and it is likely that Freud's lack of awareness of these interventions, as interventions, kept him from analyzing this part of the transference and resulted in the persistence of the "Father Complex," which he mentioned in a letter to Jung (McGuire, 1974). Because little was understood at that time of what became known as preoedipal love and development and, later, developmental requisites for self-consolidation, it is natural that Freud's emphasis would center on the child's hostile feelings toward the oedipal father who prohibited his desires. In addition, Freud had already formed this aspect of his theory six years before he met the Rat Man. Mahony (1986) tells us that Freud wrote in the margin of his manuscript of "The Psychopathology of Everyday Life," strictly for his own private use and related to his self-analysis, the following:

> Rage, anger and consequently, a murderous impulse is the source of superstition in obsessional neurotics: a sadistic component, which is attached to love and is therefore directed against the loved person and repressed precisely because of this link and because of its intensity [p. 156].

Freud's emphasis was probably also determined by his intense desire to confirm what was already his strong conviction about the origin of Lanzer's illness.

Despite Freud's belief that insight "cured" the Rat Man, it is likely that the most powerful therapeutic effects came precisely from the second level of analytic discourse and made possible whatever benefits were derived from Freud's didactic interpretive work.

THE BEGINNING OF TREATMENT

Treatment begins on October 2 with a pledge on Ernst's part to free associate. Freud invites him to begin in any way that he wishes and reports the following:

He had a friend, he told me, of whom he had an extraordinarily high opinion. He used always to go to him when he was tormented by some criminal impulse, and ask him whether he despised him as a criminal. His friend used then to give him moral support by assuring him that he was a man of irreproachable conduct, and had probably been in the habit, from his youth onwards, of taking a dark view of his own life. At an earlier date, he went on, another person had exercised a similar influence over him. This was a nineteen-year-old student (he himself was fourteen or fifteen at the time) who had taken a liking to him, and had raised his self esteem to an extraordinary degree, so that he appeared to himself to be a genius. This student had suddenly become his tutor, and had suddenly altered his behavior and begun treating him as though he were an idiot. At length he had noticed that the student was interested in one of his sisters, and had realized that he had only taken him up in order to gain admission into the house. This had been the first great blow of his life [Freud, 1909, pp. 159–160].

The central theme for Ernst is his need to establish a secure tie to an older man in order to sustain a positive sense of himself. This requisite developmental need serves to establish an idealizing selfobject transference (Kohut, 1971). He also brings his expectation and fear that Freud will disappoint and humiliate him as his friend and the tutor had. This is transference understood as the organization of experience and, more specifically, as problematic, affect-laden schemas (Wachtel, 1980; Stolorow and Lachmann, 1984/85; Fosshage, 1990). Given his expectation of humiliation, it is not surprising to discover, later in the treatment (Freud, 1909, p. 205), that the beating and humiliation Ernst experienced when he was three coincided with the fatal illness of an older sister and was a time when he desperately needed understanding and support from his father.

Ernst proceeds in the session, "without apparent transition," to relate his sexual history. He remembers a scene with a pretty young governess when he was four or five. He asks her if he can come under her skirts "to cry" (Mahony, 1986, p. 5), and she agrees. He fingers her genitals and the lower part of her body, which strike him as "very queer." After this, he is tormented with a persistent wish to see women naked. He recalls various scenes from childhood in which he caught glimpses of his sisters or servants in various degrees of undress. He also recalls a scene that occurred when he was around seven and he and his brother were sitting with the governess, the cook and another servant-girl: "The young women were talking, and I suddenly became aware of Fraulein Lina saying: 'It could be done with the little one; but Paul [Ernst] . . . is too clumsy, he would be sure to miss it' " (Freud, 1909, pp. 160–162).

Again, a scene of humiliation and a young woman's preference for one of his siblings over him organizes his associations. It seems that Ernst is consistently led back to the same feeling of inadequacy and insecurity with those he cares about. He tells Freud that, by age six he had already suffered from erections and complained about them to his mother. Feeling exposed and humiliated, he developed, at the same time, the "morbid" idea that his parents knew his thoughts and explained this to himself by imagining that he had actually spoken the words out loud without being aware of it. Certain girls pleased him immensely, and he had a "very strong wish to see them naked." He had an uncanny feeling, though, that something bad would happen if he thought such things and that he must do "all sorts of things" to prevent it from happening. In reply to Freud's request for an example of his fears, he states, "For instance that my father might die." Here, in the first session, Ernst's feeling that his thoughts and impulses are intensely destructive and dangerous is apparent. He continues that thoughts about his father's death have been with him from an early age and continue to be a source of great depression. It is at this point in the narrative that Freud learns that Ernst's father, with whom his obsessional fears are currently occupied, died some years before.

In his description of this session, Freud gave his view of the dynamics that accounted for the symptoms the patient described. The child was under the domination of a component of the sexual instinct, the desire to look, or scopophilia. Opposition to this desire arose from a source later connected to father's prohibitions, for every time he had the desire, he could not help fearing that something terrible would happen. In Freud's words, Ernst's conflict could be stated as follows: "If I have this wish to see a woman naked, my father will be bound to die" (Freud, 1909, p. 163). Protective measures followed—rituals and superstitions designed to ward off the impending evil.

An alternative way of framing Ernst's difficulties is to focus on his expressed feeling of inadequacy and repeated attempts to fortify his sense of self specifically by sexually connecting to certain women. His conflict centers on his need for self-vitalizing (selfobject) activities and his father's prohibition against them. To engage in these activities is tantamount to killing or losing father and father's needed support. Additionally, Ernst's conflict is a concretization of his belief that his inner world is shocking and, if exposed, will be destructive to others. Thus, the fact that his revelations do not shock or harm Freud constitutes, in itself, a significant therapeutic experience.

Freud (1909) felt that Ernst suffered from a full-blown childhood neurosis and that before his sixth year conflicts and repressions had occurred that were overtaken by childhood amnesia. These left behind as a "residuum" (p. 164) the particular content of this obsessive fear. Freud further underlined for his readers that in every chronic obsessional neurosis beginning in early childhood, one always discovers lascivious wishes connected with uncanny apprehensions and an inclination to the performance of defensive acts. Finally, he noted how clear the connection between infantile sexuality and obsessional neurosis. It is also worth noting, given Freud's formulation, how clear the connection between guilt and obsessional neurosis is and what a "dark view" of his life Ernst does, in fact, have.

Thus ends the published account of the first session. In it are all the threads that Freud will eventually weave into a remarkable developmental tapestry: conflicts around sex and aggression, compromise formations that defend against these conflicts, and the early experiences in which these conflicts arose. Present also are the transference and countertransference paradigms that will ultimately be played out between the two men: Ernst's belief that he is a despicable criminal, his consequent fear of abandonment, and his repeated attempts to repair early damage to his sense of himself as a man through a relationship with an idealizable father.

In his second session with Freud, Ernst relates the experience that brought him to analysis. It occurred during the previous August on military maneuvers. He was troubled with all kinds of fears and obsessional thoughts, but these had quickly passed as he became involved in the exercises. One day, on a short march, Ernst lost his pince-nez and wired his optician in Vienna to send another by post. During the same march, he was positioned between two officers, one of whom, a Czech captain, was of no small importance to him. Apparently, the captain represented another father surrogate, but this time not one Ernst looked to for reassurance. He describes him as follows: "I had a kind of dread of him, for he was obviously fond of cruelty" (Freud, 1909, p. 166).

The captain told Ernst the story of a Chinese torture:

> You take a man, as young and strong as possible, whose muscles are very resistant . . . you strip him . . . you make him kneel down on the ground and bend over his back, and secure him in chains which are fixed onto iron collars that fit tightly on his wrists, ankles, and the back of his neck and knees. . . . Then in a big pot you put a very big rat that's been deprived of food for a couple of days in order to stimulate its ferocity. And this pot with this rat inside you apply hermetically like an enormous cupping glass onto the prisoner's buttocks, with the help of strong straps attached to a leather belt going around his loins. . . . You introduce into the hole of the pot an iron rod, reddened at the fire of a forge. The rat wants to flee the burning of the rod and its dazzling

The Rat Man   115

light. . . . It panics, scrambles about, jumps and leaps, circles the walls of the pot, crawls then tears with its feet and bites with its sharp teeth . . . looking for an exit through the rummaged bleeding skin . . . [Mahony, 1986, p. 13].

The tale has a powerful effect on Ernst, we believe, for two reasons. First, it mirrors his sense of himself as angry and destructive. He seems to identify both with the torturer and possibly with the trapped, panic-stricken rat. Second, the story involves a frighteningly sadistic humiliation, pain, and destructiveness that leads to death. Ernst also identifies with the terror-stricken victim. Transferentially, Ernst undoubtedly fears his own rage and Freud's potential retaliation, themes which reappear later in the analysis. He also fears "Captain" Freud's possible cruelty, as he feared the captain and must have feared, at times, his unpredictably violent father. The "sadist" and the "victim" are the two possible positions within this relational configuration, each of which has its own terrifying note.

The hour is fascinating, for, as Kanzer (1952) notes, here the transference seems to be already in full flower. Again, the second level of the discourse, consisting of enacted communications, is even more dramatic and affect laden than the interpreted level. As Ernst is telling his story of the torture, he becomes so agitated that he rises from the couch and must walk around. He is unable to use words to maintain his equilibrium. Freud senses this and tries to help him by supplying details that he cannot verbalize. He reassures Ernst that he is not, like the captain, fond of cruelty and tells him that he will try to guess the full meaning of any hints he gives him.

[H]e expressed himself so indistinctly that I could not immediately guess in what position—. . . "a pot was turned upside down on his buttocks . . . some rats were put into it . . . and they . . ."—he had again got up and was showing every sign of horror and resistance—". . . bored their way in . . ."—into his anus, I helped him out [Freud, 1909, p. 166].

Ernst continues that the idea flashed through his mind that this torture was happening to someone very dear to him—his lady. Simultaneously the thought occurred to him that it is also happening to his father. He wards off both these ideas with gestures and phrases of repudiation. Kanzer (1952) feels that Ernst has "seduced" Freud into "guessing" in a way that parallels the story of the torture, suggesting that Ernst felt "bored into" when Freud finished his sentence for him. It is just as likely, in our view, that Ernst felt understood—both in words and in deeds. On the second level of discourse, these enactments can be understood as a dialogue in which the patient says, "I'm not sure I can do this by myself. It's disorienting and frightening, and I'm sure that what I'm thinking and feeling is unspeakable," and Freud responds, "You will not have to do this alone. To the extent that I can help you, I will. These are not unspeakable things, you see, I will speak them too." If Ernst's anxiety is raised at this point, it is probably because Freud has assumed the role of the father who knows Ernst's thoughts. But this anxiety is most likely reduced when, again, the worst does not happen. Freud does not die because he knew Ernst's thoughts, nor does he reject Ernst or find him detestable. It is, therefore, *in the second level of discourse that a significant disconfirmation of a terrifying and disorganizing fantasy occurs.* This disconfirmation most likely helped to establish greater trust, a sense of safety, and a self-soothing connection in the treatment situation. Some confirmation that this is the case seems evident in the fact that Ernst is able to continue to bring material and remain engaged in the process despite his "horror and resistance." The rest of the session concerns Ernst's story about securing a second pince-nez and some confusion when it arrived at the post office. He is not sure who paid the postage for him and how he can repay them.

In the third session, Ernst is still conflicted over how and whether to repay the debt. This probably reflects a conflict evoked in the transference over whether to trust Freud, the wished-for, idealized father, or flee from the possibility of being disappointed and humiliated by "Captain" Freud, the sadistic, malevolent father. Many months later, when the "resistance" is at its height, Ernst again considers leaving treatment and going to Vienna and paying the debt. Without addressing this issue, however, he seems to resolve the conflict enough to deepen the treatment further in the next session, when he turns to the central issues of loss, guilt, and reparation concerning his father's death.

Session four represents an important shift in the analysis. Ernst relates, at length, the story of his father's death some years before. With this session, the material moves from disguised, disconnected concretizations of inner experience to a significant event and its aftermath in the patient's subjective world. Ernst, it appears, nursed his father during his long illness. At some point, he asked the attending physician when the danger to his father's life might be considered over and was told, "the evening of the day after tomorrow." It never occurred to him that his father might die during this period, and late that night he went to bed for an hour's rest. He awakened at one in the morning to be told that his father had died. Ernst reproached himself for not being with his father when he died, and the reproach was intensified when he learned that his father had asked for him during the night.

Ernst was not initially tormented by this; successfully denying his father's death, he maintained his father's presence, expecting him to appear at any moment and thinking about him constantly. Any knock on the door would make him think, "Here comes father." If he heard an amusing story, he would think, "I must tell father that." It was not until 18 months later, when an aunt died, that the feelings were evoked once again and he began to torment himself terribly and to treat himself as a "criminal." Ernst's inability to integrate his loss and mourn effectively undoubtedly originated in an earlier loss, the death of his sister when he was three years old. Aided by neither parent, and being so young, he must have been unable to integrate and mourn her loss. Three memories suggest that he turned at that time to his father for help with his distress. In the first, he sees his father carry young Camilla to her bed. In the second, he asks, "Where is Camilla?" and goes into her room, where he finds his father sitting in an arm chair and crying. He does not respond to the little boy in any way. In the last memory, he sees his father bending over his weeping mother. There are no memories recovered in which either parent comforts the little boy. As Freud (1909) commented, "Death was brought close to him" (p. 264).

Just as he turned to his father after Camilla's death, Ernst turned to a friend after his father's death. He explains that he got through the terrible ordeal only because his friend insisted that his self-reproaches were grossly exaggerated. At this point in the analysis, the second level of discourse is ruptured. Even though with this story the patient has alerted Freud that his sense of himself as a criminal is intolerable, Freud interprets to Ernst that his sense of guilt is justified but is connected to an incident that is not actually significant. Freud further elaborates that Ernst must, in some way, have acted like a criminal in relation to his father or he would not be feeling this so strongly. Without the second level of discourse to sustain the tie and, through it, his self-esteem, Ernst is overwhelmed by Freud's interpretation. By the end of the session Ernst is disappointed and profoundly shaken.

Ernst begins the fifth session filled with doubts and clearly feeling less connected to Freud. He asks how the information that he is guilty of something in relation to his father could possibly be therapeutic for him. Freud suggests that finding the real source of his guilt will be helpful, but Ernst is not convinced. He replies that the crime must be a truly horrible one that violates his own moral principles, not just some external rules, and that a crime like that could only occur in a man whose personality has already disintegrated. He asks if there is really any chance of reintegrating his personality under such circumstances. Taking a rather moralistic stance, Freud responds that Ernst's personality is split into a conscious "moral self" and unconscious "evil self." Ernst expresses his doubt that anything can really be done about a situation like that. At this point, Freud (1909) seems, again, to sense the need to restore the tie between them:

> I did not dispute the gravity of his case nor the significance of his pathological constructions; but at the same time his youth was very much in his favor as well as the intactness of his personality. In this connection I said a word or two upon the good opinion I had formed of him, and this gave him visible pleasure [p. 178].

In other words, on the second level of discourse, Freud gives him the reassurance he requires and lets him know that he is not really a "criminal" except in some infantile fantasy. Hope is recovered and by the end of the session, through these enactments, Freud has restored the rupture between himself and the patient with direct reassurance of his respect and concern.

Obviously feeling better, Ernst comes to his session the next day having tried to remember some childhood behavior toward his father about which he is, in Freud's sense, "guilty." He has retrieved a memory. He reminds Freud that, beginning around age seven and persisting through childhood, he believed his parents could guess his thoughts. When he was 12, he fell in love with a little girl who he thought would be kind to him should he experience some misfortune. As an instance of misfortune, his father's death came to his mind. He rejected the thought at once. Freud points out to him that every fear is really a wish, but Ernst objects strenuously that he repudiated the idea simply because the thought was so terrible. An argument ensues. On the second level of discourse, a change is occurring that began to be evident in the fifth session. Ernst, so frightened of his own aggression, has become comfortable enough to disagree, even argue, with Freud without intense fear of retaliation or loss. A kind of adversarial selfobject transference (Lachmann, 1986; Wolf, 1988) has developed that must be self-defining for Ernst and helps him begin to integrate and resolve some of his intense ambivalence toward parental figures. Freud's capacity to tolerate this transference and Ernst's even greater anger later in the treatment, is a testament to his affection for Ernst. To Ernst (unlike to Dora), Freud really does offer himself as a tolerant and understanding surrogate father in this analysis and creates a highly therapeutic situation for the young lawyer.

Soon, Freud becomes convinced that, because Ernst's "resistance" is so intense, his death wish for his father must have originated much earlier than this memory from his 12 year. Ernst, still searching, recalls that a similar thought went through his mind six months before his father's death. He was in love with a woman, Gisela, but financial obstacles made it impossible to marry her. He thought that if his father died he might be rich enough to marry his lady. The day before his father's death, the thought came to him once more, this time, in the following form: " 'Now I may be going to lose what I love most,' and then had come the contradiction: 'No, there is someone else whose loss would be even more painful to you' " (Freud, 1909, p. 179).

Freud decides it is time to educate Ernst further on several basic tenets of his theory, first, that every fear is really a wish and every thought in the unconscious is the exact opposite of that in consciousness. Ernst becomes very agitated by this information, but Freud is relentless. Ernst finally insists that it is impossible for him to believe that his father's death has been his longstanding desire. Freud now softens his approach by explaining that it is precisely the intensity of Ernst's love for his father that does not allow any hatred. The hatred, he continues, must have a source and Ernst's own words suggest that the source is early—probably during the period of childhood when he began to fear his thoughts would be guessed by his parents. Ernst "admits" that this seems plausible, but he is not really convinced and continues in a "disconnected" way to insist that he and his father were best friends and that he had not even really felt sensual toward his admired lady as an adult. In fact, he triumphs, he was more sensually moved as a child. Freud has him now!

> At this point I told him I thought he had now produced the answer we were waiting for. . . . The source from which his hostility toward his father derived its indestructibility was evidently something in the nature of sensual desire, and in that connection he must have felt his father in some way or other an interference. A conflict of this kind, I added, between sensuality and childish love was entirely typical. . . . It was not until he was once more seized with erotic desires that his hostility reappeared again owing to the revival of the old situation [p. 182].

Freud further explains that the persistence of the wish confirms that this incident occurred very early, before Ernst's sixth year and the session ends.

In the seventh session, Ernst is still greatly disturbed by the thought that he has such violent wishes toward his father. He recalls an incident in which he enticed his younger brother, of whom he was quite jealous, to look down the barrel of a toy gun and shot him in the forehead. He was immediately filled with remorse, for though he had not hurt his brother he had certainly meant to hurt him. He also points out that he has had conscious, hostile feelings toward Gisela, which does not fit the formula very well. Finally, he reminds Freud of the intensification of his illness since his father's death. Freud agrees, and tells him that he regards the sorrow Ernst feels at his father's death to be the main source of the intensity of his illness, a point on which both patient and analyst can finally agree.

Presently Freud discovers what he believes to have been the real precipitating cause of the intensification of Ernst's illness. After his father's death, his mother attempted to arrange a marriage with a distant relative from a wealthy family. Such a marriage would provide Ernst with a connection to the family firm and a brilliant opportunity professionally. The family plan, as Freud sees it, stirred up a conflict in Ernst as to whether he should remain true to his admired lady or marry the girl assigned to him, as his father had married his mother. Ernst resolved the conflict, Freud feels, by falling ill and avoiding a decision altogether. For Freud, what appeared to be the consequence of the illness was, in reality, its cause. This additional information about the plan suggests that the stronger prohibiter of Ernst's attempt to marry and make a life for himself is, in fact, his mother, making it difficult for Ernst to move on in his life with a sense of his own "center of initiative." To the extent that he needed his father's support to feel more effective, he is placed in an untenable situation. Not only was his father a prohibiter of the marriage to Gisela, but also attempts to identify with his father would lead him to marry the girl assigned to him. And he would not be able to stand up to his mother and marry a woman of his own choosing. His only way out, of course, is to find a father surrogate, more powerful than his mother, who will support *his* goal. As we shall see, this is precisely what Freud ultimately does in the analysis, although it occurs on the second level of discourse and is never brought into the interpretive field. To follow this thread of the treatment, we must now move to the original record of the case, for it is only the first seven sessions that Freud describes in detail in his published account.

THE ORIGINAL RECORD OF THE CASE

On October 11, Freud asks Ernst to bring him a picture of his "lady," an enactment that can only be understood as part of the second level of the analysis. Freud is taking an essentially fatherly interest in Ernst's affairs of the heart. He even drops him a postcard to remind the young man of his request. In the very next analytic hour we learn that Ernst's spirits rose after the last session; he went to the theatre and then, for no reason that he can understand, he kissed a servant girl and then "attacked" her. Apparently Freud means by this that Ernst made love to her, for we hear that Ernst came quickly to his senses and went to his room. Still, we have seen an immediate burst of interest in women following Freud's friendly interest in Ernst's lady.

During the week, Ernst brings a family story that seems to correspond to Freud's construction of an incident between Ernst and his father before Ernst was six years old over which the child might have harbored a grudge. Ernst, however, does not remember the incident at all; he has simply heard it told by his mother.

> When he was very small—it became possible to establish the date more exactly owing to its having coincided with the fatal illness of an elder sister—he had done something naughty for which his father had given him a beating. The little boy had flown into a terrible rage and had hurled abuse at his father even while he was under his blows. But as he knew no bad language, he had called him all the names of common objects that he could think of, and had screamed: "You lamp! You towel! You plate!" and so on. His father, shaken by such an outburst of elemental fury, had stopped beating him, and had declared: "The child will be either a great man or a great criminal!" The patient believed that the scene made a permanent impression upon himself as well as upon his father. His father he said never beat him again; and he also attributed to this experience a part of the change which came over his own character. From that time forward he was a coward—out of fear of the violence of his own rage. His whole life long, moreover, he was terribly afraid of blows, and used to creep away and hide, filled with terror and indignation, when one of his brothers or sisters was beaten [Freud, 1909 pp. 205-206].

It seems likely that Ernst's misbehavior, which involved biting someone rather than any sexual acting out, was an expression of his upset and distress over his sister's illness. The beating may well have provoked a grudge in the child, who seemed to be saying that his father was like an inanimate object—a lamp or a plate—completely unresponsive to his needs. It certainly left a permanent impression, for Ernst refers to himself as a criminal many times in the course of the treatment—a negative self-schema he apparently internalized and that organized much of his experience. Freud, however, remains sure that the child's misdemeanor was really sexual in nature and that it was simply the mother's "censorship" that repressed the sexual aspect of the child's conduct in the retelling. Here we see clearly how Freud's interest in establishing the father as the normative prohibiter of Ernst's sexual desires guides what is significant to him in the childhood story. His wish to confirm his theoretical ideas leads him to alter the story of Ernst's misbehavior, and he does not explore the adequacy of the father's response or its subjective meaning for the boy. Still, whether one sees the incident in drive terms or within a more relational matrix, it is clear that this was a core event in the young child's life. It probably left little Ernst in a state of rage, toward his father, his mother and even his sister, who had abandoned him, without meaning to, by falling fatally ill. He apparently connected his rage to her death and, aided by his father's pronouncements, set firmly in his psyche the belief that he was a murderer and that his anger was dangerous and unacceptable. It is a remarkable achievement that Freud was able to engage Ernst in the analytic process and systematically reach back into childhood until he found the developmental sequence that could account for so much of the patient's symptomatology and adult illness. It is also worth noting that Ernst's sense of himself as a criminal in adult life preserved a needed psychic tie to his father after his father's death.

By the end of October, a strong idealizing transference has been established with Freud, and Ernst brings a dream from the previous January. Ernst cherished this dream as though it were a prized possession:

> I was in a wood and most melancholy. The lady came to meet me, looking very pale. 'Paul [Ernst], come with me before it is too late. I know we are both sufferers.' She put her arm through mine and dragged me away by force. . . . We came to a broad river and she stood there. I was dressed in miserable rags which fell into the stream and were carried away by it. I tried to swim after them but she held me back: 'Let the rags go.' I stood there in gorgeous raiment. He (Ernst) knew that the rags meant his illness and that the whole dream promised him health through the lady. He was very happy at the time . . . till other dreams came which made him profoundly wretched [Freud, 1909, p. 268].

The powerful, manifestly evident dream content (Fosshage, 1983) and the fact that Ernst brings this prized possession at this time to the analysis indicate that he is hopeful and positive about his progress. On October 27, he gives Freud a detailed account of his relationship with Gisela. Until now he has been extremely reluctant to talk about her. Gisela, it seems, has refused him at various times, and he recalls his father saying to him "Don't go up there [to her house] so often. You'll make yourself ridiculous" (p. 269). Ernst clearly needs a male figure to encourage him and to believe he is capable of winning the girl he loves. Following this memory, a period of questioning his father's character ensues. Ernst is unsure, for example, if his father was faithful to his mother and remembers a time when his father came home to Vienna only once a week. Ernst is surprised at his own questions, for he has not been aware of critical feelings toward his father before. His relationship with Freud evidently is secure enough for him to begin to examine his negative feelings toward his father as well as his love for him.

The work of the analysis seems to be going well, for on November 17 Freud reports that Ernst is again in a period of rising spirits. He is "cheerful, untrammeled and active, and is behaving aggressively toward a girl—a dressmaker" (p. 278). By November 22, however, a negative transference has begun to bloom, and Ernst comes to his session in a deep depression. He soon admits that he is in a crisis. He has had a frightful thought, something too terrible to tell Freud, and he feels that Freud should "turn him out." Here we see Ernst's characteristic fear that his thoughts and feelings about his "father" are unforgivable. He expects to be ejected from the relationship. It is only after what Freud describes as a 40-minute struggle and his assertion that for Ernst to leave the treatment would be an act of aggression that Ernst is able to proceed. He reveals that his thought concerns seeing Freud's daughter naked and a memory of sexual play with one of his sisters. He then discloses a fantasy that seems directly related to the story of the rats and its peculiar horror and fascination for him. He thinks of his mother's naked body, particularly the lower part of her body. Her genitals have been eaten up by Ernst and the other children. This fantasy may relate to Ernst's and the other children's ravishing and, at times, destructively experienced, attempts to connect to their mother. It may also relate to an earlier period of psychological crisis for Ernst, whose younger brother was born when he was just entering the phase of gender differentiation at 18 months. Feeling abandoned by his mother and trying to sort out his new understanding of gender differences, he was probably preoccupied with looking at women's genitals and stomachs in an effort to understand what it means to be a boy or a girl, how babies are born, and what he had done to make his mother abandon him. Since this is also a period (18–24 months) of newly found exploratory-assertive (Lichtenberg, 1989) expansiveness in the toddler, his mother's lack of availability may have contributed to the emergence of a fantasy that self-assertion and independence on his part would always lead to loss.

These issues, of course, are not taken up in the treatment. The crucial therapeutic experience here is again at the second level of discourse, the enactment of Ernst's fear of revealing his inner world to his father for fear he will be "turned out" and the disconfirmation of this fantasy when Freud responds with interest and inquiry.

The next day, on November 22, the fruits of this therapeutic experience are evident, for Ernst comes to his session with a "fresh transference" (Freud, 1909, p. 283), the thought that Freud's mother is dead. This ushers in a period of exploration of Ernst's anger and mistrust of his mother. Ernst walks around the room, this time out of fear that Freud will beat him.

Throughout November, the treatment is filled with what Freud calls "disgusting rat stories" and "anal sadistic fantasies" in which Ernst does various things to family members, both his and Freud's. The content is complex and simply summarized by Freud, but Ernst's inner world seems to unfold dramatically and be filled with thoughts, feelings, and fantasies that Ernst believes to be revolting and criminal. His expectation of punishment, however, is not fulfilled. In fact, this father surrogate is more and more interested in understanding and sorting out his internal dramas. Memories of being ashamed of his father appear, and he recalls that his mother often called her husband coarse and a "common fellow." In early December, we learn that Ernst is actively pursuing his dressmaker. Around this time, he develops a wish to marry Freud's daughter though this wish remains, apparently somewhat disguised (Freud, 1909, pp. 292–293). Ernst's wish may reflect, among other things, his feeling that Freud is a "good father" and he would really like to be part of his family.

Ernst's feelings of inadequacy as a man enter the treatment, and he tells Freud on December 10 that one of his testicles is undescended. He seems to feel that he is therefore less manly, for he also gives up the idea of marrying Freud's daughter and is in fact "much afraid" of meeting her (p. 295).

By December 12 the treatment takes an important turn when the subject of Ernst's mother finally takes center stage. We learn at the same time that his potency with the dressmaker "is excellent." His new-found sense of his masculinity may have made it possible for early, unhappy memories of his mother to emerge. He remembers being very young and seeing his mother lying on a sofa. She sat up and took something yellow from under her dress and put it on a chair. At the time he wanted to touch it, but it was "horrible." Later the thing turned into a secretion (p. 293). Ernst then has a fantasy that every female member of Freud's family is choking in a sea of revolting secretions. His fear of engulfment and his anger with his mother seem evident in this session, which marks an important step forward in the treatment (although Freud greatly underemphasized the role of Ernst's relationship with his mother in his illness). Following this session, on December 14, we read that things are progressing well with the dressmaker but that a "hostile current" toward the mother persists and is manifest in Ernst's exaggerated consideration for her (p. 296). By December 19, Ernst's anger toward, and powerful identifications with, his mother are explored, for Freud writes that Ernst says he gets "everything in him that is bad" from his mother. The process of disentangling psychologically from Rosa seems to come to a head around December 21, Freud writes, "He has been identifying himself with his mother—in his behavior and treatment transferences" (p. 298).

As for his behavior, Ernst is being "silly," "disagreeable," and "critical" of others, characteristics apparently typical of his mother. It seems fair to assume, although the related material is scant, that during this period Ernst is able to integrate and resolve some of his anger, disappointment, and fear of his mother. Most likely, given his increasingly assertive behavior with the dressmaker, he has become less dependent on his mother and less fearful of her. Like a proud father, Freud writes at one point that Ernst stood up to his mother in a "manly" way on a matter concerning his finances. By the end of December, Ernst is psychologically strong enough to confront a central fantasy of his illness.

Early in the session on December 23, Ernst is very upset because the physician who attended his sister and father is dying. Ernst is experiencing the same distress he experienced following his father's death, and he has the notion that his wishes are killing the doctor. He also thinks that an earlier wish of his actually kept his cousin alive during the previous year on two occasions. Freud apparently interprets to Ernst that the origin of his feelings of omnipotence can be found in the first death in the family, that of his sister, Camilla. Freud reminds him of his three memories of her death, and Ernst makes the following correction in his account of the first one.

> He saw her being carried to bed, not by her father, and before it was known that she was ill. For her father was scolding and she was being carried away from her parents' bed. She had for a long time been complaining of feeling tired, which was disregarded. But once, when Dr. P. was examining her, he turned pale. He diagnosed a carcinoma to which she later succumbed. While I was discussing the possible reasons for his feeling guilty, he took up another point. . . .

> When he was twenty years old, they employed a dressmaker, to whom he repeatedly made aggressive advances, but whom he did not really care for, because she made demands and had an excessive desire to be loved . . . she asked him to assure her that he was fond of her . . . he flatly refused. A few weeks later she threw herself out of the window. He said she would not have done it if he had entered into the liaison.
>
> The next day he felt surprised that after making this discovery he had no remorse, but he reflected that it was in fact already there. Excellent [Freud, 1909, pp. 299–300].

Freud is clearly delighted with the work he and Ernst are doing during this session, and it does seem that the critical issue for Ernst, his belief that his wishes and feelings kill other people has been brought to light and accepted by Ernst. He even adds a confirming memory of his own to Freud's initial interpretation. The original record ends in January, and, for our purposes, it is unnecessary to describe more of the material. We believe that this session of December 23 is made possible precisely because the theme has not simply been delivered interpretively but has been enacted in the transference–countertransference over the last few months in the second level of the discourse. Ernst can accept the reality of his conviction of intense destructiveness and ultimately transform it because he has relived it in the treatment with a different outcome. He has idealized Freud but also treated him at times with contempt, abuse, fear, and rage. He has probably wished for Freud's death as he did for Freud's mother's death in the report. As we said at the beginning of the chapter, Freud survives. He survives so well and with such a good feeling toward Ernst that, on December 28, his notes read: "He was hungry and was fed" (Freud, 1909, p. 303). Here, in the second level of discourse, after all that has been said and done, Freud is not only friendly toward Ernst, he is *nurturant.* He is the tender, supportive, affirming father Ernst never experienced. The little boy's need for nurturance and affection from someone who is "like him" has only recently received real attention from psychoanalysts (Kohut, 1977, 1984). As Kaftal (1991) notes, "Although the yearning of men for their fathers is recognized in psychoanalytic theory, the wish for the nurturing father has been underemphasized. The underemphasis causes the analyst to miss, or misunderstand, important transferential constellations" (p. 305).

Kaftal argues convincingly that it is only in the context of a secure, stable bond with the early father that the heroics and dramas of the oedipal period can be safely played out. Without this tie, men are raised with a pervasive experience of "otherness" in which their "early experience and affectivity [are] trapped forever in the world of women" (p. 305). For the Rat Man, we feel, Freud provided precisely this bond, which enabled him to reexperience and rework aspects of his relationship with his father, to disentangle finally from his mother, and to feel more positively about himself as a man. Most of the therapeutic work occurred at an enacted level of discourse and was, unfortunately, not interpreted. Following his treatment, Ernst was able to marry Gisela but died shortly after in the Great War, as Freud (1909) writes, "like so many other young men of promise" (p. 249).

THE RELATIONAL MATRIX

Throughout our discussion of the treatment we have noted Freud's view of Ernst's early development and its relationship to his illness. Freud (1909) believed that between the ages of three and five infantile masturbation reaches its height and is the clearest index of the child's sexual constitution. Infantile sexuality is made up of autoerotic activity that combines with traces of object love to form the nuclear complex of the neurosis (pp. 202, 208n). As a general rule, the father is placed in the position of being the opponent of the child's sexual pleasure, which consists largely of masturbation. As Mahony (1986) notes, Freud's formula in the case of the Rat Man combines a constitutional factor with a single trauma at age three. Little Ernst, an extremely sexual child by nature, behaved in a naughty way by masturbating and was punished by his father. The punishment stopped the behavior but set up in the child a "grudge" that was never overcome. A full-blown neurosis ensued that, as Ernst entered latency, was repressed and reappeared in adult life when erotic interests emerged. Ernst feared that his forbidden hostile wishes would harm his father and repressed his hostile feelings for him. His central conflict as an adult was between his lady, representing sexual satisfaction, and his prohibiting father, whom he loved. In the analysis, Freud focused primarily on Ernst's death wishes for his father and consequent guilt, which resulted in the denial of his father's death. This is a much abbreviated statement of Freud's formulation of the case. In it, he emphasizes the oedipal father who prohibits the child's sexual activity and those conflicts which inevitably occur, given the child's love and hate toward the same person.

How does our understanding differ from Freud's understanding of the Rat Man's early experience and later illness? First, we emphasize the child's capacity and need for various forms of relatedness beginning very early in life. Second, we see the developmental difficulties as beginning earlier, in Ernst's relationship with his mother, and taking shape over time as the child attempted various solutions with different family members and their surrogates. When those around him failed to provide needed selfobject experiences, he was thrown back on his own limited resources and whatever self-protective capacities he possessed. Central to our understanding is the idea that symptoms are always an attempt to repair damage to the subjective sense of self and to the relationships in which the individual is embedded. Aside from emphasizing Ernst's relationship with his mother to a greater degree than Freud, we believe that the oedipal problems with his father arose for Ernst, in their unique form, precisely because of earlier parental failure during the toddler period when the father is of critical importance to the boy's growing sense of himself as an adequate and lovable male. Heinrich Lanzer, in our view, did not, as a father, affirm and nurture his son. Nor did he welcome and support Ernst's sexual and assertive strivings.

Since the case and all the details in it are complex and extend over a lifetime, a short review of what we consider to be the significant developmental sequences may be helpful. Ernst was the fourth of seven children born to a middle-class couple in Vienna. His father, Heinrich, was a genial but relatively uneducated, coarse man given to unpredictable outbursts of violence. Lack of predictability emotionally is, of course, detrimental to children, who often experience themselves as bad and feel responsible for traumatic events when adults lose control or are erratic in their parenting. Ernst's mother, Rosa, was raised "harshly" by relatives and seems to have been an emotionally withdrawn woman, often critical and controlling. When Ernst was 18 months old, his brother, Robert, was born Ernst probably felt displaced by his brother and abandoned by his mother, who must have turned much of her attention to the new baby. Confirmatory references to Ernst's intense and persistent jealousy toward Robert appear many times in the treatment.

This maternal loss occurred as Ernst entered the initial stage of gender differentiation, a time when children first recognize that boys and girls are different. Recognition, at this age, is primarily focused on genital differences due to the child's concreteness. The combined trauma of feeling displaced, sorting out what it means to be a boy, and curiosity about changes in his mother's body since she had just given birth most likely impaired Ernst's budding sense of masculinity and intensified a wish to look at women, especially the lower parts of their bodies. It is also not unusual for children who feel emotionally abandoned at this age to sexualize ties to others out of intense loneliness and confusion (Kohut, 1977). Sensual and sexual pleasure intensify the needed ties (Stolorow, Brandchaft, and Atwood, 1987; Lichtenberg, 1989). In addition, recent research suggests that children who experience trauma, particularly their mother's withdrawal, during this developmental period, often try to preserve the maternal tie through global, defensive identification (Coates, Friedman, and Wolfe, 1991). This is probably what occurred with Ernst and accounts for the intensity of his identifications with his mother (see The Original Record of the Case, sessions of December 8, 14, 21; and Zetzel, 1966). Although such identifications often lead to gender identity disorders, Ernst was saved from this by turning to his older sister, Camilla, as a mother substitute. Her ability to provide some of the maternal mirroring and responsiveness Ernst required helped him through this second year. He nevertheless was left with a poorly consolidated sense of himself as capable and masculine and with global identifications with his mother, which, coupled with his father's parental failures, account for many of his symptoms, feelings, and strivings, for example, his feeling that he did not measure up, particularly in comparison with his brother; his repeated attempts to identify with a strong man; and his need to see his penis in mirrors in order to reassure himself that he was potent and undamaged.

Alongside the development of the gendered self in the toddler, another important new experience occurs in the second year. With the acquisition of mobility, the child enters a period of increased exploratory-assertive expansiveness (Lichtenberg, 1989). It is critical that both parents be responsive and available at this time so that the child does not believe that this expansiveness will precipitate abandonment. The mother, particularly, needs to anchor and affirm the infant, who typically tries his wings exuberantly, suddenly realizes that he is out in the world unprotected, and rushes back to her for reassurance that she is still there. Children at this age typically have fears of loss. It appears that Ernst could not understand, as he needed to, that exploratory-assertive expansiveness would not lead to abandonment.

Ernst and his sister, Camilla, to whom he turned as a mother substitute, were apparently so close that she once told him that she would kill herself if he died (Freud, 1909, p. 264). Unfortunately, over the next year, eight-year-old Camilla became fatally ill, thus creating a second traumatic abandonment for the little boy. During this period of his sister's illness Ernst received the beating from his father just when he needed support and understanding. He reacted to this beating with rage and was understandably angry and resentful at both his parents for their withdrawal during Camilla's illness. Shortly after, Camilla died. It is this event, we believe, that dealt the most devastating blow to Ernst. The loss of Camilla left him without the needed, self-sustaining maternal connection and confirmed absolutely the little boy's fantasy that his rage was dangerously destructive and lethal to those close to him. A few memories of Camilla's death from the Original Record suggest that Ernst tried to turn to his father for consolation and support after his sister's death, but his father could not respond (Freud, 1909, pp. 264–265). This frustration intensified his lifelong search to repair, through a responsive father, damage to his sense of self.

Ernst probably suffered from depression from this point forward, and his "naughtiness" and heightened sexual activity can easily be seen as desperate attempts to revitalize his depleted sense of self. When Ernst asked the governess, for example, if he could come under her skirts "to cry" (Mahony, 1986, p. 5), his needs to be comforted and responded to as special were probably at the forefront of his motivational priorities, but sexualized to intensify the needed experience. These early events and cumulative traumas triggered rageful feelings and set the stage for Lanzer's later obsessions and compulsions. His profound need for a father, coupled with what he felt was his lethal rage, led to the self-protective and self-maintaining denial of his father's death. Both are expressions of his destructively experienced rage and attempts to control that rage. He probably dealt with Camilla's death in a similar fashion since he desperately needed her vitalizing support and nurturance and apparently received little help with his grief from the adults around him.

Ernst was a man on a lifelong quest to restore self-vitalizing connections to lost loved ones. His choice of the "lady" seems to reflect an attempt to recover a psychic tie to his sister, Camilla, for we learn in the Original Record that Gisela was chronically ill and quite delicate, as Camilla was. He tried to restore the needed father through other men who were older and whom he admired and, when he failed, called up the dead father in a desperate attempt to restore and maintain himself. In the end, Ernst is more like Orpheus descending into the underworld to find his Eurydice than Oedipus in love with his mother and battling his father. Freud, as surrogate, provided some of the developmentally needed nurturing and mirroring responses of the father and was a strong male accepting of Ernst's angry and sexual feelings. This acceptance enabled Ernst, however briefly, to modify negative self-schemas by transforming his attitudes toward anger and sexuality and to consolidate, overall, a more positive and cohesive sense of self.

THE ANALYTIC DISCOURSE REVISITED

To return, briefly, to our discussion at the beginning of the chapter, we now ask how successful, using Ornstein's (1990) criteria, Freud's analysis of the Rat Man was. Did the treatment deepen Dr. Lanzer's exploration of his inner life? Perhaps not as much as we would like, but certainly the answer here must be yes. The analytic road was an extremely rocky one for Freud and Ernst, with deep ruptures in the selfobject bond occurring when Freud insisted on finding in Ernst's experience his own predetermined ideas of what should be there. At the same time, he took a genuine interest in Ernst's life, his symptoms, and his feelings and tried to explore these with his patient. When the ruptures threatened the treatment, Freud recovered the tie usually through some act of concern, affection, or generosity. One sees the material move from initially fragmented, symptom-focused sessions that required inquiry and exploration to clarify Ernst's affective experience to current triggers and genetic antecedents. In this sense, the treatment certainly deepened Lanzer's exploration of his inner life.

Did the patient feel verbally or nonverbally understood? Here, the second level of discourse carried the day. Though there is much argument and disagreement about Freud's verbal interpretations, and his most central hypotheses (Ernst's death wishes for his father and his early misconduct as sexual misbehavior) were never fully accepted by Ernst, in the nonverbal, enacted sphere, it seems that Ernst did feel understood often enough. In addition, he felt understood by a man he idealized, giving the moments of understanding greater therapeutic effect. The unquestioned force of Freud's personality, his confidence in his work, and his very real affection for the patient probably helped Ernst bridge those areas where he felt less understood.

Finally, were the patient and the analyst on the same wavelength? Unfortunately they do not seem to have been much of the time. It is possible that Freud's single-minded insistence on Ernst's violent wishes toward his father made it very difficult for Ernst to feel that he and his analyst were moving, cognitively and emotionally, in the same direction. It may be that, though angry, even violent, feelings for his father were certainly present, Ernst's intense disappointment in him and his feeling that he was a disappointment to Heinrich was more to the point and would have evoked the affectively rich conviction in Ernst that Freud sought. Only in one session, on December 23, does the reader sense this mutuality in the treatment. Here Freud and Ernst were on the same wavelength. Freud interpreted that Ernst's feeling of "omnipotent" destructiveness had becomes essentially fixed with the death of his sister, and Ernst for the first time completely accepted an interpretation *and* supplied a relevant confirming memory of his own. One hopes, that today, with a greater emphasis on empathy as a mode of observing and feeling into the patient's state, sessions like this one are the norm rather than the exception. Freud himself seemed to agree that this session exemplifies the best kind of analytic work, for it was only after this session that he commented directly on the process itself. He wrote, *Excellent!*

REFERENCES

Blos, P. (1985), *Son and Father.* New York: Free Press.
Coates, S., Friedman, R. C. & Wolfe, S. (1991), The etiology of boyhood gender identity disorder: A model for integrating temperament, development, and psychodynamics. *Psychoanal. Dial.,* 1:481–524.
Ellman, S. (1991), *Freud's Technique Papers.* Northvale, NJ: Aronson, pp. 290–311.
Fosshage, J. (1983), The psychological function of dreams: A revised psychoanalytic perspective. *Psychoanal. Contemp. Thought,* 64:641–669.
_____ (1990), Toward a reconceptualization of transference: theoretical and clinical considerations. Paper presented to American Psychological Association, Div. 39, April, New York City.
Freud, S. (1909), *Notes Upon a Case of Obessional Neurosis. Standard Edition,* 10:155–318. London: Hogarth Press, 1955.
Kaftal, E. (1991), On intimacy between men. *Psychoanal. Dial.,* 1:305–328.
Kanzer, M. (1952), The transference neurosis of the Rat Man. *Psychoanal. Quart.,* 21:181–189.
Kohut, H. (1971), *The Analysis of the Self.* Madison, CT: International Universities Press.
_____ (1977), *The Restoration of the Self.* New York: International Universities Press.
_____ (1984), *How Does Analysis Cure?* ed. A. Goldberg & P. Stepansky. Chicago: University of Chicago Press.
Lachmann, F. (1986), Interpretation of psychological conflicts and adversarial relationships: A self-psychological perspective. *Psychoanal. Psychol.,* 3:341–355.
Lichtenberg, J. (1989), *Psychoanalysis and Motivation.* Hillsdale, NJ: The Analytic Press.
_____ Lachmann, F. & Fosshage, J. (1992), *Self and Motivational Systems.* Hillsdale, NJ: The Analytic Press.
Lipton, S. (1977), The advantages of Freud's technique as shown in his analysis of the Rat Man. *Internat. J. Psycho-Anal.,* 58:255–273.
Mahony, P. (1986), *Freud and the Rat Man.* New Haven, CT: Yale University Press.
McGuire, W., ed. (1974), *The Freud/Jung Letters* (Bollingen Series 94). Princeton, NJ: Princeton University Press.
Ornstein, P. (1990), How theory shapes technique: A self psychology view. *Psychoanal. Inq.,* 10:478–497.
Stolorow, R., Brandchaft, B. & Atwood, G. (1987), *Psychoanalytic Treatment.* Hillsdale, NJ: The Analytic Press.

―――― & Lachmann, F. (1984/85), Transference: The future of an illusion. *The Annual of Psychoanalysis,* 12/13:19–38. New York: International Universities Press.

Wachtel, P. (1980), Transference, schema, and assimilation: The relevance of Piaget to the psychoanalytic theory of transference. *The Annual of Psychoanalysis,* 8:59–76. New York: International Universities Press.

Winnicott, D. W. (1971), *Playing and Reality.* New York: Basic Books.

Wolf, E. (1988), *Treating the Self.* New York: Guilford Press.

Zetzel, E. (1966), Additional notes upon a case of obsessional neurosis. *Internat. J. Psycho-Anal.,* 47:123–129.

Donna M. Orange
THE RESTORATION OF SCHREBER'S STOLEN SELF
(Notes on an Autobiographical Account of a Case of Paranoia, 1911)

> Such a father as this was by no means unsuitable for transfiguration into a God in the affectionate memory of the son from whom he had been so early separated by death *(Freud, 1911, p. 51)*.
>
> [God's] actions have been practiced against me for years with the utmost cruelty and disregard as only a beast deals with its prey *(Schreber, 1955, p. 252)*.

Today we know Schreber, like Freud's other cases, because Freud wrote about him. Unlike the others, Schreber was never seen by Freud. This circumstance places Freud and a modern reader at the same starting point, except that we now have both Freud's (1911) "Psycho-Analytic Notes on an Autobiographical Account of a Case of Paranoia" and considerable biographical research on Schreber, on his family, and on his physician Flechsig. No one has access to the array of nonverbal data on which the empathic-introspective method relies so heavily in clinical psychoanalysis (Schwaber, 1983). What, in common with Freud, we do have, is a substantial autobiographical account of a psychosis, Schreber's (1955) *Denkwurdikeiten eines Nervenkranken,* or *Memoirs of my Nervous Illness.*

This chapter does not add to the biographical research, nor even second-guess Freud. Rather it provides a rereading of the *Memoirs* from the perspective of psychoanalytic self psychology, that is, from within the tradition originally articulated by Heinz Kohut (1971, 1978, 1984). Thus this chapter focuses on Schreber's self-experience from a relational/self-experience perspective. Most of Schreber's self-experience consisted of his inference from, and organization of, his experience of being treated in particular ways by others. Recent research on Schreber's family by psychoanalysts (Niederland, 1984) and by historians (Israels, 1989) supports more than a small developmental "kernel of truth" in Schreber's beliefs. In addition, Schreber intended his account of his delusions to describe his treatment in the various asylums. Indeed, Schreber wrote the *Memoirs* themselves as an effort to organize and to communicate his own experience so he could be declared legally competent to manage his own affairs and to live outside the asylum. They are, in part, the work of a judge writing to a judge; that is, Schreber placed himself in an intersubjective field where he could find himself acknowledged and respected. The final section of this chapter examines this self-restorative process, the selfobject character of his book, and in particular the selfobject functions of the judge and court.

SCHREBER AND HIS *MEMOIRS*

Born in 1842, Daniel Paul Schreber was the second son and third of five children born to Daniel Gottlob Moritz Schreber and Pauline Haase. Moritz Schreber, author of books on medical gymnastics and on child-rearing practices, was best known after his death for the *Schrebergarten* and *Schreberverein,* family gardens and educational associations, respectively, which Moritz Schreber had no direct part in founding but which came, more or less by accident, to bear his name. Moritz Schreber died when his son Daniel Paul was 19. Daniel Schreber's mother was nearly unknown until Israel's (1989) biography was published. It now appears that she was a major figure for him throughout her long life. He became a jurist and rose quickly through the court system to become a prominent judge in Leipzig. He married Sabine Behr in 1878, a year after his older brother, Gustav, committed suicide by gunshot at age 38. In 1885, Schreber became a candidate for the Reichstag (the imperial Diet, or legislature) from Chemnitz, where he held the post of *Landgerichtsdirektor,* the rank below president of the district court (Israels, 1989, p. 156).

His first period of nervous disorder, as he termed it, or of hypochondria, as his psychiatrist, Dr. Paul Emil Flechsig, called it, occurred almost immediately after he lost this election. In the words of the clinic's psychiatric reports, "He imagines that he has lost thirty to forty pounds in weight. Has in fact gained two kilogrammes. Complains that he is being purposely deceived about his weight" (Baumeyer, 1956, pp. 61–62). By Schreber's (1955) own account, the first period passed "without any occurrences bordering on the supernatural" (p. 35). After six months in Flechsig's clinic in Leipzig, he returned to his wife and to his work for eight years. In 1893, he was appointed *Senatspraesident* in the *Oberlandsgericht* in Dresden, and within weeks of taking up this position he was back in Flechsig's clinic for six months. He was then transferred, after a two-week stay in the Lindenhof clinic in Coswig, to the Sonnenstein public asylum at Pirna, near Dresden, for the following eight years. The *Memoirs* chronicle this second period of illness. Schreber left Sonnenstein in 1902 but became extremely agitated in 1907 after his mother's death and entered a clinic in Dosen, where he died in 1911.

Schreber began the *Memoirs* first "to acquaint my wife with my personal experiences and religious ideas" (p. 1n) so she would understand his "various oddities of behavior" after his release from Sonnenstein. The project gradually gained, in his mind, a larger and larger intended audience, which expanded to include the courts, which could find him competent to manage his own affairs and to live outside the asylum; Flechsig, his former psychiatrist; and finally an educated public who might find the work of scientific and religious value. Schreber's "personal experiences and religious ideas" became inextricably linked because the religious ideas became his settled way of understanding and organizing his personal experiences.

Schreber began his account with general ideas about religious metaphysics and soul murder, and followed with this introduction to his third chapter:

> I will first consider some events *concerning other members of my family,* which may possibly be related to the presumed soul murder; these are all more or less mysterious, and can hardly be explained in the light of usual human experience [the further content of this chapter is omitted as unfit for publication] [p. 61].

We are left to surmise what this chapter contained. Schreber's other references to his family and to Flechsig usually mentioned early ancestors of his relatives or Flechsig's forebears.

Schreber then turned to the history of his illness, including the information given earlier in this chapter. He added that just after his appointment as *Senatspraesident* he awoke one morning thinking "that it must really be rather pleasant to be a woman succumbing to intercourse" (p. 63). He also reported a sense of feeling burdened by his new position and needing to earn the respect of the much older judges over whom he had to preside. He began to sleep badly and consulted Flechsig, who initially raised his hopes of a cure by sleeping drugs. When this did not work and Schreber looked for a means of suicide, Flechsig advised Schreber's admission to his asylum, where the same pattern repeated: failure of sleeping drugs, then suicide attempts. Finally he was made to sleep with chloral hydrate. His wife stopped visiting, and Flechsig, in his patient's experience, could no longer look Schreber straight in the eye when Schreber asked if he would recover. From then on, Schreber lived in the world of voices, divine miracles, and fleeting-improvised people.

In the first phase, according to Schreber's account, he understood that the Order of the World had been disturbed and that he had to cooperate with God in resisting his own unmanning, the transformation into a woman equivalent to the destruction of his self. He found, however, that his resistance was accompanied by divine interventions like the compression-of-the-chest miracle; the writing-down-system; the appearance and disappearance of his stomach; the opening and closing of his eyes by miracles; the head-compressing machine; the coccyx miracle, which prevented him from staying in one place or position; the breaking of his piano strings; the system of unfinished sentences; and, of course, the constant torment of the voices.

Gradually Schreber became convinced that the way to make these tortures stop was to cooperate in his transformation into a woman, that is, to accept a completely passive role in his own life and thus to placate God, who, Schreber came to believe, was actually hostile to him. By accepting the sexual identity designated for him, he would be able to redeem the world by giving birth to a new race.

FREUD'S ACCOUNT

Freud (1911) welcomed Schreber's *Memoirs* as a wonderful piece of evidence to support his own theory linking paranoia and homosexuality. As his title, "Psychoanalytic Notes Upon an Autobiographical Account of a Case of Paranoia (Dementia Paranoides)," indicates, he saw Schreber as "a case of paranoia" and as a clear confirmatory example of what he termed the "remarkable fact that the familiar principal forms of paranoia can all be represented as contradictions of the single proposition: 'I (a man) love him (a man)' " (p. 63). This theory-bound reading of the *Memoirs,* together with Freud's tendency to exonerate fathers once he had minimized or disavowed the seduction theory (Bloch, 1989), undoubtedly shaped his understanding of Schreber. Still, Freud's essay contributed significantly to the understanding of psychosis.

First and most important, Freud made the shift from symptom to meaning. Rejecting the psychiatric custom of listing symptoms and inferring a diagnostic category, or of detailing delusions and concluding that the patient is insane, Freud insisted that symptoms and delusions have meaning. They refer, in other words, to something in the patient's experience or in the way the patient organizes experience. Though he may have made gratuitous assumptions about the content and meaning of Schreber's experience, assumptions that probably limited his access to other meanings, he did consistently regard the psychoanalytic task as understanding the content and structure of the patient's subjective world.

More particularly, he saw Schreber's sense of being emasculated (his soul murder or loss of self) as central to his experience both of his threatened self and of the threatening others. He read "the end of the world" as referring to the destruction of Schreber's subjective world. Freud understood that the requirement that Schreber should redeem the world was a secondary, reactive, or even perhaps restorative aspect of his delusions. In addition, Freud saw that Schreber's fear of sexual abuse was central to his experience (p. 44) and was probably involved in the "soul murder," though Freud was unable to guess at any special reasons for Schreber's conviction that he was likely to be so abused. Further, Freud saw clearly the parallels and identifications drawn by Schreber among God, Flechsig, the sun—all three, in Freud's view, referred to Schreber's father—and recognized Schreber's mixture of hatred, love, and puzzlement toward them.

In fact, Freud was particularly well attuned to an important part of the subjective meaning of Schreber's belief that he must be transformed into a woman. Schreber had to become a woman so that he could feel like a woman—a person, in the eyes of both Freud and Schreber, who derives pleasure from being done to, from adopting a passive attitude, from submission. In addition, Freud and Schreber both saw "female" as equivalent to "emasculated." Since Freud understood Schreber's God as the father, he thus recognized that Schreber felt compelled to take up a compliant passivity so extreme as to involve a change in physical sex characteristics. Because by this time Freud was locating pathology solely in the patient, he could not go further and ask what kind of child rearing might have produced the experience of such an extreme requirement of passivity or self-loss. Nor could Freud ask why Schreber had to accept the loss of selfhood so completely that he could no longer experience this loss as soul murder but had to feel it as redemptive.

Freud (1911) understood, however, that "the delusional formation, which we take to be the pathological product, is in reality an attempt at recovery, a process of reconstruction" (p. 71). Freud recognized, as did Schreber's physicians, that Schreber was more "sane" in his general behavior as his delusions became more fully articulated and organized. Finally, Freud saw the *Memoirs* as Schreber's attempt at self-rehabilitation by attempting to resolve his disputes with God/father. Freud commented on Weber's view of the *Memoirs* as "unblushing": "Surely we can hardly expect that a case history which sets out to give a picture of deranged humanity and its struggles to rehabilitate itself should exhibit 'discretion' and 'aesthetic' charm" (p. 37, n. 1).

Among the limitations of Freud's essay, already alluded to, is his method: the use of Schreber as a case to illustrate and support a theory, thus precluding Schreber's appearing as a person with a history of relationships, reflected in the self-states described in the *Memoirs*. Freud's commitment to a one-person, or intrapsychic, view of human nature and of psychopathology made it difficult or perhaps impossible for him to present Schreber's childhood or adult environments, or his treatment relationships, as structuring his inner world. Though Niederland (1984) views his own researches into the work of Moritz Schreber as support for Freud's dynamic formulation, Freud did not himself consider it important to use available information about either Schreber's family or Flechsig's treatment philosophy in his own account. Nor did Freud, as far as we know, attempt to meet Schreber, still alive when Freud was writing about him. Perhaps this omission on Freud's part can be attributed to a concern that such researches would undermine or complicate his use of Schreber as a case to illustrate a one-person theory of paranoia.

We do have evidence that Freud thought about the effect of early environment on Schreber. Lothane (1989) quotes a letter from Freud to Ferenczi dated October 6, 1910:

> What would you say to Doctor S. senior performing "miracles" as a physician? But who was otherwise a despot in his household who "bellowed" [i.e., yelled and scolded] at his son and understood him as little as the "lower God" understood our paranoiac [Lothane's translation, p. 215].

We do not know why Freud chose to exclude these ideas from his published work on Schreber.

Second, Freud, despite his remarkable shift from symptom to meaning, sometimes confused symbol and meaning, or collapsed meaning into simple reference. He took symbols like unmanning as referring to castration, when Schreber made it clear that the much more serious and more real threat was soul murder or soul stealing. Stolorow, Brandchaft, and Atwood (1987) term such a collapse of meaning into symbol "concretization." Other examples in Freud's account—lapses probably owing to his desire to support his own theory—are the assumption that Schreber transformed his father into God because "such a father as this was by no means unsuitable for transfiguration into a God in the affectionate memory of a son from whom he had been so early separated by death" (Freud, 1911, p. 51). Here Freud saw the reference or denotation of the symbol but missed the emotional meaning. Schreber's God, a tyrant who regulated every part of life, was a tormentor. Or, again, while Freud recognized the distinction Schreber drew between Flechsig himself and "the Flechsig soul," between the objective and the subjective realities, and knew each had a separate reference, he bypassed the question of what experiential meaning Schreber's complaints against the Flechsig soul might carry. Freud apparently assumed that these were transference distortions of the behavior of an unequivocally benevolent physician. In addition, Freud saw Schreber's "megalomania" as compensatory for the insult of being turned into a woman, but he could not—and here we cannot blame him, perhaps, for not seeing with Kohut's eyes—that the compensation in narcissistic grandiosity was for the complete loss of self that becoming a woman signified and that had been required of him as a child.

Third, Freud's interpretation, identifying the psychosis with an "outburst of homosexual libido," relied on drive-theory assumptions about human motivation that self-psychological thinking has replaced with premises that attribute motivational primacy to self-consolidation and to relational concerns. Freud's Schreber is a self-enclosed system of energy transformations. A related, though nonidentical, assumption—about homosexuality as one kind of libido—led Freud to believe that Schreber was homosexual, despite all evidence to the contrary. Not only did Schreber never behave as a homosexual, there is no evidence whatever that he thought of himself in that way. Freud, nevertheless, identified "feminine" and "homosexual" and took "it must be rather pleasant . . ." as all the evidence he needed. For Freud, passivity or receptivity constituted femininity, and femininity was equivalent, in a male, to homosexuality. Feeling attracted to same-sex partners was not required. As Lothane (1989) points out, Schreber gave no sign of sexual attraction to men. To Freud, this had to be unimportant: homosexuality was an intrapsychic condition, not a relational matter, for Freud.

Finally, to return to the limitations of the one-person theory, Freud apparently missed the possibility that Schreber actually had been and was being persecuted and thus was not entirely delusional. (Freud, 1911, did, of course, insert his famous enigmatic caveat, "It remains for the future to decide whether there is more delusion in my theory than I should like to admit, or whether there is more truth in Schreber's delusion than other people are as yet prepared to believe" [p. 79], but did not explore the implications of this statement.) Among those who have explored the possibilities, Lothane (1989) draws a convincing picture of the ways Flechsig may have mistreated Schreber and construes Freud's reticence not only as political, but as resulting from Freud's steadfast disinterest in the relational context of Schreber's difficulties.

Altogether, Freud's account directs us to the meanings in Schreber's psychosis, then systematically obscures these meanings. It has thus become the task of psychoanalytic commentators and researchers to get closer to Schreber's own experience, a task for which self psychology sees itself as especially well suited because of its commitments to experience-near theorizing and to understanding the patient from the patient's point of view.

In Kohut's (1978) view, Freud's (1911) central insights in his writing on Schreber, were that " 'the *step back* . . . *to narcissism*' is characteristic of the psychoses, and that 'The delusional formation . . . [is not the central pathology but] . . . an attempt at recovery, a process of reconstruction . . .' " (pp. 71–72). In his comments on Niederland's work on Moritz Schreber, Kohut (1978) remarked that the historical data may throw light on the essence of Schreber's psychosis: "the narcissistic fixation and regression" (p. 307). Kohut believed that

> the secret of Schreber's psychosis is bound up with his father's personality—adding the important fact . . . that the mother was subordinated to, submerged by, and interwoven with the father's overwhelming personality and strivings, thus permitting the son no refuge from the impact of the father's pathology [p. 307].

Kohut went on to explain that the father's pathology consisted of a special kind of psychotic character in which reality testing is generally present, but which, as it was in Hitler, is organized around a central *idée fixe:*

> The absolute conviction father Schreber had toward his ideas, the unquestioning fanaticism with which he pursued them, betrays, I believe, their profoundly narcissistic character, and I would assume that a fear of hypochondriacal tensions lies behind the rather overt fight

against masturbation. His fanatical activities, too, although lived out on the body of the son, belong to a hidden narcissistic delusional system. The son, in other words, is felt as part of the father's narcissistic system, and not as separate [p. 307].

Thus Kohut shifted the emphasis in understanding Schreber to the relational world of his childhood and to its bearing on his adult self-experience.

POST-FREUDIAN PSYCHOANALYTIC ACCOUNTS

Beginning with his 1951 paper, "Three notes on the Schreber case," and continuing through the second edition of *The Schreber Case* (1984), Niederland has provided the readers of Freud and Schreber with what he regards as the "kernel of truth" in Schreber's complaints. His researches have led him to believe that the "miracles" Schreber felt perpetrated on him were thinly veiled references to his father's child rearing methods. Niederland searched the books of Moritz Schreber and found pictures and descriptions of various pieces of apparatus—intended to correct improper posture or prevent its emergence—which resemble the "compression-of-the-chest-miracle," the "head-being-tied-together-machine," and others. He quotes extensively from Moritz Schreber's works passages that suggest an effort to control every part of a child's physical and mental life so that the child will develop so much self-control that he will not even feel externally coerced. No further discipline, the father thought, should be necessary after the fifth or sixth year of life. Niederland suggests that, like other 19th-century parents, Schreber's father was especially concerned with preventing children from masturbating. Altogether, Niederland has assembled a horrifying picture of the probable world of Schreber's childhood, which not only makes his later fragmentation under stress understandable, and many details of his report interpretable, but also leaves the reader wondering how Schreber managed to function as long as he did. Niederland's book makes the older brother's suicide completely unsurprising.

At the same time, having marshalled such a mountain of evidence against what he sees as Schreber's persecutory childhood environment, Niederland repeatedly and explicitly supports Freud's view that Schreber was a "case of paranoia" to be explained in terms of intrapsychic conflict between love and hatred for the father, that is, rejection of his unconscious homosexual desire for the father and, later, for Flechsig. Indeed, Niederland believes, his researches provide evidence for Freud's interpretation by showing that Schreber had reason both to hate and to love his father and that the content of Schreber's *Memoirs* makes even more sense than Freud had thought.

To a reader unconcerned with protecting Freud and his theories, Niederland's conclusions are puzzling. He does not see that he has seriously undermined Freud's attempt to exonerate the father and to place the cause of paranoia in the patient. If the parallels Niederland draws are correct, early environment shaped Schreber's subjective world beyond any extent Freud could consider after he replaced the seduction theory. Niederland's relentless pursuit of historical meanings in Schreber's *Memoirs* makes his reluctance to draw the obvious conclusions from his own work puzzling.

Schatzman (1973) has no such hesitation. He, like Shengold (1989), straightforwardly accuses Moritz Schreber, with the full cooperation of his wife, of the soul murder, by prolonged physical and emotional abuse, of his sons. Schatzman agrees with Freud that the God of the *Memoirs* is Schreber's father, a deity who, Schreber only gradually comes to realize, intended to destroy his mind. He details, again by extensive reference to Moritz Schreber's books, the systematic ways the child, from infancy, was robbed of self-determination precisely in the name of self-determination. The child was programmed to want and not want precisely what the parents determined that the child should want and not want. This, to Schreber's father, was self-determination. (Schatzman provides a telling partial list of titles of Moritz Schreber's books: *The Cold-Water Healing Method, The Systematically Planned Sharpening of the Senses, The Harmful Body Positions and Habits of Children, Including a Statement of Counteracting Measures.*)

More recently, Lothane (1989, 1990), in the interpersonalist tradition, has made a convincing case for regarding Schreber's psychosis as precipitated by his treatment by Flechsig and other psychiatrists as well as by his wife's efforts to have him declared incompetent to manage his own affairs. Less convincing is his attempt "to vindicate both Schrebers, father and son" (Lothane, 1989, p. 206). Lothane regards his own method as historical (fact not fancy) in contrast to what he see as the hermeneutic or theory-bound method of Freud. He notes that the *Memoirs* seem to contain both Schreber's account of what actually happened to him ("On the 1st of October 1993 I took up office as *Senatspraesident* to the Superior Court in Dresden") as well as his interpretation—cleverly disguised as delusional to avoid accusations of libel by Flechsig—of events ("Divine rays above all have the power of influencing the nerves"). Lothane apparently

The Restoration of Schreber's Stolen Self

believes there is a "just the facts" story about Schreber, as if any story could be told without interpretation (see Orange, 1992). He thus dismisses the works of Niederland and Schatzman as "unproven inferences and constructions" (p. 209), and Freud's views as hermeneutics.

Lothane's (1989, 1990) own interpretation of Schreber's story sees the psychosis as nondelusional, as an extremely anxious response to Schreber's here-and-now situation and especially to his treatment by Flechsig. According to Schreber and Lothane, Flechsig committed soul murder on Schreber by assisting Schreber's wife in having him declared incompetent, thus "unmanning" him, by hypnotizing him and thus robbing him of his reason, and by sending him, at the end of six months, to Sonnenstein, a public asylum for untreatable cases. Only then, according to Lothane, did Schreber's behavior become "insane." Schreber's diagnosis was, in this view, iatrogenic psychosis. It is interesting, Lothane thinks, that Schreber never accused Weber, chief psychiatrist at Sonnenstein, of soul murder. Weber, he thinks, did seriously mistreat Schreber by opposing his release when Schreber's behavior, by Weber's own account, had been reasonable, civil, and courteous for a long time.

Lothane's collection of information about Flechsig and his use of it to corroborate Schreber's statements in the "factual" parts of the *Memoirs,* are striking enough to make self psychologists wonder if more respectful treatment might not have prevented Schreber's full deterioration into a desperate, suicidal, bellowing madman who believed no one around him was real. Apparently Flechsig, a psychiatrist of his own historical time, was interested only in biological treatments. What Lothane does not consider is how Schreber's early experience in his family preconditioned his experience of the stresses of his adult life—"overwork," Schreber called it—as well as of his mistreatment by Flechsig, by Weber, and possibly by his wife. Lothane is well aware of intersubjective process between patient and psychiatrist, but misses the way a child may experience the relational world of the family and then organize experience accordingly. In what follows, I try to take the traumas of Schreber's childhood and of his adulthood equally seriously. Schreber illustrates the clinical truism that abused children frequently become abused adults. What made Schreber extraordinary, besides Freud's interest in him, was his capacity and determination to tell his story and thus to heal himself by freeing himself from unjustified confinement. Why his attempt at self-restoration worked only partly and temporarily is a topic for later in this chapter.

SCHREBER'S RELATIONAL EXPERIENCE

Schreber's self-experience, the primary concern of a self-psychologically oriented analysis, can only be understood as the product of his experience of the intersubjective context, the emotional environment, that produced his self-experience. Although we have no direct access to the relational worlds of his childhood or of his adulthood, we do have his eloquent account of his experience and of his interpretation of his psychiatric treatment. Without claiming to know the "facts" about either Schreber's childhood or his treatment, we can consider the "organizing principles" (Stolorow et al., 1987) he inferred from his relational experiences.

Schreber (1955) viewed his psychiatrist and at least some of his caretakers as persecutors. He felt them to be attempting to murder his soul, to rob him of his reason, to "unman" him, for the sake of their own needs. He felt that they needed to get away from him, whose own needs, "the attraction of my nerves," he believed, were too much for people around him. So, he thought, they gave him sleeping medicines, but inconsistently, so they could get away from him—not an implausible guess. They were thus responding to their own needs, not to his.

> Always the main idea was to "forsake" me, that is to say abandon me; at the times I am now discussing [just before he was sent away from Flechsig's asylum in 1894] it was thought that this could be achieved by unmanning me and allowing my body to prostituted like that of a female harlot, sometimes also by killing me and later by destroying my reason (making me demented) [p. 99].

The beginning of this experience of persecution was a sense of being misunderstood. In early November 1893, Schreber came to Flechsig complaining of sleeplessness and was given a combination of drugs that not only did not help him sleep but made him so anxious that he started to attempt suicide. By Schreber's account, the psychiatrists, seeing his entire difficulty as a biologically based sleep disturbance, tried alternately to treat him with weaker sleeping drugs and with chloral hydrate. He felt that no attempt was made to understand him as an anxious living person:

> It is my opinion that Professor Flechsig must have had some idea of this tendency, innate in the Order of the World, whereby in certain conditions the unmanning of a human being is provided for.... *A*

The Restoration of Schreber's Stolen Self

fundamental misunderstanding obtained, however, which has since run like a red thread through my entire life. It is based upon the fact *that within the Order of the World, God did not really understand the living human being* and had no need to understand him, because, according to the Order of the World, He dealt only with corpses [p. 75; emphases Schreber's].

God . . . saw human beings *only from without;* as a rule his omnipresence and omniscience did not extend within *living* man [pp. 59–60].

Schreber's indictment suggests that massive failures in empathic understanding, together with a complete inattention to the patient's subjective world, precipitated his turn from overwork and anxiety to psychosis. God, Flechsig, and Moritz Schreber had devoted themselves to an Order of the World, a scientific empiricism, in which the subjective world of the living human being could have no place. They could comprehend only beings with no feelings. Schreber here meant that he had never been understood as a living human being with needs and feelings of his own but had been seen, throughout his life, "only from without." He felt used and misunderstood by those who should have been his caregivers and protectors.

Misunderstanding turned, in Schreber's experience, into abandonment. Schreber felt that others saw him as a hopeless case and thus that he must commit suicide. When his wife, who had been visiting him daily, taking him out, and attempting to raise his spirits (p. 68), took a four-day vacation, he had a night of "a quite unusual number of pollutions," which Freud took to mean an outburst of homosexual libido and Schreber saw as decisive in his turn for the worse. After that time he saw his wife rarely, felt her not to be real, and began instead to communicate with supernatural powers. He felt abandoned by everyone. There is, by the way, no mention in any of his hospital records of any attempt by his wife, his mother, or his siblings to secure his release from the hospital at any time. The significance of the night of emissions may be that the combined abandonments meant complete loss of control: Moritz Schreber had believed nocturnal emissions, and, of course, all masturbation, could and must be prevented.

Abandonment was also integral, not simply sequential, to the experience of misunderstanding. Misunderstanding can result from abandoning the subjective world, the experience of the patient or child. For Schreber, Flechsig's treatment of him constituted such an abandonment that he sometimes felt invisible: "something in the nature of a wizard had suddenly appeared in the person of Professor

Flechsig . . . I myself, after all a person known in wider circles, had suddenly disappeared" (p. 97). At other times he felt that he must have leprosy, the disease of abandoned outcasts, or the plague. Later he felt required to think continuously, for fear God would misunderstand and regard "my mental powers as extinct" (p. 166). A partial function of the bellowing, paradoxically, was to interfere with God's abandonment of or withdrawal from him. It was both indicator of madness and a cry for help. "It remains a riddle to me that the cries of help are apparently not heard by other human beings: the sound which reaches my own ear—hundreds of times every day—is so definite that it cannot be a hallucination" (p. 166). He was, however, deeply ashamed of his own needs. "The genuine 'cries of help' are always instantly followed by the phrase which has been learnt by rote: 'If only the cursed cries of help would stop' " (p. 166). We may speculate that in Schreber's family there had been no way for a child to cry for help and that both as a patient and as a child he felt abandoned, unsupported, and unvalidated (in his terms, misunderstood) in his extreme distress.

Closely related to the experience of others as abandoning may have been Schreber's sense of their unreliability. People, he felt in the years before writing his account, do not even persist in being. They are *fluchtig hingemacht,* or fleetingly made-up, "cursorily improvised" in McAlpine and Hunter's translation. People were not real; they were made-up contraptions. We can only speculate on the origins of this prominent feature of Schreber's experience of the human world. Perhaps Moritz Schreber's children never knew whether they would find him playful and affectionate or punitive and repressive. The father's books suggest that both attitudes are central to childrearing. Or perhaps Schreber's experience of his psychiatric treatment was that it included considerable improvisation and little consistency. Schreber may have felt the massive unreliability in his environment as its unreality. Another possibility is that Schreber's upbringing had deprived him of any sense of his own reality as a center of experience and initiative and led him to say that others were unreal because he felt so unreal himself. He may have felt himself to be a made-up contraption like the people in the illustrations in his father's books on medical gymnastics (Niederland, 1984, pp. 81, 95). In any case, it is likely that his sense of the unreliability and unreality of human beings—particularly of those who should have been consistently helpful, like parents and physicians—contributed to his sense of abandonment and vice versa. Increasingly, he understood both involvement with others and abandonment as intended to contribute to the destruction of his reason.

From misunderstanding and abandonment, soul murder continued to its central business of "unmanning." Lothane (1989) points out that, in German, "the word *Entmannung* has two basic meanings: the concrete one of gelding or castration, and the metaphorical one of loss of virile power, vigor, and pride" (p. 237). I agree with Lothane's view that Schreber consistently used the word in the second sense; I would add only that he felt the "loss" as a robbery and a betrayal. Consider the following:

> [A] plot was laid against me (perhaps March or April 1894), the purpose of which was to hand me over to another human being after my nervous illness had been recognized as, or assumed to be, incurable, in such a way that my soul was handed to him, but my body—transformed into a female body and, misconstruing the above-described fundamental tendency of the order of the World—was then left to that human being for sexual misuse and simply "forsaken," in other words left to rot [p. 75].

Schreber's understanding of the intersubjective reason for the efforts to murder his soul was that others saw him as a threat, as dangerous. He often spoke of the "miracles" directed against him as attempts to reduce his power to attract the nerves of God. He suspected that God—whom I take to stand for Moritz Schreber and, at times, Flechsig—had a manifest need to dominate, a need that covered a profound vulnerability.

> God Himself must have been or be in a precarious position, if the conduct of a single human being could endanger Him in any way and if even He Himself, if only in lower instances, could be enticed into a kind of conspiracy against human beings who are fundamentally innocent [p. 59].

Parenthetically, this sense of being a threat to his older colleagues in his new position as *Senatspraesident* may have been one precipitant for his second period of illness. In Flechsig's clinic, he was likely to have questioned his treatment and thus seemed a threat to the established psychiatric hierarchy; as a child he may have known from experience that his father would not tolerate explicit or implicit questioning of his authority. Whatever the origins of this sense of others as threatened by his "nerves" (read: feelings, needs, ideas), Schreber's conviction that others felt him as dangerous runs throughout the *Memoirs*.

Another part of the soul murder was Schreber's sense of being used a guinea pig, a subject in endless experiments. Moritz Schreber supported his child-rearing theories by claiming he had tested them on his own children. Flechsig may have tested his biological theories of psychiatry on the patients in his university hospital. Schreber as patient thought he was surrounded by "tested souls." Experiments, of course, must be replicated: "God cannot learn by experience" (p. 155).

To be an experimental subject is, of course, not to be a person in one's own right, but to exist only to validate others' theories and to support the narcissistic needs of the experimenter. Indeed, Schreber's primary complaint was that people attempted to destroy his reason and change his awareness of his own identity (p. 99), a common effect of child rearing by narcissistic parents (Miller, 1981).

The principal vehicle for the destruction of Schreber's soul or self, was, in his experience and expectation, sexual abuse. In his last months in Flechsig's clinic, "the most disgusting was the idea that my body, after the intended transformation into a female being, was to suffer some sexual abuse, particularly as there had even been talk for some time of my being thrown to the asylum attendants for this purpose" (p. 101). Now, whatever our estimate of the likelihood of sexual abuse of patients in Flechsig's asylum, Schreber's own sense of vulnerability and of being used was clearly tied to the experience of sexual abuse. He may have identified this vulnerability and the accompanying shame as equivalent to becoming female. If Schreber had been sexually abused as a child—not impossible in a family where children were experimental subjects—he would understandably experience any threat of sexual abuse as "unmanning," depriving of all autonomy, and as central to the stealing of his soul.

The sense of being used as an experimental subject may also have contributed to Schreber's messianic convictions. He believed God was creating a new race of humans out of his nerves, "new human beings out of Schreber's spirit" (p. 110). Schreber's father, particularly, had grandiose hopes for the transformation of the species by his child rearing methods and may have often told his children of these dreams. For the mental patient Schreber, exposure to the experiment-over-treatment preference at Flechsig's clinic may have evoked a central organizing principle: transformation into a passive and vulnerable (i.e., female) person gives your life meaning—you contribute to the salvation of the world. Unmanning, he thought, might be "with the purpose of creating new human beings" (p. 117). Taking charge as *Senatspraesident* would have opposed this meaning too much and probably contributed to the evocation of his fantasy about how lovely it might be to be a woman succumbing to intercourse.

SCHREBER'S SELF-EXPERIENCE

Schreber's self-experience was organized by his relational experience both as a child and as an adult. His experience of persecution led him to see himself as dangerous to others and to explain the persecution and the miracles as attempts to control him because he was dangerous. His experience of what he called soul murder led him to experience himself as empty, as both vulnerable and invulnerable (p. 212), as helpless and unfree, as unprotected (p. 117n), and as female. His experience as an experimental subject led him to think of himself as important only if he could be used for some larger purpose like the salvation of the world. These dimensions of his self-experience clearly emerged from his relational experiences.

In addition, Schreber's self-experience was the exact opposite of cohesive. He spoke of the partitioning of souls, of nerves strung out across the heavens, and commented that he was inclined "to believe that the natural unity of the human soul used to be respected" (p. 109). His sense of fragmentation displayed itself in his difficulty knowing who did the writing in the writing-down-system, why he was housed separately from the other patients (later he learned that it had been because of his bellowing). He thus felt his fragmentation both as spatial and as temporal. Possibly because his relational experience had been traumatically inconsistent and, perhaps, with Flechsig, desperately disappointing, he had considerable difficulty feeling himself as continuous in time. He reminds me of some highly intelligent and creative patients who protect themselves from overwhelming trauma through dissociation, with the resultant loss of continuity of experience of self and others. The confusion involved in this fragmentation may be integral to the soul-murder process. Since the usurpation of the child's subjectivity is the essence of soul murder, Schreber had no basis for knowing anything.

Schreber's self-experience during his confinements also took on an intensely negative coloration. No only did he feel small, vulnerable (female), and without protection from the rays (p. 117n), but he also saw himself as stupid. Cognitively, he always knew he had been a prominent judge, but this knowledge did nothing to hold at bay the voices that tormented him. When fellow patients would insult him, "the stupid twaddle of the voices 'has been recorded,' 'Why don't you say it (aloud)?', 'Because I am stupid,' or even 'Because I am afraid,' etc., tells me that it is still God's purpose that I relate these insulting forms of speech to myself" (pp. 199–200). He felt ashamed and humiliated by his condition and by his confinement. The voices often called him "wretch"—"an expression quite common in the basic language to denote a human being destined to be destroyed by God and to feel God's power and wrath" (p. 124).

A particularly evocative expression of Schreber's negative self-valuation was his conviction, during his first period of "nervous illness," that he had lost weight. To have weight, as philosopher Robert Nozick (1989) points out, is to be real and substantial, to have to be taken into account. In Nozick's words,

> the weight of something is its internal substantiality and strength. It may help to think of its opposite. What is meant when a person is called a 'lightweight'? It might be impact and importance that are being talked about here, but usually, I think, what are meant are those qualities that importance is (or should be) based upon. People are commenting on how substantial the person is, how considered his thoughts, how dependable his judgment, how that person holds under buffeting or deeper examination. A weighty person is not blown by winds of fashion or scrutiny. The Romans called it *gravitas* [p. 178].

This description probably fitted Schreber the jurist well and points to the magnitude of his felt loss.

The notion of weight involves that of importance, a more relational matter, that is, having-weight-for-someone. In fact, Schreber's specific concern was about validation:

> I believe I could have been more rapidly cured of certain hypochondriacal ideas with which I was preoccupied at the time, particularly concern over loss of weight, if I had been allowed to operate the scales which served to weigh patients a few times myself [p. 62].

For self psychology, the self-experience of having weight, making a difference, emerges from the relational experience of having importance in the eyes of early caretakers, of mirroring responses to the child's own emerging selfhood. Now we know that Moritz Schreber's children were important to him, but from his writings we may infer that this importance resided in their value as experimental subjects and as exemplars of his child-rearing methods. As mentioned earlier, he intended to eradicate every trace of the child's own will. The wishes and desires of children carried no weight with him, and his son, despite his impressive accomplishments, internalized a profound sense of himself as a lightweight. Schreber experienced himself and others as merely fleeting and improvised. As an asylum patient, the weightless Schreber was given to fits of bellowing, as if to impress his existence and presence—his weight—on his world and on God. For years, to experience himself as having any weight, he had to see others as fleeting-improvised Lilliputians. This view of the weight loss experience may also lend intelligibility to Schreber's conviction that he was becoming a woman, a person of lesser weight and of little importance in 19th-century German society. He usually described his transformation into a woman as a process of shrinking. In his experience he replaced his quantitative loss (of weight) with a qualitative loss (of manhood).

Before we leave Schreber's self-experience as related in the *Memoirs*, we may note the absence of any obvious sadness in Schreber's words themselves. Schreber portrayed himself as feeling angry, humiliated, frustrated, abandoned, and destroyed, but never as sad. Perhaps the emotion that was thoroughly eradicated in his childhood, by the demand to be always cheerful, was sadness. Or perhaps he had to drop this emotion from his repertoire in order not to commit suicide like his brother. In any case, his losses were considerable: home, wife, position and respect, autonomy, peace of mind. But instead of feeling these losses, he said that he lost weight and masculinity.

SCHREBER'S EFFORTS AT SELF-RESTORATION

From the beginning of his illness, Schreber displayed a remarkable determination to restore, repair, and reclaim his stolen self. Not content with just surviving, he struggled to reestablish himself as a person of weight in his own eyes, in the eyes of God, and in the human community. His efforts included his activities, his paradoxical-passive efforts, and the paranoia itself seen as self-reparative response to narcissistic injury (soul murder).

Under the heading of activities, we may consider his piano-playing, his chess, his learning of poetry, and, of course, his writing of the *Memoirs*. The piano playing, chess playing, and the poetry learning were intended to convey to God, seen now as persecutor, that Schreber's soul had not been entirely destroyed. They also functioned to ward off the voices and the miracles that otherwise tormented him.

The writing of the *Memoirs* even more clearly attempted to restore Schreber to the status of a person in the human community. I suspect, however, that even his earliest attempt to write an account of his illness was sporadically curative and shows his intense desire to articulate and communicate his experience. If Miller (1990) is correct, abused children without a validating witness can neither experience their own pain nor experience themselves as abused. Schreber was partly healed by his own process of attempting, by writing, to find such witnesses. He proclaimed both that he suffered and that crimes had been perpetrated on him. Censored portions of his book were likely cut precisely because he there indicted his abusers by name, thereby claiming his own status as a human being. The *Memoirs* not only expressed his distress and outrage at the way he had been treated and at his own mental state; it also signified his finding sufficient self-respect to challenge his tutelage. He overcame his feelings of weakness, helplessness, and shame enough to confront those who would keep him in a less-than-human status. That he should have found the courage to engage in such an action of self-reclamation makes it probable that with adequate human support he might have recovered faster, more thoroughly, and more permanently.

We can explain the restorative effect of these activities by reference to the self-psychological notion of selfobject experience. Anything functions as selfobject to the extent that it contributes to the cohesiveness, continuity, and positive valence of a person's self-experience. For Schreber, the writing of his book apparently served such selfobject functions. By telling his story, even metaphorically, he tried to make a coherent, continuous, and cohesive whole out of what he felt to be absurd, confusing, and fragmenting. Both the story he told and the action of telling it transformed him from a bellowing madman into a learned, cultured, and genteel person who ate dinner and discussed various topics at the table of the director of the asylum. The story, submitted to the courts and to the director, also demanded recognition of the transformation. Hence the writing itself not only served as a selfobject experience for Schreber, but was clearly intended to evoke additional selfobject experiences from his wife, from the medical establishment, and from the larger community.

Paradoxically, Schreber also attempted, from the time of his commitment to Sonnenstein, to repair himself by surrendering to the requirements he felt had been placed on him. The literary critic E. Barry Chabot (1982) has pointed out a significant continuity to Schreber's desire to sleep, his catatonia, and his acceptance of the female soul-voluptuousness. Each meant to him the possibility of release from torture by giving in to externally imposed requirements for the sake of a larger purpose. Initially, Schreber said that a person who could not sleep would surely have to commit suicide. Later he found that even with nocturnal sleep he was tormented by voices that demanded his complete immobility and by miracles that made every position he took uncomfortable. (One is reminded of the father's devices and exercises to control children whether waking or sleeping.) For many months, Schreber tells us, he sat for hours a day without moving. When he understood at last that God—not just "little Flechsig"—was tormenting him and demanding both his mental and physical passivity, then he realized as well that he must actively cultivate the mental/physical state of female soul-voluptuousness, the ultimate acquiescence. All three—sleep, catatonia, and soul-voluptuousness—were attempts to rescue the self from torment. The last, however, became even temporarily healing when Schreber could understand its larger salvific meaning. Unfortunately he somehow, by the very acceptance of his passive role, both actively cooperated in his own destruction and rescued a vestige of himself, a kind of compromise sanity. We, of course, can see that this solution could not be stable for Schreber because it depended on compliance, on nonbeing, rather than on being a self. It was acceptance of the soul murder.

Finally Schreber's very paranoia constituted a prolonged effort at self-reparation. What he called soul murder was a lifelong narcissistic injury, an insult to the self, a cumulative trauma. His system of beliefs—delusions, many would call them—transformed his sense of vulnerability and stupidity into a grandiose belief that only he had access to ultimate religious truth. His helplessness became the power to attract the nerves of God. His confusion became a privileged access to meaning. His sense of profound insignificance became a mission to redeem the world precisely by adopting the role of insignificance assigned to women. A self-psychological reading of Schreber must enthusiastically support Freud's (1911) view that "the delusional formation, which we take to be the pathological product, is in reality an attempt at recovery, a process of reconstruction" (p. 71).

Schreber did not simply write a summary of his delusions; he wrote his story with a beginning, a middle, and an ending. The beginning is lost to us because censors cut the sections referring to his family. The middle describes the miracles and other torments, along with Schreber's attempts to survive by resistance to the soul murder. The ending recounts the change, development, or transformation of his experience. By his account, once he accepted the fate dealt to him, he no longer found himself alone among cursorily improvised contraptions. He found other people real and himself significant. His book communicates this understanding of the process of the provisional and partial restoration of his stolen self.

REFERENCES

Bacal, H. & Newman, K. (1990), *Theories of Object Relations: Bridges to Self Psychology*. New York: Columbia University Press.

Baumeyer, F. (1956), The Schreber case. *Internat. J. Psycho-Anal.*, 37:61–74.
Bloch, D. (1989), Freud's retraction of his seduction theory and the Schreber case. *Psychoanal. Rev.*, 76:185–201.
Chabot, E. B. (1982), *Freud on Schreber*. Amherst: University of Massachusetts Press.
Freud, S. (1911), *Psycho-Analytic Notes on an Autobiographical Account of a Case of Paranoia (dementia paranoides)*. Standard Edition, 12:3–82. London: Hogarth Press, 1958.
Israels, H. (1989), *Schreber*. Madison, CT: International Universities Press.
Kohut, H. (1971), *The Analysis of the Self*. New York: International Universities Press.
―――― (1977), *The Restoration of the Self*. New York: International Universities Press.
―――― (1978), *The Search for the Self*, Vols. 1 and 2, ed. P. Ornstein. New York: International Universities Press.
―――― (1984), *How Does Analysis Cure?* ed. A. Goldberg & P. Stepansky. Chicago: University of Chicago Press.
Lothane, Z. (1989), Schreber, Freud, Flechsig and Weber Revisited: An inquiry into methods of interpretation. *Psychoanal. Rev.*, 76:203–262.
―――― (1990), Panel on Schreber at American Academy of Psychoanalysis. On tape.
Miller, A. (1981), *Prisoners of Childhood*, trans. R. Ward. New York: Basic Books.
―――― (1990), *The Untouched Key*, trans. H. & H. Hannum. New York: Anchor Doubleday.
Mitchell, S. (1988), *Relational Concepts in Psychoanalysis*. Cambridge, MA: Harvard University Press.
Niederland, W. (1951), Three notes on the Schreber case. *Psychoanal. Quart.*, 28:151–169.
―――― (1984), *The Schreber Case*. Hillsdale, NJ: The Analytic Press.
Nozick, R. (1989), *The Examined Life*. New York: Simon & Schuster.
Orange, D. (1992), Subjectivism, relativism, and realism in psychoanalysis. In: *New Therapeutic Visions: Progress in Self Psychology, Vol. 8,* ed. A. Goldberg. Hillsdale, NJ: The Analytic Press.
Schatzman, M. (1973), *Soul Murder: Persecution in the Family*. New York: Random House.
Schreber, D. (1955), *Memoirs of My Nervous Illness*, trans. & ed. I. Macalpine & R. Hunter. Cambridge, MA: Harvard University Press.
Schwaber, E. (1983), Construction, reconstruction, and the mode of clinical attunement. In: *The Future of Psychoanalysis*, ed. A. Goldberg. New York: International Universities Press.
Shengold, L. (1989), *Soul Murder: The Effects of Childhood Abuse and Deprivation*. New Haven, CT: Yale University Press.
Stolorow, R., Brandchaft, B. & Atwood, G. (1987), *Psychoanalytic Treatment*. Hillsdale, NJ: The Analytic Press.

Barry Magid
SELF PSYCHOLOGY MEETS THE WOLF MAN

(*From the History of an Infantile Neurosis,* 1918)

In reviewing the case that Freud (1918) chose to call "From the History of an Infantile Neurosis," but that has become famous as the case of the Wolf Man, we have at our disposal, as in no other instance, additional accounts of the patient's life and treatment, not only by the famous patient himself, but by others who knew and treated him over many later years. Serge Pankejeff—to give the Wolf Man his real name—published the memoirs of his life and his recollections of Freud. These, along with Freud's original case; Ruth Mack Brunswick's "Supplement"—her account of her reanalysis of the Wolf Man; and Muriel Gardiner's memoirs of her long association with him, have been conveniently gathered into a single volume, *The Wolf-Man by the Wolf-Man* (Gardiner, 1971). Finally, we have the record of the extensive interviews conducted by the German journalist Karen Obholzer (1982), which she published after Serge's death as *The Wolf-Man Sixty Years Later.*

Together these accounts provide a longitudinal picture unique in the annals of psychoanalysis. We get to see not only the patient through Freud's eyes, but Freud through the eyes of his patient. Despite the fact that Serge's memoirs and his interviews with Obholzer were set down many years after publication of his case made him self-consciously famous as an icon of psychoanalytic literature, we nonetheless are given unique access to what he himself came to see as the most significant aspects of his life story, the origins of his difficulties, and the substance of his treatment. As Freud's title indicates, his was a very focused account of the case and was directed very specifically at validating his theories of the neurosogenic role of infantile sexual conflict as evidence against what he called "the twisted re-interpretations which C. G. Jung and Alfred Adler were endeavoring to give to the findings of psychoanalysis" (Gardiner, 1971, p. 153).

The broader scope of the Wolf-Man's own recollections thus allows us a glimpse at the material through which Freud sifted in writing his account, and we can see many elements that he chose to underplay or leave in the background. We shall, of course, keep in mind that what Serge wrote or recalled decades later cannot be identical to what he told Freud. However, just as we grant a subjective validity to a patient's account of his parents many years after the fact, so we must grant to Serge's later memoirs the subjective validity of what he himself came to see as most important in his own story and his treatment. We cannot say now that this is what Freud was "really" like with his patient; rather—and not insignificantly—we can say that this is what Freud and analysis seemed like to this particular patient.

I will proceed, therefore, not only to review Freud's published case material, but also, where possible, to weave together with it Serge's description of some of the same material, which I think will present his story in a somewhat different light. This is particularly the case as we look at the stories Serge tells of his parents, if we look at them in the light of our current knowledge of selfobject development, and not exclusively as Freud did, in terms of psychosexual development.

I will begin by reviewing the clinical picture that presented itself to Freud in 1911 and suggest how an initial diagnostic impression of the then 24-year-old patient might have been formulated from a self-psychological perspective. We will see how attention to a selfobject dimension of the story gradually alters our perspective on Freud's reconstruction of the details of Serge's childhood; what it does to our understanding of the famous dream that gave him his psychoanalytic nickname; and how the transference and treatment, both with Freud and Brunswick, are newly understood. Indeed, we will necessarily speculate at length on the nature of what I believe are the strong selfobject elements in Serge's transference to Freud. Freud literally relegates discussion of the transference to a footnote to his case, and with the famous exception of the tactic of the forced termination, is not here concerned with issues of technique. However, Serge's own account of how he viewed Freud and his experience of his two analyses will enable us to add this additional dimension to our overview.

DIAGNOSIS

Our conclusions about the Wolf-Man's diagnosis will ultimately be inseparable from the full ongoing review of the entire genetic and psychodynamic picture that Freud draws of his patient. We can, however, begin to outline some of the main features of the case that first presented itself to Freud and see what different impressions emerge in the light of self psychology.

Freud initially described his patient as "a young man whose health had broken down in his eighteenth year after a gonorrheal infection, and who was entirely dependent on other people" (Gardiner, 1971, p. 154). Serge's own account of himself in the period prior to meeting Freud was that his life felt "empty" and "unreal," that "people seemed to me to be like wax figures or wound-up marionettes with whom I could not establish any contact" (Gardiner, 1971, p. 50). Elsewhere he speaks of "a veil" between himself and life. Prior to seeing Freud, he had had chronic feelings of depression that had led him to seek a variety of treatments and to spend "a long time in German sanatoria, and at that period classified in the most authoritative quarters as a case of 'manic-depressive insanity' " (p. 154). But Freud maintained that his patient never displayed any overt break with reality that would warrant that diagnosis: "I was never able . . . to detect any changes of mood which were disproportionate to the manifest psychological situation either in their intensity or in the circumstances of their appearance" (p. 154).

Freud concluded, rather, that his patient suffered from "a condition following on an obsessional neurosis which has come to an end spontaneously, but has left a defect behind it after recovery" (p. 154). It is worth noting how Freud puts the essence of the Wolf Man's problem—the obsessional neurosis—in his *past,* enabling an investigation of the childhood symptoms to serve as the treatment of the more incapacitating adult problems that, despite their range and severity, are viewed merely as the sequelae of an incomplete, spontaneous recovery from the earlier illness. In his ongoing argument with Adler and Jung, Freud took pains to demonstrate that it was not some problem in mastering the difficulties of his *adult* situation that was the source of the Wolf Man's illness—despite the evident failure of this young man to develop satisfying relations with women or find a career. Rather, the diagnosis is framed as it is to show that

> the occurrence of a neurotic disorder in the fourth and fifth years of childhood proves, first and foremost, that infantile experiences are by themselves in a position to produce a neurosis, without there being any

need for the addition of a flight from some task which has to be faced in real life [p. 198].

If we, however, look at the symptoms that Serge presented as a young man, rather than as a child, as the basis of a clinical diagnosis, we will find much that is suggestive of a narcissistic personality disorder. Although Kohut (1971) cautioned that the only true criterion for that diagnosis was the emergence in the course of an analysis of the pathonomonic transference configuration, nonetheless he outlined the principal symptomatic manifestations of a structural defect in the self that points our attention in the direction of the narcissistic disorders. As applied to Serge's case, these included, in addition to the dominant symptom of recurrent, empty depressions and the experience of a "veil" separating him from others (a feeling of depersonalization often relievable only by the administration of enemas), disturbances in the sexual sphere evidenced in his tendency toward obsessive infatuations and a habit of following women in the street; difficulties in the social sphere as shown in chronic work inhibitions and his failure to develop professional ambitions and skills; and, finally, a lifelong tendency to hypochondria and somatization, which reached almost delusional proportions in times of self-fragmentation.

Although Freud did not include it in his case report, Jones (1955) records that Freud wrote to Ferenczi on February 13, 1910, describing his first session with Serge, during which his new patient allegedly "offered to have rectal intercourse" and "defecate on his head" (p. 274). When Obholzer (1982) showed Serge this passage in Jones's biography years later, Serge was flabbergasted and vehemently denied it ever happened. "It's nonsense, utter nonsense," he said. "That fellow [Jones] must have a screw loose" (p. 170).

By placing his account of the meeting with Freud immediately after a description of the child Serge's compulsion to say "God-shit" and other blasphemies, Jones was inviting the interpretation that his "offer" to Freud was somehow a continuation of the anal obsession, even though that particular symptom had not, in fact, persisted into adulthood.

Fish (1989) has offered an alternate reading of Freud's letter in which the new patient expressed the fear that Freud was a "Jewish swindler . . . [who] wants to use me from behind and shit on my head" (p. 526). It is possible that Freud, writing to Ferenczi, reflexively interpreted the fear as disguising an underlying wish. Certainly it seems dynamically more plausible to assume that Serge, who throughout his life was to remain skeptical about doctors, would approach Freud with trepidation, arising out of his narcissistic vulnerability, even as he yearned to idealize him.

Prior to meeting Freud, Serge had become progressively dependent on a series of doctors who became virtually his sole companions, and he seemed destined to drift fecklessly from spas to sanatoria as long as the family fortune remained intact. While staying in a Munich sanatorium recommended by Kraeplin, the wealthy young patient was invited to attend a fancy dress ball for the staff and nurses. As he recalled in his "Memoir" (Gardiner, 1971),

> Watching the dancers I was immediately struck by an extraordinarily beautiful woman. She was perhaps in her middle or late twenties and thus a few years older than myself. This did not disturb me, as I always preferred more mature women [p. 49].

He thought the other dancers were "frolicsome" or "clownish," but the woman kept "a serious expression the whole time," adding to her "exotic" and "enigmatic" appearance. He learned that she was a "most conscientious nurse and was highly regarded by the doctors and patients." He was also "particularly" interested to learn of her Spanish background, which gave him a clue to her exotic Mediterranean features. Whereas he had until that moment felt life "empty" and "unreal," suddenly "I embraced life fully and it seemed to me highly rewarding, but only on the condition that Therese would be willing to enter into a love affair with me" (p. 50).

Therese exhibited several features important to the young Serge. She was an older woman and a nurse, a nurturing, caretaking figure. In addition, as an "exotic" foreigner, she was sexually exciting. There would always, for Serge, be something about women of a lower class that allowed them to be the objects of his sexual infatuations. It may have been that someone exotic was perceived as the antidote to his own inner deadness. Also, her social inferiority may have allowed Serge to escape, in fantasy, from his own neurasthenic sense of inferiority, into a position of self-importance and grandiosity. But his dual susceptibility to infatuation and dependency left him in a precarious situation—needing the enlivening stimulation of Therese's sexually charged attention and also always at the mercy of her whims and demands lest his life line be threatened.

His thwarted selfobject needs seem to be able to be reinstated only in the context of a series of dependent and masochistic ties, both in this period of his youth, through his relationship with Freud and Brunswick, and into his old age, as Obholzer (1982) was to discover. His psychological fragility forever kept Serge at the mercy of those who could promise some enlivening mixture of excitement, idealization, attention, and nurturance. With his family opposed to marriage to Therese, as well as her own ambivalence at marrying her young patient, keeping their relationship in perpetual turmoil, Freud's acknowledgment of the positive aspects of the relationship and the eventual possibility of marriage (after analysis, of course!) helped forge Serge's initial ties to him.

Serge's father had suddenly died at the age of 49 the previous year, and Freud's willingness to assume control of such matters as determining the proper timing of his patient's visits to Therese and pronouncing when Serge would be ready to marry certainly must have helped reawaken Serge's transferential yearnings for a powerful, idealizable father figure in the transference.

Freud's description of the initial years of treatment as having "produced scarcely any change," his patient seemingly "unassailably entrenched behind an attitude of obliging apathy" (Gardiner, 1971, p. 157), may also indicate, as Gedo and Goldberg (1973) noted, the establishment of an unrecognized mirror transference. Freud felt that his patient required "a long education to induce him to take an independent share in the work. . . . His shrinking from a self-sufficient existence was so great as to outweigh all the vexations of his illness" (p. 157). It was to break this seeming log jam that Freud hit upon the idea of forcing a date for the termination of treatment: "I was obliged to wait until his attachment to me had become strong enough to counterbalance his shrinking . . . [then] I determined the treatment must be brought to an end at a particular fixed date" (p. 157). As Fish (1989) showed in his analysis of Freud's rhetorical style in writing this case history, we should be put on alert by the odd and paradoxical elements of Freud's description of his method: the patient requires an "education"; is both somehow "induced" and "independent"; and all the while Freud blithely maintains the appearance of neutrality. ("Readers may at all events rest assured that I myself am only reporting what I came upon as an independent experience, uninfluenced by my expectation," p. 158.) In fact, Freud's use of the forced termination seems to have been a last-ditch effort to force the facts of this difficult case to conform to his expectations about the centrality of infantile sexuality in neurogenesis. Only under the pressure of this deadline will his patient accede to the reconstruction of the primal scene as the key to his illness and of the famous dream.

Serge's mother, we are told by Freud, began to suffer from abdominal disorders at a young age, and as a result "she had relatively little to do with the children" (p. 159). She is described as preoccupied by her own illness, and Serge is said to remember an incident "certainly before his fourth year, while his mother was seeing off the doctor to the station. . . . He overheard her lamenting her condition" (p. 159). In his own memoirs, Serge added some other important details to this picture. He recalls, "I had, as an infant, Titian-red hair. After my first haircut, my hair turned dark brown, something my mother deeply regretted. She kept a little lock of the cut-off Titian-red hair, as a sort of relic her entire life" (Gardiner, 1971, p. 5). Also, he, significantly, remembers that it was only when he himself fell ill as a child that his mother would rowse herself to pay special attention to him: "[Then] she became an exemplary nurse. . . . I can remember as a child I sometimes wished I would get sick, to be able to enjoy my mother's being with me and looking after me" (p. 9).

His mother, then, was generally unavailable, either ill or hypochondriacally self-absorbed, as her son would turn out to be. (She ultimately lived to the age of 89.) Her apparent neglect of her growing son except when he was also ill perhaps formed the basis for an archaic, masochistic merger. He would go on to marry a nurse and to claim for himself some measure of self-importance as one of the world's most famous patients. Although his mother had idealized him as a red-haired infant, he evidently felt acutely her subsequent lack of interest. As might be expected, he therefore sought to compensate for her unavailability by turning even more strongly to idealizing his father.

When we reflect on the degree of deprivation the young Serge must have felt, it is all the more remarkable that in Freud's account his mother's most significant role turns out to be as the sexually vigorous participant in a reconstructed primal scene. The Wolf-Man's own experience of her as a largely absent figure, to whom he could connect only in illness, is superseded in Freud's narrative by the oedipal mother required by his theory of neurosis.

Freud's description of Serge's early relationship with his father begins with an acknowledgment of their initial deep affection for one another and then attempts to explain their subsequent estrangement against a background of sexual conflict and castration fears. In contrast to Freud's oedipal scenario, I offer a picture of Serge's development organized around his needs for mirroring and idealization.

Freud summed up the initial positive phase in their relationship as follows:

> In the earliest years of the patient's childhood this relation had been a very affectionate one. . . . His father was very fond of him, and liked

playing with him. From an early age he was proud of his father and was always declaring that he would like to be a gentleman like him [Gardiner, 1971, p. 162].

We can flesh out this picture with some of the material collected in "Recollections of My Childhood," which Serge wrote in his old age (Gardiner, 1971).

Amid an aristocratic family environment in which he and his sister were often left in the care of servants, opportunities to be with his parents took on a heightened significance, and many stood out in his memory years later. Many of these memories were indeed prideful and full of joy, as Freud describes. For instance, Serge recalls pony rides when his father would "take me up front of him on his saddle . . . this made me feel like a grownup riding on a big 'real' horse" (p. 6). In contrast to this opportunity to feel big and grownup like his father is the memory that immediately follows in the "Recollections," in which he is riding with his English governess, this time in a "closed carriage [while] she tried to teach me a few English words, repeating several times the word 'boy'" (p. 6). Clearly, it was a special and exhilarating experience to feel like a man while riding with his father, compared with being just a boy with his governess in a carriage.

He also recalls with pleasure that it was his father who taught him the Russian alphabet and to read. And he remembers a special game called "Don't Get Angry, Man" that they used to play for a while every evening:

> One spread out a gameboard which was a map of European Russia, and everyone had a wooden figure, something like a chessman. . . . I enjoyed this game tremendously, probably partly because we played it with my father, whom at this time I dearly loved and admired. . . . Often he told us many things about the cities and regions on the map . . . [p. 8].

But these special proud and admiring moments were not to last. Unfortunately, the evening games with his father soon came to an end because "he had no more time for them. . . . When he no longer played with us the game was less interesting and less fun, and we stopped playing altogether" (p. 8).

Other memories, also not included in Freud's narrative, further illustrate the disappointments around this time to Serge's emergent exhibitionism and his attempts to idealize his father:

> When I was about four years old, probably as a Christmas present, [I] was given a little accordion. . . . I was literally in love with it, and could

not understand why people needed other musical instruments, such as a piano or violin, when the accordion was so much more beautiful [p. 10].

In this account of the specialness of his instrument we can certainly hear the child's sense of his own specialness and his phase-appropriate, grandiosity seeking parental mirroring. But, instead, the accordion was to be the cause of a traumatic rupture in the relationship with his father. As Serge recalled:

> It was winter, and when darkness fell I sometimes went to a room where I would be undisturbed and where I thought nobody would hear me, and began to improvise. I imagined a lonely winter landscape with a sleigh drawn by a horse toiling through the snow. I tried to produce the sounds on my accordion which would match the mood of this fantasy. . . . One time my father happened to be in an adjoining room and heard me improvising. The next day he called me into his room, asking me to bring along my accordion. On entering, I heard him talking to an unknown gentleman about my attempts at a composition which he called interesting. Then he asked me to play what I had been playing the previous evening. The request embarrassed me greatly because I was unable to repeat my improvisations "on command." I failed miserably and my father angrily dismissed me. After this painful failure I lost all interest in my beloved instrument, left it lying around somewhere in my room, and never touched it again. With this my whole relationship to music was destroyed [p. 10].

Not just his relationship to music, but his relationship to his father, was undergoing a traumatic disruption. Several other factors make this incident, I believe, worth examining at some length. First, its occurrence just around his fourth birthday, which is when, we will remember, Freud will date Serge's famous dream about the wolves. Second, the elements of his private fantasy and play being suddenly and involuntarily exposed to the critical gaze of his father and his guest; elements we see repeated in the famous dream. And, last, we see here a paradigm for a different source of the estrangement from his father.

Another incident, compounding his traumatic deidealization, occurred when his father attempted to inoculate some 200,000 sheep belonging to their estate against an epidemic that had broken out. In Serge's words, "The result was a catastrophe. All the inoculated sheep died, as the wrong serum had been delivered." Shortly after, when Serge was five, he "learned that my father had sold our estate. I cried and felt most unhappy that our life on the estate where we were so close to nature, had come to an end" (p. 11).

Because Freud did not recognize an ongoing developmental need for idealizable selfobjects, he did not give these early traumas the attention that we would today in the light of Kohut's work. Freud treated Serge's attempts to identify with his father as a more primitive need ("in conformity with a small child's narcissism") than his maturing sexual drives. Thus, "in conformity with his higher stage of development, identification was replaced by object love" (p. 171).

THE DREAM OF THE WOLVES

> I dreamt that it was night and that I was lying in my bed. (My bed stood with its foot towards the window; in front of the window there was a row of walnut trees. I know it was winter when I had the dream, and nighttime.) Suddenly the window opened of its own accord, and I was terrified to see that some white wolves were sitting on the big walnut tree in front of the window. There were six or seven of them. The wolves were quite white, and looked more like foxes or sheep dogs, for they had big tails like foxes and they had their ears pricked like dogs when they pay attention to something. In great terror, evidently of being eaten up by the wolves, I screamed and woke up [Freud, 1918, p. 173].

Freud tells us that "the patient related the dream at a very early stage of the analysis and very soon came to share my conviction that the causes of his infantile neurosis lay concealed behind it" (p. 177). He goes on to say that

> in the course of the treatment the first dream returned in innumerable variations and new editions [but] it was only during the last months of the analysis that it became possible to understand it completely, and only then thanks to spontaneous work on the patient's part [p. 181].

Freud's description of the process of interpretation in this case is quite disingenuous, as Fish (1989) has pointed out, and at odds with what Freud himself tells us elsewhere. Freud states that this patient "required a long education to induce him to take an independent share in the work" (p. 157). Even in this one sentence we note an odd tension between "induce" and "independent." The process of "sharing my conviction" is also thus a result of "a long education." Because, Freud says, "The first years of the treatment produced scarcely any change" he at last resorted to the technique of setting a fixed date for termination. Under this "inexorable pressure . . . [Serge's] resistance and fixation to the illness gave way. . . ." (p. 157).

Thus, the so called *spontaneous* work on the patient's part came about only as a result of "inexorable pressure." An odd use of "spontaneous" indeed! Freud tells us that "all the information, too, which enabled me to understand his infantile neurosis derived from this last piece of the work, during which resistance temporarily disappeared..." (p. 157).

The picture that emerges is of Freud's elaborately weaving an interpretative schema that Serge must at first be educated in and then progressively comply with, in all its implications, no matter how far-fetched they seem, as the price for maintaining his desperately needed selfobject ties to Freud.

Freud's elaborate "deciphering" of the dream to reveal the underlying primal scene Serge was said to have witnessed at age one and a half is well-known and need not be reiterated here except in outline. Freud's commentary on each of the elements of the dream is given in a footnote that extends across three pages of Gardiner's (1971) collection (pp. 186–188). Briefly, then, Freud deals with the dream elements as follows: "it was night" is a distortion of "I had been asleep"; "Suddenly the window opened of its own accord" means "suddenly I awoke"; "the big walnut tree" represents a Christmas tree, and also "a high tree is a symbol of observing, of scopophilia"; "six or seven wolves" has to do with "the fact that the number of participants in the primal scene, two, is increased is a distortion in the service of resistance"; "They were sitting on the tree" relates to his grandfather's story, in which they were beneath the tree, and by being transposed up into the tree, they both are in a position to look and point to further reversals in the latent content; "They were looking at him with strained attention" is a reversal of his own looking at the primal scene; "They were white" refers back to his parents' white bedclothes; "They sat there motionless" is a reversal of the agitated movements of sexual activity; "They had tails like foxes" is a denial of castration; "The fear of being eaten up by the wolves" is a fear of the underlying wish for sexual satisfaction by his father. To all this Freud adds the final elements of the reconstructed scene: Serge, ill with malaria, is sleeping in his parents' bedroom, when he awakens and sees them copulate three times in the position Freud calls coitus a tergo, "which alone offers the spectator a possibility of inspecting the genitals." The boy finally interrupts his parents by passing a stool. (Freud remarks here, "This method is the same in every case"!)

Mahony (1984) has thoroughly reviewed the many objections that have been raised to Freud's conclusion that this dream reveals the actual details of Serge's witnessing his parents' intercourse. We might, first of all, cite the Wolf Man's own comments to Obholzer (1982): "The whole matter is improbable, because children in Russia slept with the nurse in her room and not with the parents in their room" (p. 36). (Always the compliant analysand, however, he adds for Freud's sake, "But there could have been an exception once, how can I know" [p. 36]. This is hardly the voice of a patient who has come to share his analyst's convictions.)

As to Serge's actually viewing the sex act itself, Mahony endorses Viderman's conclusion:

> The position is the least favorable to observe the female genitals, unless the child enjoyed the optimal position neither behind nor before the couple but at their very junction . . . a coitus a tergo already in progress [is] a position which no longer allows any observation of the partners' genitals covered up by each other [p. 52].

Mahony concludes: "The amount of perceptual acrobatics in Freud's reconstruction is staggering, for the observability assigned to the Wolf-baby's angle of vision would exceed the ingenious staging of any pornographic film producer" (p. 52).

The assumption that a feverish one-and-a-half-year-old awakened from a delirious, fitful sleep and was able to watch with "strained attention" his parents having intercourse three times in half an hour—without crying out and only interrupting at the very end by passing a stool—strains our credulity in the service of preserving Freud's reconstruction. Mahony (1984) facetiously adds that we must imagine the father to be a "husky Rusky" outscoring the mythic heroes of *Playboy* (p. 51).

For Freud, the correctness of this reconstruction was synonymous with its capacity to incorporate the myriad details of the case into a dynamically coherent whole. The dream, which presented itself early in a long and often seemingly fruitless analysis, was at last made to give up its meaning in a way that made sense of the whole case. It is important to note that the recovery of the details of the primal scene were a *"reconstruction,"* not a recollection by the Wolf-Man of a previously repressed memory: "These scenes from infancy are not reproduced during the treatment as recollections, they are products of construction" (p. 194); and

> it seems to me absolutely equivalent to a recollection if the memories are replaced (as in the present case) by dreams the analysis of which invariably leads back to the same scene. . . . It is this recurrence in dreams that I regard as the explanation of the fact that the patients

gradually acquire a profound conviction of the reality of these primal scenes [p. 195].

What this means is that the patient is gradually drawn into an interpretative scheme that gives shape to his experience and that at last the "facts" are indistinguishable from their interpretation. This question of "evidence" for the correctness of the interpretation is crucial, because as Fish (1989) pointed out, it reverses our accepted notions of hypothesis and evidence. The primal scene, which Freud claims to have uncovered, is not a newly discovered fact about Serge's childhood; it is, in Freud's own words, an *assumption* that is necessary to make sense of all that has gone before. Freud demands of us—and demanded of the Wolf Man—that we

> assume as an uncontradicted premise that a primal scene of this kind has been correctly educed technically, that it is indispensable to a comprehensive solution to all the conundrums that are set us by the symptoms of the infantile disorder, that all the consequences radiate out from it, just as all the threads of the analysis have led up to it. . . . It must therefore be left at this (I can see no other possibility): either the analysis based on the neurosis in his childhood is all a piece of nonsense from start to finish, or everything took place just as I have described it [p. 199].

We are now in a position to assert that, given the choice, the whole primal scene-based story was simply nonsense from start to finish. We are able to do so because we are no longer dependent on the story, as Freud was, to make sense out of the dream or the whole of the Wolf Man's neurosis. In proposing a reinterpretation of the dream along other lines, and by elucidating the selfobject dimensions of Serge's problems, we are not merely offering an alternative view to Freud's; for the possibility that there *could* be an alternative, equally cogent explanatory scheme eliminates the very basis of Freud's argument—that the primal scene is necessary to make sense of the case.

In fact, if we stay close to Serge's own associations to the dream and view them in the light of what we have been told already about his troubled attempts to idealize his father, a far more straightforward interpretation emerges. Take first, "The tree was a Christmas tree." Since Christmas was also Serge's birthday, we can see how it became involved in his early fantasies of specialness, epitomized by the expectation of double presents. But Christmas was also a time of special vulnerability. As Freud rightly put it: "We know that in such circumstances a child may easily anticipate the fulfillment of his wishes ... the content of the dream showed him ... the presents which were to be his hanging on the tree. But instead of presents they had turned into—wolves" (p. 180). But Freud, searching for an underlying sexual conflict, then goes astray, presuming a repressed wish for sexual satisfaction by the father and leading everyone off on his wild goose chase for the primal scene.

Serge's fear of his father, however, was based not on sexual conflict but on narcissistic vulnerability. The staring wolves concretize two incidents we know of that traumatized him in his attempts to idealize his father. His first association to why the wolves were white (pp. 174–175) told us of the incident where his father, who had hitherto proudly shown off his flocks of sheep to his son, had inadvertently inoculated them incorrectly, causing many to die. Wolves were also featured in his recollections of his humiliations by his sister. He recalls screaming at the sight of the wolf about to swallow Little Red Riding Hood and tells us straightforwardly again, "Probably the cause of this outburst of rage was not so much my fear of the wolf as my disappointment at Anna for teasing me" (p. 7). Finally, I suggest that the element of "staring" gives us the connection with another traumatic event, his father's humiliating him for being unable to play his accordion in front of company. The Wolf Man recalled that the incident "embarrassed me greatly. I failed miserably and my father angrily dismissed me" (p. 10). Exposed to his father's withering glare, Serge not only loses a chance to show off, but sees his father transformed into a dangerous persecutor.

The terrifying stare of the wolves would thus appear symbolically to concretize the malignant transformation of the mirroring he wished to receive. As a "self-state dream," as described by Kohut (1977), this dream seems to be an attempt "to deal with the psychological danger by covering frightening nameless processes with nameable visual imagery" (p. 109). Rather than being an elaborate disguise of a hidden sexual wish, this dream seems to "encapsulate the danger to the self and reflect a concretizing effort at self-restoration," as Atwood and Stolorow (1984) have described the workings of the dream as a "guardian of psychic structure" (p. 103).

For Freud, however, we should recall, this dream was seen to be not an agent for maintaining psychic structure, but a "new trauma, like an interference from the outside analogous to the seduction" (Gardiner, 1971, p. 250). Prior to the dream, young Serge was thought to have retreated to an anal-sadistic level of organization in response to the castration threats from Nanya. The dream forcibly brought back to his attention the possibility of genital intercourse, but once again the castration threat undermined this precarious new level

Self Psychology Meets the Wolf Man

of organization; repression set in, and the new awareness was replaced by an animal phobia.

In fact, in addition to the animal phobia, Serge also developed, as another sequela to the dream, a fear of being stared at. The recollection of this fear, which Freud did not report, emerged in the Wolf Man's reanalysis with Ruth Mack Brunswick and lends further weight to our reinterpretation of the dream as an attempt to cope with a traumatic disruption of his exhibitionistic needs.

Given that, according to Freud, this dream not only was the first to be reported in the analysis, but also was one that would recur in various permutations throughout the analysis—and would years later recur in yet another version as the first dream reported to Brunswick—I venture to suggest that the dream carried significant transference meaning, as well as being simply the recounting of a childhood event. Rank in 1926 more baldly challenged Freud by declaring that the dream was strictly transferential and not, in fact, a recollection of any childhood dream. For Rank, the bed simply equalled Freud's couch, the wolves were photos of Freud's disciples looking down from the waiting-room wall, and so on (Mahony, 1984, p. 138). Rank—correctly, I believe—saw through the implausibility of Freud's interpretation and also correctly attempted to use the dream to untangle the uninterpreted aspects of the Wolf Man's transference relationship to Freud. However, now that we are able to reconstruct a new and far more plausible origin for the dream focused on Serge's selfobject development, we need not resort, as Rank did, to a wholesale denial of the childhood origin of the dream in order also to discern the ongoing transferential elements in it.

Thus, it is reasonable to surmise that the experience of lying down on Freud's couch, under the analyst's penetrating stare, contributed to Serge's recall—and later to the recurrence—of an old childhood dream in which passivity and staring were such prominent elements. We should recall that in "My Recollections of Sigmund Freud" (Gardiner, 1971), the Wolf Man remembered that Freud's "most impressive feature was his intelligent, dark eyes, which looked at me penetratingly" (p. 137).

Given this patient's profound archaic needs both for the mirroring of his grandiosity and for attaching himself to a stabilizing, idealized figure, might not his experience with Freud have recapitulated both the hopes and the disappointments we know occurred with his father? And especially given that Freud's interpretations demanded the Procrustian mapping of Serge's subjective experience of his narcissistic needs onto Freud's schema of oedipal conflict and the primal scene, might not the analysis indeed have recapitulated the trauma that he suffered under his father's stare? George Atwood (personal communication, 1990) has pointed out that Freud's interpretation of the young Serge's retreat into sexual passivity and phobias as a result of the castration threat posed by his father, and the Wolf Man's acquiescence to this interpretation as underlying the wolf dream in the face of Freud's threat of termination, reveal in their parallelism the unrecognized transferential pattern that had emerged between Freud and his patient.

The Wolf Man was repeatedly required to accommodate his own subjective reality to the powerful influence of Freud's vision in order to maintain the desperately needed selfobject tie. On one level, this enabled him to preserve a modicum of self-cohesion by submissively attaching himself to the powerful selfobject, but the validity of his own perception was repeatedly sacrificed in the process. The Wolf Man's tie to Freud was thus essentially masochistic, a desperate style of connection that he would resort to throughout his life.

This view of the Wolf Man's masochism, in contrast to Freud's, in which a wish to be sexually gratified by the father is central, focuses instead on the painful submission or truncation of one's self as the price perceived as necessary for sustaining selfobject ties. As defined by Stolorow, Atwood, and Brandchaft (1988), masochism becomes structuralized as an invariant organizing principle in the form of a

> conviction that the subjugation of one's own distinctive affective experience is an absolute requirement for maintaining needed ties. This configuration . . . is repeated in analysis whenever critical information concerning the impact of the analyst on the patient is interpreted solely as reflecting the patient's malignant intrapsychic mechanisms [p. 509].

In his old age, during the long series of interviews he granted Obholzer (1982), the Wolf Man was permitted a much greater degree of autonomy in expressing his own opinions than was ever afforded in any of his analysis with Freud, precisely because he was not made to fit them into any predetermined theoretical schema. Here we at last hear how little plausibility Freud's reconstructions had for his patient, even though at the time the need to idealize Freud overrode all other considerations. Serge told Obholzer:

> In my story, what was explained by dreams? Nothing, as far as I can see. Freud traces everything back to the primal scene which he derives from the dream. But that scene doesn't occur in the dream. When he interprets the white wolves as night-shirts or something like that, for example, linen sheets or clothes, that's somehow farfetched, I think.

That scene in the dream where the windows open and so on and the wolves are sitting there, and his interpretation, I don't know, those things are miles apart. It's terribly far-fetched [p. 35].

And we must not forget that this interpretation and reconstruction was all taking place under Freud's imposed deadline for the termination of the analysis. Thus his patient was left in what we can only imagine was a turmoil of fear of abandonment and a desperate state of frantic placation and compliance.

THE DREAM OF THE ESPE

The masochistic nature of the Wolf-Man's ties to Freud are given even more explicit expression in another dream that Freud reports, the dream of the "Espe."

"I had a dream," he said, "of a man tearing the wings of an Espe." Freud, correcting him, said that the actual name of the insect in German is *Wespe* (wasp). Whereupon Serge had the insight, "Espe, why that's myself" (Gardiner, 1971, p. 236). (That is, S.P., which were his initials.)

Freud interpreted the dream as follows: "The Espe was of course a mutilated *Wespe*. The dream said clearly that he was avenging himself on Grusha for the threat of castration" (p. 236). Freud's understanding of this dream is based on his earlier deductions concerning Serge's witnessing of the alleged primal scene, and it is instructive to see the use to which he puts it. The train of associations and interpretations that Freud says "clearly" reveals the castration threat behind the dream runs for some six pages of text. It goes roughly as follows: the opening and closing of butterfly wings in a V-shape; the memory of being suddenly frightened by a butterfly; the Roman numeral V, meaning five, a time of day Serge often became depressed; the word for butterfly in Russian being *babushka* (granny); butterflies seeming in general to be like women and girls, whereas beetles and caterpillars were like boys, so "there could be little doubt that in the anxiety scene (of the butterfly) a recollection of some female person had been aroused"; Grusha, Serge's nursemaid kneeling to scrub the floor with a short broom made of a bundle of sticks beside her; John Huss burned at the stake by a bundle of firewood like the sticks of Grusha's broom; the association of fire, enuresis, and the shame of urinary incontinence; the nursemaid appearing "physically debased" by her posture while scrubbing the floor, which made her, in Freud's view, a "surrogate" for "all his later love objects" (i.e., women of inferior position); Grusha's projecting buttocks and horizontal back while scrubbing appearing to be identical to the position his mother took during the primal scene; the association of Grusha's posture and his mother's during sex finally producing in Serge a seizure of sexual excitement that culminates in his attempted seduction of her (by urinating on the floor) and her reply of a castration threat (see pp. 231–237).

Freud's interpretation thus seizes on all the associations he can muster to the sexual connotations of the butterfly/wasp, which culminate in Serge's attempted reenactment with Grusha of the primal scene he had allegedly witnessed approximately a year previously (Freud dates the primal scene at a year and a half, the incident with Grusha at two and a half), the castration threat he received from her now being reversed by the action in the dream.

The first thing we might say about this long interpretive train is that it starts off by completely ignoring Serge's own insight—that *he,* S.P., is the Espe/Wespe. Freud, in fact, *after* his long reconstruction of the various childhood scenes, introduces the dream itself as *evidence* for his having correctly deduced the existence of the primal scene and its aftermath. We have here, once again, as Fish (1989) noted, the phenomenon of Freud offering as evidence what is, in fact, a hypothesis or interpretation that justifies itself by supposedly making the whole story of what came before hang together.

But with this dream, even more than with the dream of the wolves, one does *not need* the reconstructed primal scene to explain what is going on in the dream. One need merely follow up on Serge's own insight. Someone is tearing his wings off. If, in line with our earlier diagnostic conclusions, we see Serge as seeking to reestablish in the transference his selfobject needs for mirroring and idealization, then it is not unreasonable to see this dream report—at least initially—as the report of a narcissistic injury. We might speculate that the image of having one's wings torn off connects with his being deprived of his ability to fly—a common enough image of grandiosity. Whether the tearing off of the wings ultimately had the connotation for Serge of undercutting his exhibitionistic needs or, indeed, as Freud thought, operated at the level of a castration threat, we cannot say, although our overall picture is increasingly one of thwarted narcissistic needs. But certainly we would want to explore the immediate imagery of the injury to see if the patient perceived the hands that are doing the mutilating to be the hands of the analyst. Freud, in his desire to use the dream as a confirmation of his interpretative reconstruction, overlooked the transferential aspect of the dream. Indeed, this dream reinforces our perception of the Wolf Man's tie to Freud as persistently masochistic. Serge's selfobject needs, unrecognized by Freud, seem to have been consistently sacrificed to Freud's theoretical agenda. In order to maintain a desperately needed idealized tie to his analyst, Serge had to put up with repeated narcissistic injury.

Freud's account of the disruptions in Serge's life from ages three and a half to four (i.e. from the dates Freud gives for the "seduction" to the time of the wolf dream) centers on the vicissitudes of Serge's sexual aims as they were supposedly affected by his sister's behavior and his Nanya's response to his masturbating. The seduction by his sister, Freud says, "had given him the passive sexual aim of being touched on the genitals" (Gardiner, 1971, p. 169). Nanya's threat ("children who did that—i.e. masturbated—got a 'wound' in that place," p. 169) reportedly resulted in his giving up masturbating and, according to Freud,

> his sexual life, therefore, which was beginning to come under the sway of the genital zone, gave way before an external obstacle, and was thrown back by its influence into an earlier phase of pregenital organization . . . the boy's life took on a sadistic-anal character [p. 170].

His sadistic behavior consisted in tormenting his hitherto beloved Nanya, as well as cruelty to small animals and insects and fantasies of beating horses. This was also the summer of his angry tantrums and naughty behavior.

Alongside Freud's explanation of the change in Serge's behavior, I would like instead to place the emphasis on the other disruptions in Serge's relationships. He was abandoned for the summer by his parents; he was undergoing traumatic failures in his attempts to idealize his father; his positive relationship with Nanya was disrupted by her empathic failure to accept his childhood sexual play; and his sister both tormented him and threatened to usurp his role as their father's favorite. All these factors taken together represent a profound disruption of Serge's selfobject world and would in themselves account for the regressive fragmentation in his behavior. Freud's exclusive emphasis on sexual issues obscures the selfobject dimension and rather than seeing the child as rageful and frustrated over the disruption of the family, leads to an interpretation that Serge masochistically attempted to *provoke* his father's beating. Freud, in fact, refers to these provocations as "seductions" of his father, with the aim of simultaneously gratifying masochistic sexual longings and, through punishment, setting his sense of guilt to rest (p. 172). The implications of this form of interpretation are far reaching and provide the basis for significant empathic ruptures, when the analyst insists on taking the stance that the patient's responses to narcissistic injury are provocations to induce a sadistic response in the analyst or in others. The consequences of this line of thinking have been well elucidated by Brandchaft and Stolorow (1984).

The obsessional neurosis, which Freud took to be the core of all the symptomology that was to persist through Serge's adult life, was said to have first made its appearance at age four and a half, following the wolf dream and the onset of the animal phobias. The immediate precipitant was Serge's being instructed by his mother and Nanya in the story of Christ. Serge was naturally predisposed to identify with Jesus, given that his own birthday was Christmas Eve and the family ritual included his receiving double presents on that day. In his memoirs, Serge confirmed that it was his mother who had first taught him about religion, and this instruction must have provided one of the infrequent opportunities for him to be close to the normally distant and preoccupied parent.

Serge's fascination with the New Testament story coalesced around two particular features: first, the evident mistreatment of his son by the supposedly omnipotent God the Father in allowing the Crucifixion; and second, the paradox of Jesus' dual nature as both man and God. In the first instance, we discern a parallel with Serge's own recent traumatic deidealization of his father. In the second instance, the boy was perplexed over whether Christ had a behind and needed to defecate, a seemingly very undivine need. Trying to resolve the question, he reasoned: "since Christ made wine out of nothing, he could also have made food into nothing and in this way avoided defecating" (p. 206). Serge's attempt to reason this problem out is reminiscent, I think, of Little Hans's similar attempt to figure out how women urinate if they don't have "widdlers." And, as Anna Ornstein points out, the confusion that Hans's father inadvertently produced by misunderstanding the nature of his predicament, and instead focusing on a sexual issue, derailed his attempts at mastery and may have contributed to the onset of his phobia.

Serge developed the compulsive habit of thinking "God-shit" and "God-swine" (p. 209). Freud interprets this as a "genuine compromise product" (p. 209) that arose out of his retreat to anal eroticism in the face of the castration threat aroused by the wolf dream. Serge's other symptom at this time was a compulsion to exhale ritually at the sight of beggars or cripples. The onset of this other symptom, which Freud dates later, at age six, was said to have been instigated by Serge's visit to his father in a sanatorium, when he had been away sick for several months. For Serge, breathing out already had the connotation of expelling evil spirits and was part of his attempts to atone ritually for his blasphemous thoughts. The symptom thus seem to have been part of an effort to repair the confusion and fragmentation that resulted from the broken selfobject bond with his father. God the Father—or for Serge, his father the God—had not only failed to protect his son, but also persecuted him; not only failed to be perfect, but, like Christ, turned out to be a man with defects, defecations, and illnesses.

Freud wanted to trace the source of the ritual exhalations to the boy's attempt to imitate his father's heavy breathing, overheard during the alleged primal scene; but this connection was not reported in any of Serge's own associations and seem to have been based purely on Freud's own need to establish a sexual origin for the etiology of the symptom.

The obsessional piety and its attendant compulsions disappeared when Serge was assigned a new German tutor at the age of ten. This figure served as a powerful new father-surrogate who stimulated an "enthusiasm for military affairs, for uniforms, weapons, and horses . . . as well as all things German." Freud said that this attachment proved to be "of great advantage to the transference during the treatment" (Gardiner, 1971, p. 212). In this rare reference to the transference in this case report, Freud acknowledges the value of this idealization but will ultimately exploit it for "leverage" when he becomes frustrated and forces the termination.

The tutor evidently provided a much-needed restorative selfobject function, and the childhood symptoms abated. Such figures, however, were only temporarily available in his life, and in their absence a regression to a more dependent, depressed, and masochistic level of organization occurred. Indeed, in his later life, the Wolf Man was able to maintain selfobject ties almost solely through a masochistic surrender to the other. This mechanism unfortunately seems to have characterized his relationship with Freud, where his own reality was continually sacrificed to the necessity of making his experience conform to Freud's preordained theories of sexuality; as well as in his subsequent reanalysis by Brunswick; and in his relationships with his wife and other women who seemed perpetually to be able to browbeat him into submissive dependence. Rather than representing the core of his subsequent problems, the childhood neurosis seems to be merely one example among many of the outbreak of symptoms in the face of selfobject disruptions. The masochism that characterized the Wolf Man's relationships was not primarily an expression of a retreat to anality to avoid oedipal conflict; rather it became the only available vehicle for selfobject connection to a series of controlling and withholding figures.

THE REANALYSES

Although Freud ended his patient's analysis in 1914 "regarding him as cured" (Gardiner, 1971, p. 262), Serge's involvement with Freud and with psychoanalysis was far from over. Severe symptoms were to recur throughout his long life, and these occasioned, first, reconsultations with Freud after the war, and then a resumption of analysis by Ruth Mack Brunswick beginning in 1926.

Both Freud and Brunswick attributed the further symptoms to unresolved transference issues—issues whose interpretation was notably absent from Freud's published case study, focused as it was almost exclusively on the reconstruction of the childhood trauma. In a footnote to the case, added in 1923, Freud stated, "After a few months' work, a piece of the transference which had not hitherto been overcome was successfully dealt with." He noted that Serge had told him that "immediately after the end of the treatment he had been seized with a longing to tear himself free from my influence" (p. 262). In the absence of further discussion of the transference, we are left with the distinct impression that what needed to be "overcome" in this unresolved remnant was Serge's longing for independence and that the resolution was in fact a resubmission to Freud's authority. The pattern of relinquishing his own independent, subjective reality in order to reestablish vital selfobject ties needed to ward off impending disintegration was, in fact, the transference theme unrecognized and unresolved by both Freud and Brunswick.

Following World War I, Serge's relationship to Freud was further complicated by a dramatic reversal in their economic relationship. Serge was transformed by the revolution in Russia from a millionaire aristocrat to a penniless emigré who eventually was to secure a meager livelihood as a clerk in a large bureaucracy. For the next six years, Freud undertook to raise an annual allowance for his former patient, one on which Serge increasingly became dependent and that obviously precluded any renewed outbreak of his "longing" to tear himself free from Freud. In addition, Freud treated his famous patient for free after the war and arranged for Ruth Mack Brunswick to do so as well.

The breakdown that led to Serge's reanalysis appears to have been precipitated by the appearance of Freud's cancer and the traumatic disruption of the idealized selfobject tie that this entailed. As chronicled by Brunswick (1928), Freud had his first operation on his mouth in April 1923. Although Brunswick describes it as "minor," Serge was evidently "shocked at Freud's appearance" that summer when he went to receive his annual stipend. In the autumn, Freud was again operated on, and the full seriousness of his illness, she continues, "was known to all of us, including the Wolf Man" (p. 268).

Later in November 1923, when Serge's mother arrived from Russia, he observed an unusual black wart on her nose, one that several doctors had apparently suggested she have removed, which she refused to do. In February 1924, Serge became hypochondriacally preoccupied with his own nose. He became obsessed with the need to have various blackheads, enlarged pores, and obstructed sebaceous cysts surgically treated. His mother returned to Russia in May, and shortly afterwards he found a new pimple on his nose that, when scratched out, left a large hole that, he was convinced, disfigured him.

During this period there was also a recurrence of other symptoms indicating a progressive self-fragmentation: his psychosomatic constipation returned; he developed a "marked fatigue"; and he began following women in the streets and visiting prostitutes.

He consulted a physician about a persistent cough and was convinced that as a result of his prescriptions he would get worse and develop pneumonia. When the doctor mentioned in passing that he himself was suffering from a kidney problem, Serge thought to himself, "How agreeable it is that I, the patient, am really healthy, when he, the doctor, has a serious illness" (Brunswick, 1928 p. 270). He also had a series of consultations with a "Professor X," a dermatologist who had treated him for obstructed sebaceous cysts when he was in analysis with Freud. Although the treatment dissatisfied him and for a long time left his nose bright red, he returned to Professor X when a new pimple appeared that—along with a movie he had just seen called "The White Sister"—reminded him of his sister, who had committed suicide and who had also often worried about pimples on her face. Plunged into a suicidal depression about his seemingly mutilated appearance, he rushed to Professor X, who surgically excised the infected gland, causing a stream of blood to gush forth. The sight of his blood brought about an intense wave of ecstasy that temporarily stimulated him out of his depression.

This remission was only temporary, however, and he became obsessed anew with the scar that the procedure left on his nose. Also at this time he underwent a similarly obsessive series of consultations with a number of dentists (including a Dr. Wolf!). Finally, in the summer of 1926, the day after calling on Freud to receive his allowance, he went to yet another dermatologist, who, after examining the small white line on his nose that was the trace of Professor X's surgery, remarked that "scars never disappear." Once again Serge plunged into despair. Nervously carrying with him at all times a little mirror to examine his nose, he was also now plagued with the obsessively recurring thought, "How could Professor X, the foremost dermatologist in Vienna, have been guilty of such an irreparable injury to a patient?" It was in this state that he was referred to Ruth Mack Brunswick for reanalysis.

In 1926, Brunswick was 26 years old and had been in analysis with Freud for four years. In addition, she was serving as Freud's personal physician and analyst to Dr. Schur, who would also attend to Freud's medical needs. It is worth noting that she herself suffered from symptoms similar to the Wolf Man's, including psychosomatic disorders, hypochondria, and unresolved dependency issues that would lead to drug abuse and keep her in treatment with Freud until 1938 (see Mahony, 1984). Deeply entangled in Freud's life and influence herself, she evidently had strong countertransferential needs to attest to the complete validity of Freud's original interpretation of the case. Her work was to be merely a "supplement" to Freud's case— "nothing new whatsoever made its appearance in the analysis with me"—and she repeated Freud's interpretation that the new illness represented "an unresolved remnant of the transference" (Brunswick, 1928, p. 265). Nonetheless, she was deeply shocked at the condition of the patient whom Freud had pronounced cured.

She was shocked not only by the severity of his new symptoms, but by his apparent attitude towards Freud and psychoanalysis. Brunswick (1928) writes, "In the analysis, his attitude was one of hypocrisy.... Any mention of Freud was passed over with an odd, indulgent little laugh." He refused to discuss his nose, but instead "talked at great length about the marvels of analysis as a science, the accuracy of my technique, which he professed to be able to judge at once, his feelings of safety at being in my hands, my kindness in treating him without payment" (p. 280). The hypocrisy in all this is evidently that while praising analysis in the abstract, he refused to get down to work!

She felt him to be "walled off" and "unusually closed to suggestion" (p. 280). But in what sense is suggestion supposed to be part of analytic technique? The Wolf-Man simply wasn't acting the part of a good patient. Unprepared to see any of his behavior as aspects of a narcissistic transference, Brunswick concluded that it all was fundamentally a resistance to treatment. Further, his sense of entitlement in accepting money from Freud while concealing his possession of some remaining family jewels, she saw as simply dishonest. She does not mention her own feelings about treating him for free upon hearing about the jewels.

The Wolf Man evidently accepted the free treatment as his due, "as a token of a father's love for his son" (p. 282). She further notes, "With this attitude went certain ideas of grandeur," especially his sense of an "unusual intimacy with Freud . . . far more friendly than professional" (p. 282). Even Freud's advice not to return to Russia after the war to recover his fortune—advice the Wolf-Man believed turned out to be disastrously wrong, furthering his sense of entitlement to reparations—was seen as motivated by Freud's great *personal* concern for him.

But while Brunswick was beginning to feel stalemated by her patient's avoidance of the conflictual material she thought he should be addressing, the Wolf Man was insisting how satisfied he felt with his new analyst and showing evidence of transferring his idealizations of Freud to her. Indeed, he said he was *better* off than he had been with Freud; Freud's personal influence was too strong and she was more objective. Now he had all the benefits of Freud's knowledge without directly coming under his influence.

He brought her as the first dream of his new analysis yet another version of the famous wolf dream, only now instead of white, the wolves were gray. She attributed this change to his seeing Freud's gray police dog on his numerous visits.[1] This modification of the dream to incorporate Freud's dog directly, however, does further underscore the capacity of the childhood dream to be the carrier of ongoing transferential issues, as does its recurrence as a first dream in the new analysis. For the Wolf Man, the dream's new reference to Freud corroborated "his statement that all his difficulties came from his relation to the father; for this reason, he added, he was glad to be in analysis with a woman" (Brunswick, 1928, p. 280).

In this new opening phase, he thus seems to be quickly establishing an idealization of his analyst, while both preserving the earlier idealization of Freud and at the same time trying to come to terms with the degree of influence that his selfobject needs left him open to. These processes were not to be permitted to unfold at their own pace, however, simply because Brunswick, given the theoretical apparatus available to her at the time, could not help but see the Wolf Man's narcissism, his grandiosity, his entitlement, his idealizations, as anything but resistances to underlying *conflictual* material. Keeping in mind Freud's strategy of the forced termination to cut through what he had earlier seen as a stagnating treatment, Brunswick likewise resolved to undertake a frontal assault on her patient's narcissistic "resistances." She reasoned:

> So long as he combined his two techniques of satisfaction, on the one hand blaming Freud for the loss of his fortune and therefore accepting

---

[1] Alas for Rank's radical thesis, this pet was not a member of the household before World War I.

all possible financial aid from him, and, on the other hand maintaining, on this basis, his position as favorite son, it was impossible to make progress in treatment. . . . My technique therefore consisted in a concentrated attempt to undermine the patient's idea of himself as the favorite son, since it was obvious that by means of it he was protecting himself from feelings of a different nature [p. 284].

Two features of her account are especially worth noting. First, not only was the patient's narcissism seen as purely defensive, his presumed underlying anger at Freud was categorically assumed to be unrelated to any actual behavior on Freud's part or even to the Wolf Man's subjective experience of his treatment. The Wolf Man was indeed at this time denying he felt any anger toward Freud. But rather than denying a repressed instinctual wish, he was trying to sustain an idealizable image of Freud, lest his own anger, or even a simple desire to assert the validity of his own perceptions, disrupt the selfobject tie. He therefore split his perception of his connection with Freud into two distinct aspects, the professional and the personal. His anger at his professional mistreatment was displaced onto figures such as Professor X while preserving an idealizable Freud by virtue of the great *personal* attention and assistance he was shown.

Second, we should note that Brunswick's denial of the Wolf Man's specialness involved doing considerable violence to the facts. The Wolf Man was undeniably special to Freud, and his case was already being hailed as a masterpiece. If Freud's seeing his patient for free and arranging for Brunswick to do so as well was not unique, then the annual stipend to the Wolf Man surely was. Freud's concern about the outcome of the case was such that, as Serge recalled it in a letter to Gardiner (September 14, 1970), "My re-analysis in 1919 took place not at my request, but at the wish of Professor Freud himself" (Gardiner, 1971, p. 142n). And to find time for the Wolf Man's sessions, Freud abruptly dropped Helene Deutsch from treatment. Freud made him feel like a coworker, Serge recalled, and praised him saying, "It would be good if all his pupils could grasp the nature of analysis as soundly as I" (p. 140).

In response to the Wolf Man's protestations of specialness, Brunswick bluntly pointed out his exclusion from all of Freud's family and social gatherings, denying he had anything personal in his relationship to Freud at all. He was not even a unique patient—others had been treated longer and other equally important cases published. Finally, with what was to prove to be the last straw, Brunswick declared that not only did she not discuss his case with Freud, but Freud had never even inquired after him. This, as Mahony (1984) has pointed out, was far from likely, given that she was not only in analysis with Freud at the time, but regularly discussed her caseload with him.

Her simultaneous assault on his grandiosity and on his idealized image of Freud finally capsized the Wolf Man's already precarious narcissistic equilibrium with the predictable outcome of a resurgence of his symptoms. His hypochondria deteriorated into a "full persecution mania" (Brunswick, 1928, p. 290): now he was convinced that Professor X had intentionally disfigured him. All his previous doctors, including Freud, had mistreated him and he felt that he was left both disfigured and mentally ill. Brunswick reports that during this period his personal hygiene also deteriorated, leaving him looking slovenly and harrassed, again driven to stopping compulsively to inspect his nose in every shop window.

He dreamed that his mother had taken down the holy pictures from the walls of his room and smashed them to bits; he was amazed that a pious woman could be so destructive—evidently reflecting the iconoclastic role that Brunswick had assumed despite her being Freud's devout disciple. It was during this period of intense transferential turbulence that he recovered the childhood memory that the original wolf dream had been followed by a phobia of being stared at, the trauma in the transference seemingly reactivating the memory of the childhood trauma.

His dreams now began to display his old restorative strategy of masochistic surrender: twice the image of lying at a woman's feet is reported. In the first instance, he surrenders in despair of going mad; in the second, in anticipation of having to descend from a great height by a precarious ladder out of a skyscraper window. In another dream the same night as the skyscraper dream, he is telling Freud of his ambition to study criminal law, only to be discouraged and told to study political economy instead. We can perhaps summarize the import of these various images as his fear that he must renounce any hope of justice for the narcissistic injuries done him (abandon criminal law) and submit to the analyst's sense of reality (lie at her feet/change his career) in order to preserve his psychic equilibrium (political economy).

Yet despite the severe narcissistic injuries, the traumatic deidealization of Freud, and the restorative attempts by way of masochistic submission, the analysis was not without positive aspects. Perhaps because he perceived Brunswick as a less formidable and less overwhelming figure than the indomitably charismatic Freud, he could allow his rage to emerge in a way never reported in the original analysis, where it seems to have been expressed in a passive–aggressive resistance that led Freud to feel that the treatment was stagnating. The ambivalence that was suppressed by the sheer force of Freud's influence emerged, if only under highly traumatic circumstances. If Brunswick misunderstood the function of his grandiosity, she did understand his need to work through his unacknowledged anger at Freud—even if she failed to recognize any legitimate basis for it in his subjective experience. Indeed, rather than exploring the Wolf Man's sense of injury or undue influence at Freud's hands, Brunswick (1928) concluded that the stagnation in the first analysis came about because "our patient was too comfortable in the analytic situation" (p. 304)!

For the most part, Brunswick (1928) could not acknowledge that the Wolf Man's sense of being injured or mistreated had any legitimate ground in his subjective reality. She asserted instead, "We know that the persecution is in reality the hostility of the patient himself projected upon the object" (p. 299).

The hatred that emerged toward Freud during the second analysis she did not attribute to any subjectively valid sense of mistreatment in need of exploration. Rather she viewed it as a transformation of the intense love for Freud that his illness mobilized in his patient:

> The threatened death of a beloved person mobilizes all one's love. But the love of this patient for his father—represented by Freud—forms the greatest menace to his masculinity: satisfying it involves castration. To this danger the narcissism of the patient reacts with tremendous force; the love is partially repressed, partly converted into hate [p. 305].

In the end, she falls back on the patient's "primary bisexuality" as "obviously the cause of his illness" (p. 307). Because his femininity was "constitutionally . . . so strong . . . the normal oedipal complex has been sacrificed in its development to the negative oedipus complex" (p. 307). Unable to see the selfobject dimension in the Wolf Man's submissiveness, she invokes a biological origin to account for its predominance in his character.

For Brunswick (1928), the turning point in the treatment was the dream about the holy pictures, but the mechanism of cure remained obscure: "I can attribute the change only to the fact that at last the patient had sufficiently lived through his reactions to the father, and was therefore able to give them up" (p. 306), she wrote in conclusion. Rather than his making a final renunciation, I would instead point to a restorative compromise that the patient seems to achieve in a later dream. There he consults a benign doctor who asks for a fee of only 100,000 kronen. In his associations, he could not tell whether this number meant that he was once again so rich that the money meant nothing to him, or that in the new, devalued currency the doctor was indeed offering to treat him virtually for free. In the dream he is able to refuse an offer of some sheet music from the doctor, but lacks the courage to reject a gift of postcards. In a final scene, a boyishly-dressed woman analyst appears whom the patient embraces and takes on his knee.

Something of his old capacity for grandiosity and idealization seems to have been restored here, and he is at least partially in control of what is given him. The doctor is a benign figure and Brunswick is reduced to nonthreatening proportions.

He now found that a significant symptom had disappeared. For years he had been unable to enjoy reading novels; he had refused to allow himself to identify with the hero, who was really always under the complete control of the author, but neither could he identify with the author out of a sense of his own inadequacy. This sadomasochistic subtext to his reading was now dispelled, and his interest in literature, the arts, his painting and his work were all invigorated.

The pleasure he derived from these sources and from his hobby, painting, was, however, not a sufficient ground on which to establish a mature, self-affirming sense of ambition and ideals. Serge's professional life and its disappointments are given little weight in either Freud's or Brunswick's accounts of his illnesses. A failure to develop a secure and satisfying professional identity is seen as the sequela of the failure to resolve childhood conflicts, not as an ongoing and debilitating trauma to his self-esteem.

Serge had originally planned to study law but had broken off his studies when he first went to consult Kraepelin in 1908. Following his analysis with Freud, he returned to Moscow with Therese and during the winter of 1914–15 resumed his studies. He had to repeat the exams from his earlier days, which were no longer valid, but was able to pass required tests in 18 different subjects and received his degree from Odessa Law School in 1915. After the war, he was in exile in Austria and his degree was worthless. He was forced to take work in an insurance company. Although in his *Memoirs* he writes of occasional opportunities to use his talents and his pride at writing articles for professional journals, overall one gets the impression that his work, which he clung to for financial and emotional security, never could approach his notorious patienthood as source of pride and identity. Indeed, in later years, he would write to Gardiner (1971), "I am at the moment a 100% 'red-tape office man,' just the thing which I always despised" (letter of August 18, 1948; p. 337). But when Karen Obholzer called on him in his old age, he would answer the phone, "This is the Wolf-Man." His painting, which Brunswick thought a valuable sublimation, ultimately never advanced beyond providing mementos for visiting analysts.

The relative calm of the years following his treatment with Brunswick was shattered by the suicide of his wife on March 31, 1938, following Hitler's occupation of Austria. Serge found his wife's death inexplicable—she had no known Jewish blood and was not in any immediate danger—and he was plunged into despair and a fear of not being able to endure on his own. His sense of his own fragility seems to have been paramount: "The question kept hammering away in my mind: how could Therese do this to me? And as she was the only stable structure in my changeable life, how could I, now suddenly deprived of her, live on?" (Gardiner, 1971, p. 122).

Through Muriel Gardiner, Brunswick's analysand, to whom he had been giving Russian lessons and helping with her insurance policies, he recontacted his former analyst, who had already fled to Paris. With the further intercession of Princess Marie Bonaparte, he obtained a visa and traveled first to Paris and then on to London, following Brunswick for daily sessions for about six weeks in all. At the end of the summer he returned to Vienna and moved into a single-room apartment he called his "hermitage." As it happened, one of Therese's farewell letters had been addressed to a maid in their old building, a Fraulein Gaby, asking her to look after her husband after she was gone. And indeed Fraulein Gaby now came to take care of him for years to come, until her death in 1972. Serge then arranged to have his mother live with him in his former apartment, where she would remain for the last 16 years of her life. His newly constituted household and his job remained intact throughout the war, providing him with a measure of stability, even if within seemingly ever-constricting emotional bounds. When he was forced to retire from his job at age 63 in 1950, he found the loss "catastrophic" and wrote to Gardiner (September 21, 1950):

> A taedium vitae has taken hold of me, so that when I wake in the morning I shudder at the thought that I must get through a 'whole day,' from morning to evening. Like crashing waves then come fits of despair in which life seems horribly ugly and redeeming death seems beautiful [p. 339].

The following summer his condition seems to have grown so confused and fragmented that he inadvertently wandered across the border into the Russian Zone while off trying to paint, resulting in his temporary arrest and interrogation before being found harmless and released.

During his old age, he became once again entangled in an ambivalent dependent relationship with a woman named Luise, whom, as he related to Obholzer, he variously supported, promised to marry, felt guiltily tied to, and unable to escape, over the course of more than two decades. His last years were again plagued by obsessional and hypochondriacal concerns, and he remained in personal and therapeutic contact intermittently with both Gardiner and Kurt Eissler for the rest of his life. And as seen in his last interviews with Obholzer, he never resolved his ambivalent feelings toward Freud, who provided him with an identity but who never let him find his own.

REFERENCES

Atwood, G. & Stolorow, R. (1984), *Structures of Subjectivity.* Hillsdale, NJ: The Analytic Press.
Brandchaft, B. & Stolorow, R. (1984), The borderline concept: Pathological character or iatrogenic myth? In: *Empathy, Vol. 2,* ed. J. L. Lichtenberg, M. Borstein & D. Silver. Hillsdale, NJ: The Analytic Press.
Brunswick, R. M. (1928), A supplement to Freud's "History of an Infantile Neurosis." In: *The Wolf-Man by the Wolf-Man,* M. Gardiner. New York: Basic Books, 1971.
Fish, S. (1989), *Doing What Comes Naturally.* Durham: Duke University Press.
Freud, S. (1918), *From the History of an Infantile Neurosis. Standard Edition,* 17:3–122.
Gardiner, M. (ed.) (1971), *The Wolf-Man by the Wolf-Man.* New York: Basic Books.
Gedo, J. & Goldberg, A. (1973), *Models of the Mind.* Chicago: University of Chicago Press.
Jones, E. (1955), *The Life and Work of Sigmund Freud, Vol. 2.* New York: Basic Books.
Kohut, H. (1971), *The Analysis of the Self.* New York: International Universities Press.
Mahony, P. (1984), *Cries of the Wolf-Man.* New York: International Universities Press.
Obholzer, K. (1982), *The Wolf-Man Sixty Years Later.* New York: Continuum.
Stolorow, R., Brandchaft, B. & Atwood, G. (1988), Masochism and its treatment. *Bull. Menn. Clin.,* 52:504–509.

Barry Magid
THE HOMOSEXUAL IDENTITY OF A NAMELESS WOMAN
(*The Psychogenesis of a Case of Homosexuality in a Woman*, 1920)

This case, although brief, unsuccessful, and abruptly terminated by Freud himself, nonetheless provided Freud with the opportunity to outline a general approach to the problem of homosexuality. Likewise, we can use it to contrast self psychology's approach to the issue with that of Freud's and see how far we have come in grappling with a problem that is laden with political and cultural dilemmas, as well as clinical issues.

The case itself often makes for awkward reading today. On one hand, we can see Freud trying to identify and break free from the traditional cultural stereotypes that surrounded homosexuality in his day. Almost as pernicious were the quasi-scientific explanations about the role of hormones and other biological factors that were being floated about. Nonetheless, Freud's—perhaps inevitable—blindness to what now appears to be a host of cultural preconceptions about masculinity, femininity, and normality and deviance mar his attempts at objectivity.

The case revolves around an 18-year-old girl brought for treatment by her parents. Outwardly compliant, she nevertheless was being seen against her will. Freud (1920) tells us she "had aroused displeasure and concern in her parents by the devoted adoration with which she pursued a certain 'society' lady, who was about ten years older than herself" (p. 147). The parents claimed that this woman had a notorious reputation and was known to be flagrantly carrying on affairs with both women and men. Their daughter's infatuation with this woman consumed her to the neglect of everything else in her life, and she had refused to obey her parents' commands to stop seeing her. The situation reached a crisis when her father encountered the two of them walking together in public. He gave them a furious look, which immediately precipitated his daughter's throwing herself over a guard wall beside the railway line they happened to be passing. The suicide attempt had the dual effect of provoking her parents to bring her in for psychoanalytic treatment and making her ladyfriend take her attentions more seriously.

Freud admits that he was not sanguine about the prospects for the analysis. He acknowledges that the girl "was not in any way ill (she did not suffer from anything in herself, nor complain of her condition)" (p. 150). He compares the task the parents set him with that of a husband bringing his nervous, neurotic wife to treatment to restore their marriage, whereas it is only the compromise afforded by the neurotic symptoms that allows the wife to endure living with him at all, and, once cured, she leaves. Even more to the point, he cites the example of the parents of an unruly child, whose treatment results only in the child's ability to go "its own way all the more decidedly, and the parents are now far more dissatisfied than before" (p. 150). A treatment that allowed this patient to proudly avow her homosexuality would parallel the example of that child exactly, but because that outcome was not socially acceptable, Freud effectively excluded it from his mandate from the beginning of treatment and thereby ultimately alienated and lost his patient.

What Freud calls "the secret plan" (p. 151) of the typical homosexual patient, namely that the very *failure* of psychoanalysis to change his or her sexual orientation, to feel that he has now "done everything possible against his abnormality" and is thereby free to "resign himself with an easy conscience" (p. 151) to his sexual orientation, now seems like nothing so much as a desire to accept oneself, and be accepted, as one is. But this kind of self-acceptance is not here regarded as a *successful* outcome by Freud; to the contrary, it is the byproduct of the failure of the analysis.

A successful outcome for Freud, as for the girl's parents, would consist only in converting her to a heterosexual orientation. Theoretically, Freud can envision this as a real possibility since he had postulated mankind's innate bisexuality. Once the conflictual blockages to heterosexual wishes are analytically worked through, the patient will then be able to experience both heterosexual and homosexual desires and be free to choose the safer and socially sanctioned course.

Freud's alliance from the start is thus clearly with the parents, in that they both hold the same notion of what would constitute a successful outcome—a definition of success clearly not shared by the patient. Thus, despite his own awareness of the dangers of trying to comply with the parents' mandate, he closes off to himself the option of genuinely empathizing with his patient's wishes. The girl's compliance with the treatment at all was on the slimmest of footings, she did not, she said, wish to cause her parents pain and would try to cooperate. One can indeed see "the secret plan" at work. The patient presents a compliant façade, but only the failure of the analysis can bring her the outcome she desires.

Freud concludes his introductory comments to the case with an admirable attempt to dispel some then-current stereotypes about homosexuals, particularly the presumed effeminacy of the male and masculinity of the female. "The degree of physical hermaphroditism" (p. 154) is his rather archaic-sounding way of putting it. But he ends up waffling somewhat, suggesting the correlation is more common in women. He allows as how it is "conventional rather than scientific" to describe as "masculine" such traits in a woman as "acuteness of comprehension" and "objectivity" (p. 154). But he then goes on to ascribe a scientific distinction between the sexes in terms of their behavior towards their love-object. For example, he writes that his patient

> displayed the humility and sublime over-valuation of the sexual object so characteristic of the male lover, the renunciation of all narcissistic satisfaction, and the preference for being lover rather than beloved. She had thus not only chosen a feminine love-object, but had also developed a masculine attitude towards that object [p. 154].

All this now sounds as "conventionally" determined as what precedes it about objectivity and lucidity. Freud distanced himself from one stereotype only to give psychoanalytic sanction to another.

This is not to say, of course, that any observation about differences between the sexes is necessarily the result of a cultural stereotyping and that only a presumption of absolute equivalence can be free of prejudice. The work of Gilligan (1982) and Tannen (1990), for instance, seem to offer examples of legitimately documented sex differences. The crucial difference is the use to which this finding of difference is put. Gilligan and Tannen each establish new *normative* descriptions for female cognitive styles and oppose these to earlier presumptions of deviance or deficiency, when comparisons were made with males' presumably more logical, abstract reasoning abilities. Their effect is to create a greater acceptance of alternate valid modes of functioning. Freud's comparisons, on the other hand, are used to define deviancy and do not further his empathic appreciation for the appropriateness of his patient's behavior given her subjective experience.

Despite the dramatic turn of events that brought his patient precipitously to treatment as an adolescent, Freud found the history of her earlier development unremarkable, except for a memory of comparing genitals with her older brother at about the age of five. Although there is nothing in her recollection to suggest that this was anything other than an example of a very common, nontraumatic childhood exploration, much will be made to hinge on this episode later on.

At the age of 13, we are told, she developed a special attachment to a little boy of about three years of age whom she had met in the playground. Gradually she became friendly with the little boy's parents, and her interest began to focus increasingly on his young mother. Something must have seemed amiss because it provoked a "mortifying chastisement" from her father. The transformation of her interest in children and her fantasies of being a mother herself someday, to a sexualized romantic fascination with the young mothers themselves, seems to have coincided with her own mother's giving birth to a new baby boy when the patient was 16. This event, apparently, traumatically ruptured what had already been an impaired and conflicted relationship. The mother saw her daughter as a competitor in the family and "favored her sons at her expense, and kept an especially strict watch against any close relation between the girl and her father" (p. 157).

Whether the young adolescent had any particular talents, ambitions, or other goals for herself, we are not told. Freud's case history, by his own description, is a "sexual history" (p. 155), and any other potential sources for her emergent sense of identity are slighted in his account. Significantly, she remains nameless throughout the case and is known to us as well only by reference to her sexual identity.

Overall, we see her growing up in a very restrictive home, where assertiveness is the prerogative only of the sons, who are the favorites. There seem to have been few opportunities for the empathic mirroring of the assertive and sexual sides of her emerging adolescent personality, and the rejection by her mother may have left her hungry for idealizable role models.

Thus, her involvement first with the little boy's mother and then with the shady "Lady" that so upset her parents, seems to have been motivated as much by frustrated needs for mirroring and idealization as it was by sexual desire. Indeed, what Freud called the "masculine" quality of her pursuit—"the sublime over-valuation of the sexual object" and "the preference for being lover rather than beloved" (p.

154)—seems precisely to be a manifestation of her idealizing needs, not her sexual drives. Furthermore, we are told that she "illogically" courted women who were "coquettes in the ordinary sense of the word" (p. 161) and rejected without hesitation the willing advances made by a homosexual friend her own age. It is "illogical" only if one assumes, as Freud did, that what was at issue was only a matter of sexual gratification. But clearly her emergent self-identification as a homosexual carried a meaning far beyond the opportunities for sexual satisfaction, what Harris (1991), in reviewing the case, called using "love objects as points of identification as well as desire" (p. 213). The license and rebellion manifested by the "bad" crowd to which she gravitated allowed her own inhibited expansiveness—and not just her sexuality—to emerge.

Freud was no doubt correct that the birth of the new baby brother fatally disrupted her own nascent attempts to identify with her own mother. We can imagine that the family's attention was abruptly diverted away from her just at the time when her own adolescent needs were most in want of appropriate mirroring. Freud's interpretation was also that the beloved lady friend was a substitute for the mother; but rather than seeing this as we would now, as a sexualized breakdown product of the disruption of her adolescent needs for mirroring and idealization (which may or may not end up influencing her adult sexual orientation), he saw a revival of an Oedipal conflict at its root.

In Freud's account, puberty aroused in her the wish to have a male child by her father, but it was her hated rival, her mother, who bore his child instead. Furiously resentful at this defeat, she turned against her father and men in general altogether: "she foreswore her womanhood and sought another goal for her libido (p. 157) . . . she changed into a man and took her mother in place of her father as the object of her love" (p. 158). The attraction to mother—or mother-substitutes—thus becomes part of an overcompensation for the girl's hostility toward her mother.

The incident of comparing genitals with her brother is now interpreted in terms of her unwillingness to be second to him in any way. Her envy of his penis is manifested in her rebellion "against the lot of woman in general" and in her feeling that it "was unjust that girls should not enjoy the same freedom as boys." This unhealthy attitude had grown to the point, Freud sums up, where "she was, in fact, a feminist" (p. 169).

Freud also introduced the theory of "retiring in favor of someone else" (p. 159n), that is, the avoidance of an unacceptably conflictual rivalry, as one of the fundamental dynamics in the genesis of homosexuality in both men and women. He further sought to derive this mechanism from one of his anthropological conjectures about the aboriginal primal horde in which all women once literally belonged to the dominant male. Thus, rather than risk oedipal rivalry, the homosexual "retires" from the field of competition. This hypothesis in particular seems subsequently to have acquired a status quite disproportionate to the slender clinical evidence on which it was based.

In reviewing these explanations today, we might begin by noting the way Freud regularly intertwined the notions of "womanhood," "feminity," and the choice of a heterosexual object. For Freud, being a lesbian meant "changing into a man." In fact we now see these factors as operating far more independently of one another, femininity in whatever currently conventional sense may or may not be repudiated, and "womanhood" can be actively affirmed without reference to men as the love object. Conversely, the "masculine," especially to the extent that it carries with it patriarchal, hierarchical, or authoritarian connotations, may be shunned rather than embraced. Freud's account also completely omits any consideration of the dynamics by which the woman may seek to avoid the repetition of a genuinely abusive, traumatic relationship with the father or another male, whereby a homosexual orientation is established to allow selfobject connections in a relationship free from the danger of reinjury. By focusing on the intrinsically dangerous wishes and fantasies of his patients and abandoning his early seduction hypothesis, Freud left himself open to underestimating the incidence of actual abuse.

Finally, we should again note how thoroughly all issues of idealization of, and identification with, mother substitutes are reduced by Freud to defensive attempts to resolve conflictual feelings of jealousy and hatred for her mother, without any suggestion that these needs for idealization and identification could have a developmental primacy all their own, independent of their role in a sexual drama. Perhaps the clearest difference between Freud's and my own selfpsychological approach to this case lies precisely in his relentless subjugation of all issues of identity to their function within the oedipal scenario, whereas I see the process flowing in exactly the opposite direction—the libidinal transformation and sexual role development have been enlisted in the service of self-development and the preservation of selfobject ties in the face of a familial disruption. The use of a simultaneously idealized and sexualized selfobject mentor could just as well be enacted by a heterosexual adolescent, and there need be no implication here that her homosexuality is "caused" by this selfobject need.

Another fundamental difference surrounds Freud's whole notion of the "meaning" of a symptom, which is, for him, invariably to be found by uncovering its *origin*—hence the title of this case, "The Psycho*genesis* of Homosexuality in a Woman" (italics added). While not neglecting origins, I would place the emphasis on meaning as the *use,* or function, the symptom serves in the ongoing maintenance of the integrity of the Self. The difference in these emphases is particularly striking in the case of homosexuality and how it has been regarded over the years by psychoanalysts. As long as it was defined by its origins, it was inevitably pathologized. Whatever developmental or dynamic scenario was invoked, whether giving centrality to overbearing or rivalrous mothers or absent fathers, homosexuality was defined by its origins in a disturbed family constellation. The first crucial step away from this perspective was a recognition of the diverse pathways that could lead to adult homosexuality, and that, dynamically, homosexuality could be a part of a broad spectrum of structural configurations from preoedipal to oedipal. Lachmann (1975) used a range of clinical vignettes to illustrate that "sexual functioning, ego development, and object relations are not always correlated" (p. 254) and that maintaining homosexuality as a distinct diagnostic category thus made little sense.

Within Kohut's published work there was perhaps an overemphasis on a particular set of dynamics—that of homosexuality functioning either as part of an erotized means of self-stimulation to ward off depression and fragmentation, or as a part of a sexualized connection to an archaic selfobject (see the case of Mr. X [Kohut, 1977]). This overemphasis was no doubt due, in part, to the need to elucidate what was then a novel approach to the role of sexuality in the narcissistic character structure. Kohut's (1977) demonstration of a role for sexual acting out based on a desperate attempt to restore self-cohesion, and the resolution of the symptom without any reference to what would hitherto have been presumed to be its origin in the oedipus complex, added a significant dimension to our understanding of sexuality's place in the broader context of the self. This new formulation was so compelling, however, that it tended to overshadow the recognition that different functions might be served by homosexuality in different circumstances. There were in Kohut's writings simply no comparative case reports of homosexual relationships serving mature, stable selfobject functions, or of patients achieving firm, cohesive selves in the context of such relationships.

There was only the intriguing instance of Mr. Z's boyhood homosexual experiences, where Kohut (1979) allowed homosexuality to be seen in a somewhat different light. There, as a preadolescent, the patient is described as having formed an eroticized attachment to his male camp counselor. The eroticism is presented as being clearly in the service of his transferential need for an idealized father figure. "During the summer," Kohut tells us,

> in camp, he admired him not only in his function as an expert outdoorsman who taught his charges various skills but also as a spiritual leader who infused the boys with his own deep, almost religious, love for nature. Later on, when the two continued their contact in the city, the boy's admiration continued, but now shifted to the friend's moral and social philosophy and his knowledge and love for literature, art, and music [p. 404].

While the eroticization of this kind of mentor relationship is fraught with the potential for abuse, in Mr. Z's case, Kohut repeatedly assures us that it was never experienced by the patient as threatening or exploitative. Kohut nonetheless remained ambivalent about the overall value of such sexualized selfobject relationships. Positive though it was, "because of its sexualization [it] did not lead to truly structure-building, wholesome results" (p. 441). And later in the same case report, when he refers to the selfobject dimension of homosexual relations, it is to refer to the way the *archaic* (italics added) transference longings are revealed by the "description of the homosexual practices he engages in or wishes for" (p. 440).

These remarks of Kohut's have occasionally been construed so as to give rise to the mistaken therapeutic expectation that homosexuality, arising out of archaic selfobject longings in which the child turns to an eroticized substitute for the same sex parent, could be "cured" by a transferential reinstatement and working through of the early narcissistic needs and thereby have their mature satisfaction uncoupled from the earlier homosexual solution. This would be to ignore the stable, autonomous role that sexuality comes to assume over the years as part of the person's identity, as well as the fact that the evolution from archaic to mature selfobject ties may take place in a homosexual as well as a heterosexual relationship. Our primary concern should always be whether these maturer ties are capable of forming, or whether the sexuality has served an exclusively defensive, self-stimulating function. The focus on meaning as use, rather than origin, is intended to bring us firmly back to this crucial vantage-point.

In an attempt to escape the pathologizing implications of origin-based explanations for homosexuality, many homosexuals have sought to affirm its natural, biological origin—to assert that they were "born" not "made" homosexual. I think this is an unnecessary and ultimately misguided solution to the problem, regardless of the merits of the underlying genetic hypothesis, because it may close off exploration of the person's particular subjective experience around the emergence of sexual identity. In any case, the argument for a purely biological basis for such a complex configuration as sexual identity has serious conceptual flaws, according to Oyama (1985), who has investigated the confusions arising out of dichotomized "nature versus nurture" explanations.

> This association of biology (or, in many discussions, the genes) with the invariant, the intractable, or the inevitable is a serious error and one that must be undone if we are to make progress in this area. The further association of nature [i.e., the natural] with biology compounds the error [p. 3].

In part, we have been misled by simplistic computer-programming metaphors—for our generation the conceptual morass that hydraulic drive theories were for Freud's—to view the genes as an invariant, all-powerful inner master code for the organism's development. But philosophers of science like Oyama remind us that genetic codes derive their meaning from their context in the cell's life and its surround and that the development of complex systems is always interactive, not unidirectionally programmed by genes or Nature.

If we do not equate meanings with origins, then we do not have to devise or cling to a pathology-free origin theory to justify nondiscrimination or nonstigmatization. If an object choice that had its origins in the most abusive or neglectful of families permits in adulthood the development of stable selfobject bonds and, through the laying down of compensatory structure, the solidification of a cohesive self, it is in need of no further justification. Perversion, it follows, is not simply a matter of unnatural object choices; instead, it represents the addictive or fetishistic use of others as objects, in the service of defensive, rather than selfobject, needs.

Freud's inability to recognize this alternative dynamic interpretation of his patient's sexuality inevitably led to the disruption and termination of the analysis. His lack of understanding reinforced her distrust and emotional disengagement from the treatment. The lack of any meaningful alliance is revealed by Freud's telling anecdote: "Once when I expounded to her a specially important part of the theory, one touching on her nearly, she replied in an inimitable tone, 'How very interesting' " (p. 163). Obviously, there is no real exploration of the patient's subjective experience going on here. Freud is "expounding," not exploring. What is most important to him—his theory—is experience distant and unimportant to her. Sadly, as it all too often seems to have been the case, when Freud had to choose between believing his theory or believing his patient, he chose his theory. Her lack of interest thus became a resistance to be explained, but the truth of the interpretation or of the underlying theory, was never seriously questioned. We would see her resistance as resulting from the unempathic and off-target nature of the interpretation, but Freud could only conclude that his patient was unwilling to face an unacceptable and painful truth.

The most egregious example of their misalliance occurs when Freud is driven to accuse her of actually lying to him in her dreams. During a brief period when he felt that a positive transference toward him might be beginning to emerge, she brought in a series of dreams that seemed to "anticipate the cure of her inversion through the treatment," and "confessed her longing for a man's love and for children" (p. 165). Unfortunately, Freud gives us only this summary of what he considered the dreams' manifest content, not a verbatim report of the dreams themselves. In any case, this was evidently the wrong wish expressed at the wrong time according to his preconceptions. He found it too much at odds with her consciously expressed contempt for men and marriage—although, of course, in other circumstances he himself originated the idea that dreams could express wishes seemingly at odds with our conscious attitudes. Freud was somehow sure that his patient wished to deceive him with a false compliance with his expectations, as she was doing with her father, "perhaps in order to disappoint me all the more thoroughly later on" (p. 165). Freud proceeded to tell his patient that he regarded her dreams as "false" and "hypocritical" (p. 165). As might be expected, he reports that thereupon "exposition of this kind of dream ceased" (p. 165). Although it seems obvious now that her subsequent anger and withdrawal were the result of his unempathic confrontation, Freud (1920) concluded it was, rather, that "she had transferred to me the sweeping repudiation of men which had dominated her ever since the disappointment she suffered from her father" (p. 164). This was true only insofar as Freud had in *fact*—not in some transferential projection—retraumatized her by his misinterpretation, and thus reconfirmed her expectation that men inevitably abuse her. But that the traumatic reenactment was real, and not her projection, was not an alternative available within his theoretical framework.

One must also wonder at the possible countertransferential element in this exchange, since Freud's account of her basic antipathy to men and of the lying dreams occurs following her dismissal of his "specially important" interpretations as "very interesting." Freud's own narcissistic injury may have led him too quickly to the conclusion that the patient's whole intent was to render the analysis a failure. Freud was determined not to allow her that satisfaction, nor, perhaps, was he willing to risk a repetition of the rejection inflicted on him by "Dora." He himself "broke off the treatment and advised her parents that, if they set store by the therapeutic procedure it should be continued by a woman doctor" (p. 164). All in all, this is probably the best advice he could have offered. But we are not told that any referral was actually made or whether there was indeed any follow-up in this case.

The case report itself concludes with the judgment that, despite all the dynamic factors uncovered, and the disturbances in the parental relationships noted, this was probably a case of *inborn* homosexuality all along, which "as usual, became fixed and unmistakably manifest only in the period following puberty" (p. 170). Perhaps there is a detectable note of self-exoneration for Freud in this conclusion, absolving him for his failure to make any headway in the treatment. His closing remarks refer to the then current research by Steinach, who was removing and transplanting testes in an attempt to influence sexual behavior. Freud allows as how unlikely it is a woman would consent to the removal of her presumably "hermaphroditic" (p. 172) ovaries as part of the treatment of her inversion, but he characteristically assumes that her main objection to this bizarre and intrusive surgery is that it would preclude motherhood.

That the then most fashionable and "scientific" research into the biological basis of sexual orientation sounds so bizarre today should serve as a caveat that the only appropriate avenue for psychoanalytic investigation is the subjective experiences of our patients. It is the attempt to find a biological underpinning to psychological reality that has led to all the misdirected diversions of instinct theories. Such theories will inevitably be experience distant and can only lead us away from an empathic immersion in the patient's experience. When we explore the experience of our homosexual patients, we must take as our sole guide the ongoing function that sexuality serves within the self-selfobject context. A sexual orientation that makes available a range of positive, stable selfobjects is not in need of any further justification and is neither stigmatized nor redeemed by looking for its origins either in early development trauma or biological predispositions. Our explorations of a patient's personal history must always have at their center the goal of the patient's feeling more deeply and comprehensively understood. The uncovering of origins, we now recognize, is not an archaeological expedition that can be curative simply by virtue of what is brought to light. And the meaning of the various elements of our patients' lives and histories is truly to be found not in any search for their origins, but in an empathic understanding of the dynamic use that they serve.

REFERENCES

Freud, S. (1920), *The Psychogenesis of a Case of Homosexuality in a Woman*. *Standard Edition,* 18:145–172. London: Hogarth Press, 1955.
Gilligan, C. (1982), *In a Different Voice*. Cambridge, MA: Harvard University Press.
Harris, A. (1991), Gender as contradiction. *Psychoanal. Dial.,* 1:197–224.
Kohut, H. (1977), *The Restoration of the Self*. New York: International Universities Press.
_____ (1979), The two analyses of Mr. Z. In: *The Search for the Self,* Vol. 4, ed. P. H. Ornstein. Madison, CT: International Universities Press, 1991, pp. 395–446.
Lachmann, F. (1975), Homosexuality: Some diagnostic perspectives and dynamic considerations. *Amer. J. Psychother.,* 22:254–260.
Oyama, S. (1985), *The Ontogeny of Information*. Cambridge, MA: Cambridge University Press.
Tannen, D. (1990), *You Just Don't Understand*. New York: Morrow.

INDEX

A

Abandonment, 97, 128–129, 147–148, 173
Abuse, 11, 94n, 139, 144–145, 149–150, 153, 194
Adatto, C.P., 39, *82*
Adolescence, 11, 35n, 38–41, 45, 54, 73n, 194
Affect, 51–52, 68, 102, 112, 131, 172
Aggression, 40, 42, 47n, 110, 114, 127
Ambivalence, 26, 40, 110, 118, 184, 187
Anna O, 5, 9–28
Anthony, E.J., 97, *105*
Antisemitism, 27, 56–61, 72n, 74n, 75
Anxiety
 castration, 88–90, 93–98, 102, 163, 170, 173
 disintegration, 97
 separation, 98, 104, 129
Atwood, G., 129, *132*, 141, 146, *156*, 172, *187*

B

Bateson, G., 6, *8*
Bauer family, 54–56, 58. *See also* Dora
Baumeyer, F., 136, *156*
Beatus, H.R., 13, *29*

Begel, D., 48, *82*
Bernheimer, C., 33n, 35, 39, 45, 47, *82*
Bernstein, I., 39–42, 44, *82*
Bisexuality, 40, 43, 184, 190
Bloch, D., 138, *156*
Blos, P., 38, 40, 41, 79, *82*, 104, *105*, 110, *132*
Bonaparte, M., 42, *83*, 186
Bowlby, J., 98, *105*
Brandchaft, B., 129, *132*, 141, 146, *156*, 172, 176, *187*
Breuer, J., 9–10, 13, 15–18, 26, *28*
Bristow, E.J., 25, *28*
Brunswick, R.M., 157, 158, 161, 171, 177–186, *187*
Buckley, P., 31, 35, 40, *83*

C

Cathartic method, 11, 14, 18
Chabot, C., 154, *156*
Clark, R.W., 56, *83*
Coates, S., 129, *132*
Cognition, 92n, 100, 191
Collins, J., 46, *83*
Compliance, somatic, 51–53
Conflict, 143
 oedipal, 78, 89, 171, 177, 193–194
 preoedipal, 44, 54, 67
 sexual, 102, 110, 114, 119, 127, 163, 170

201

INDEX

Conversion hysteria, 17, 20, 43, 55, 60
Countertransference, 17, 35n, 41, 61
  Freud's, 34, 37n, 39, 42, 47–48, 65, 110, 114, 126, 198
Cranefield, P.F., 16, *28*

D

Decker, H.S., 33n, 35, 39, 47, 48, 53n, 54, 56–65, 74, 78n, *83*
Deidealization, 60–61, 74, 77, 165, 176, 183
Delusion, 139, 142–144, 155
Denial, 71, 75, 127, 130, 171
Depression, 14, 77, 80, 113, 130, 159, 160, 179
Deutsch, F., 54, 55, 74, *83*
Deutsch, H., 182
Dissociation, 14–17, 20, 151
Dora, 7, 31–85, 118, 199
Dreams, 6, 36, 50–51, 53, 66, 79, 122, 166–176, 181–184, 198
Dual-drive theory, 42, 54, 141, 197

E

Edinger, D., 10, 12, 19, 21n, 24, 26, 27, *28*
Ego psychology, 38, 41, 67
Eissler, K., 187
Ellenberger, H.F., 10, 11, 17–18, *28*, 56, *83*
Ellman, S., 107, 111, *132*
Empathy, 1, 4n, 33n, 38n, 74, 132, 147, 175, 200
  Freud's, 63, 69–70, 191, 198
Erikson, E.H., 26, *28*, 32n, 38–41, *83*
Erotism, anal, 170, 176
Exhibitionism, 164, 171, 174

F

Fantasy, 6, 102, 110, 116, 123
  pregnancy, 17, 25
  sexual, 47, 52, 63–66, 91
  unconscious, 50, 58
Femininity, 42–44, 73, 78–80, 81n, 141, 189, 194
Feminism
  French, 38–39, 41–44, 67, 79
  German, 21–23, 25, 27, 59–60

Fish, S., 4, *8*, 160, 162, 166, 169, 174, *187*
Flechsig, Paul Emil, 135–138, 144–145, 149–150
Fosshage, J., 107, 112, 122, *132*
Free association, 45, 49, 53, 69–70, 79, 173, 177
Freeman, L., 17, 26, *28*
Freud, A., 42, 102, *105*
Freud, S., 4, *8*, 9–17, 26, *28*, 31, 35, 41, 45, 57, 59, 71, *83*, 87–88, 92, 94, 103, *105*, 108, 110–130, *132*, 135, 138–142, 155, *156*, 157, 166, 173, 178, *187*, 189–193, 197–199, *200*
Friedman, R.C., 129, *132*
Fromm, E., 99, *105*

G

Gardiner, M., 56, *83*, 157–159, 161–167, 170–171, 173, 175, 177–178, 182, 185–186, *187*
Garrison, M., 99, *105*
Gay, P., 56, *83*
Gedo, J., 18, *28*, 162, *187*
Gender differentiation, 128–129, 191
Gill, M.M., 35, 39, 41, 44, 45, 47, 53n, *83*, 84
Gilligan, C., 191, *200*
Glenn, J., 32, 35, 38–48, 73n, 94n, *83*, 84, 103, *105*
Goldberg, A., 2, *8*, 162, *187*
Graf, Herbert, 105. *See* Little Hans
Grandiosity, 141, 150, 161, 165, 174, 181, 183–185
Greenson, R.R., 14, *28*
Grünbaum, A., 2, *8*
Guilt, 89, 94, 114, 117, 127, 175

H

Hallucination, 19n, 153
Harris, A., 193, *200*
Hertz, N., 47, *83*
Hirschmuller, A., 9–15, 17–20, 22, 24, *28*
Homosexuality, 195–197
  female, 4, 7, 39, 40n, 79, 189–199
  paranoia and, 5, 138, 141, 143

Index

Hypnosis, 15–16, 18
Hypochondria, 160, 163, 179–180, 183, 187
Hysteria, 31, 38, 42, 50–51, 53, 58, 68, 70, 72n

I

Idealization, 91, 101, 105, 163, 185, 192, 194
Identification, 47, 91, 101–102, 110, 125, 129, 166, 193–194
Inhelder, B., 92n, 100, *106*
Internalization, 77, 91
   transmuting, 73n, 101–102
Interpretation, 6, 33n, 49, 58, 70, 76, 103, 169
   Freud's, 39, 42–48, 52, 59, 72, 73n, 91, 96, 111, 126, 131, 166, 171–175, 180, 197–198
Intervention, 33, 107, 111
Israels, H., 136, *156*

J

Jennings, J.L., 31, 35, 38, *83*
Jensen, E.M., 10, *28*
Jones, E., 10, *28*, 16, 54, 56, *83*, 160, *187*

K

Kaftal, E., 126, *132*
Kahane, C., 31, 33n, 35, 39, 43–47, *82–83*
Kanzer, M., 35, 38, 41, 48, *83–84*, 115, *132*
Karpe, R., 25, *28*
Kluft, R.P., 11, *28*
Kohon, G., 44, *84*
Kohut, H., 1, 2, 5–7, *8*, 9, 22, 26n, *28*, 57n, 69, 70n, 73n, 77, 82, *84*, 88–90, 97, 99, 101–103, *105–106*, 110, 112, 126, 129, 135, 142, *156*, 160, 170, *187*, 195–196, *200*
Kris, E., 42, *83*
Krohn, A., 41, 44, *84*
Krohn, J., 41, 44, *84*

L

Lacan, J., 43, *84*
Lachmann, F., 107, 112, 118, *132*, *133*, 195, *200*
Langs, R., 39, 44, 46, 48, *84*
Lanzer, Ernst. *See* Rat Man
Lewin, K.K., 43, 44, *84*
Libido theory, 38, 40, 87, 141
Lichtenberg, J., 107, 123, 129, *132*
Lindon, J., 99, *106*
Lipton, S., 111, *132*
Little Hans, 2, 7, 32, 87–106, 176
Lothane, Z., 140–142, 144–145, 149, *156*

M

Mahony, P.J., 5, *8*, 56, *84*, 107, 111, 114–115, 127, 130, *132*, 167–168, 171, 180, 182, *187*
Malcolm, J., 47n, 48, *84*
Marcus, S., 38, 39, *84*
Masculinity, 78, 124, 189, 191, 194
Masochism, 172, 175, 177, 183
Masturbation, 88, 94–95, 127, 143, 147, 175
McCaffrey, P., 69n, *84*
McGuire, W., 111, *132*
Meissner, W.W., 41, *84*
Miller, A., 150, 153, *156*
Miller, J.P., 18, *29*
Mirroring, 25, 91, 101, 129–130, 163, 165, 170, 171, 174, 192–193
Moi, T., 39, 44, 49, 65, *84*
Moscovitz, J., 43, *84*
Muslin, H.L., 35, 39, 41, 44, 45, 47, 53n, *83*, *84*

N

Narcissism, 79, 104, 142, 166, 181–183
Narcissistic injury, 14, 100, 155, 170, 174–176, 183
Narcissistic personality disorder, 160, 195
Neurosis
   infantile, 90, 96, 113, 159, 163, 166–167, 169
   obsessional, 6, 107, 111, 114, 159–160, 176–177, 187

Neutrality, 44, 162
Niederland, W., 136, 143, 148, *156*
Nozick, R., 152, *156*

O

Oberholzer, K., 56, *84*
Obholzer, K., 157, 160, 161, 168, 172, 185, 187
Orange, D., 145, *156*
Ornstein, A., 69, 79, *84*, 99–100, 104, *106*
Ornstein, P.H., 33, 68, *84–85*, 100, 107, 131, *132*
Object choice, 43, 191, 193–194, 197
Object love, 26, 127, 166
Oedipus complex, 17, 36, 43–44, 54, 57n, 61, 63, 67–69, 74, 77–80, 87–105, 184, 195
Oyama, S., 197, *200*

P

Pankejeff, Serge. *See* Wolf Man
Pappenheim, Bertha. *See* Anna O
Pappenheim, Recha (Goldschmidt), 20–21
Penis envy, 193
Phobia, 91, 95–98, 102, 104, 171, 172, 176, 183
Piaget, J., 92n, 100, *106*
Pleasure principle, 2, 88
Pollock, G.H., 22–23, *29*
Possick, S., 48, *85*
Primal scene, 32, 162, 163, 167–174, 177
Psychoanalysis, 2–3, 5, 11, 17–18, 34n, 49
Psychosis, 135, 138–139, 141–145
Pumpian-Mindlin, E., 40, *85*

R

Rage, 14, 70, 110, 111, 115, 121–122, 130
Ramas, M., 41, 44, *85*
Rank, O., 171, 181n
Rat Man, 6–7, 32, 40n, 107–133
Reality testing, 6, 142
Reconstruction, 17–18, 69, 72, 90, 96, 162, 167–168, 172–174

Reeves, C., 17, *29*
Refugees, Jewish, 23–25, 27
Regression, 142, 177
Repression, 51–53, 68, 88–89, 91, 94, 97, 110, 113, 127, 171
Resistance, 91, 96, 116, 119, 166–167, 180–181, 194, 198
Rieff, P., 35, 38n, *85*
Rogow, A.A., 33n, 38, 39, 54–55, 74, *85*

S

Sabshin, M., 18, *28*
Sadow, L., 18, *28*
Sand, R., 32, 34n, 39, 49–53, 65, 68, *85*
Scharfman, M.A., 39, 40, 45, 46, 48, 73n, 78n, *85*
Schatzman, M., 144, *156*
Schlesinger, H., 38–40, *85*
Schlesinger, N., 18, *28*
Schonbar, R., 13, *29*
Schorske, C.E., 57n, *85*
Schreber, D.P., 5, 32, 135–136, 146–152, *156*
Schreber, Moritz, 136, 143–144, 147–148, 152
Schur, M., 56, *85*, 180
Schwaber, E., 135, *156*
Scopophilia, 113, 167
Secondary gain, 72n
Seduction theory, 54, 57, 61, 63, 138, 144
Self
  cohesive, 78, 91, 195, 197
  disorder, 11, 76, 80, 88, 90
  -esteem, 77, 79, 117, 185
  -experience, 67, 80, 135, 143, 146, 151–153, 197, 199
  restoration, 21, 136, 145, 153–155, 170
  unmirrored, 10–12, 18, 21–22
Self psychology, 1, 4–6, 65, 82, 88, 91, 97, 101, 141, 152, 157, 189
Selfobject, 73, 99, 158
  bond, 7, 26, 131, 172, 184, 194, 197, 199
  experience, 91, 105, 128, 154, 169
  function, 4, 11–13, 20, 101–102, 136, 177–178, 195–196, 199
  need, 80, 100, 113, 166, 174–175

Index

Sexuality
  female, 38, 42–44, 79
  infantile, 38, 64, 87, 94, 114, 127, 157, 162, 177
Sexualization, 72, 75, 79–80, 128, 192, 194–196
Shengold, L., 144, *156*
Silverman, M., 89, 103, *106*
Slap, J., 95, *106*
Slipp, S., 41, *85*
Soul murder, 137, 139, 141, 145, 149–151, 153, 155
Sprengnether, M., 41, 47, *85*
Stern, D., 100, *106*
Stolorow, R., 112, 129, *132–133*, 141, 146, *156*, 172, 176, *187*
Structure, compensatory, 10–11, 20, 23, 26, 77, 197
Sulloway, F.J., 56, *85*
Superego, 88, 91
Symptom formation, 15–16, 50–54, 87–88, 95, 139–140, 176–177, 195

T

Tannen, D., 191, *200*
Terman, D., 104, *106*
Termination, 116, 158, 162, 166, 172–173, 177, 181, 197, 199
Therapeutic alliance, 7, 111, 197
Thompson, A.E., 55, *85*
Transference, 33n, 47n, 53n, 61, 123
  erotized, 41, 44–46, 104
  Freud and, 20, 39, 65–67, 171–172, 178, 180

idealizing, 73–77, 79, 104, 110, 122, 126, 174–175, 177, 181–182, 196
mirror, 73n, 74, 110, 162
oedipal, 17–18
selfobject, 5, 10, 12, 14, 73n, 112, 118, 158, 160
Trauma, 51, 53, 68, 81n, 88, 198
  childhood, 78, 107, 127–130, 165, 170, 172, 175, 183

U

Unmanning, 137–141, 145–146, 149–150, 153

V

Van Den Berg, S., 41, 44, *85*
von Hameln, Gluckel, 22–23

W

Wachtel, P., 112, *133*
Weber, G., 140, 145
Winnicott, D.W., 110, *133*
Wittgenstein, L., 4, *8*
Wish, 89, 110, 119–120, 124, 131, 160
Wolf, E., 101, 118, *133*
Wolf Man, 2, 4, 6, 7, 32, 40n, 157–187
Wolfe, S., 129, *132*
Wollstonecraft, Mary Godwin, 22–23

Z

Zetzel, E., 107, 111, 129, *133*